BROKEN
PATTERNS

BROKEN PATTERNS

Professional Women and the Quest for a New Feminine Identity

Anita M. Harris

WITHDRAWN

 WAYNE STATE UNIVERSITY PRESS   DETROIT

Copyright © 1995 by Wayne State University Press,
Detroit, Michigan 48201. All rights are reserved.
No part of this book may be reproduced without formal permission.
Manufactured in the United States of America.
99 98 97 96 95   5 4 3 2 1

Library of Congress Cataloging-in-Publication Data

Harris, Anita M.
   Broken patterns : professional women and the quest for a new
feminine identity / Anita M. Harris.
      p.   cm.
   Includes bibliographical references and index.
   ISBN 0-8143-2550-5 (alk. paper).—ISBN 0-8143-2551-3 (pbk. :
alk. paper)
   1. Women in the professions—United States—Psychology.
2. Identity (Psychology)—Social aspects—United States.   3. Mothers
and daughters—United States.   4. Grandmothers—United States.
5. Sex role—United States.   I. Title.
HD6054.2.U6H37   1995
305.43—dc20   94-46292

Jacket designer: Mary Primeau
Text designer: Joanne Kinney

The women interviewed for this book are real. Their names and certain identifying
characteristics have been changed to protect confidentiality.

CONTENTS

ACKNOWLEDGMENTS

Researching and writing *Broken Patterns* has been a long and fascinating quest; many people have helped along the way, and to them I offer my heartfelt thanks. I am especially grateful to my parents. My mother, Sara Richman Harris, supported me in the creative process throughout; my father, the late Raymond Harris, M.D., in addition, suggested the spiral theory on which *Broken Patterns* is based.

Jessica Begun served as research assistant and editor in the early stages; Deb Silverman, in transcribing the interviews, first noticed the mother-daughter pattern; Joel Bernard suggested the life cycle approach; Irene Stiver shared her clinical knowledge and expertise, helping to interpret my interview findings and providing encouragement from day one. Jane Hunter provided guidance in my historical search and generously read and commented on the manuscript, as did Gordon Lewin and Mark Orton. Genevieve MacLellan has long been a friend and editor. Susan Ginsburg of Writers House offered loyalty and counsel; Helen Rich shared her keen insight on the experiences of generations of women; Donna Greenberg, Rosa Shinagel, Edward Messner, and Peggy Barnes provided steady confidence; and Sarah Blacher Cohen advised me on the publishing process.

At Radcliffe College, Matina Horner, Anne Colby, and Martha Mauzy made available to me the facilities and resources of the Henry A. Murray Research Center: A Center for the Study of Lives; Beatrice Whiting, Glen Elder, Margaret Fine-Davis, and Sally Powers read portions of the manuscript and presented valuable suggestions; the late Patricia King and the staff of the Arthur and Elizabeth Schlesinger Library on the History of Women in America offered important research assistance.

7

ACKNOWLEDGMENTS

At Simmons College, my colleagues Bonita Betters-Reed, Carole Biewener, Laurie Crumpacker, Nancy Gilson, Lynda Moore, and Raquel Halty Pfaff read drafts and discussed many of the ideas presented here; the staff of the Beatley Library graciously conducted reference searches; and Jan Stanwood and the faculty were instrumental in my receiving a financial grant through the College's Fund for Research.

At Harvard University, Dean Michael Shinagel and the late David Aloian made available the resources of Quincy House; the late Deane Lord gave me the opportunity to teach writing in the Harvard Division of Continuing Education, which led to tremendous insight into the creative process; the Nieman Foundation and Curator James Thompson allowed me the freedom to explore and my colleagues encouraged me to do so. Special thanks also to the staff of the Monroe C. Gutman Library at the Graduate School of Education.

I would also like to thank the women who shared their stories with me, and the many scholars and professional women of the past and present whose hard work made *Broken Patterns* possible.

1

INTRODUCTION

When I reached my thirties, I had a lot of questions.

I had grown up in the 1950s—an era when men worked and women wore high heels and tight skirts and had babies. I went to college in the late 1960s when drugs, sex, and politics challenged the order of our childhood: the "traditional" family, neighborhood schools, segregation by race and sex. In the 1970s, feminists exhorted us to fight for equality—to prove women could do things with . . . as well as . . . better than . . . men. By 1980, I was a successful television journalist in New York City, trying both to challenge "the system," and be promoted within it. I wanted to marry a fine, sensitive man who had a lucrative, socially-redeeming profession and plenty of time to spend with me and our children-to-be.

To all appearances, I almost had it all. My work sent me jetting around the country to interview some of the important thinkers of the day. I owned my own apartment in Manhattan and was thinking about marrying a surgical resident who had a master's degree in English literature. But something was wrong.

Early in my career, I had helped to start a weekly newspaper in order to help fight for the rights of others. I wrote an exposé of a migrant labor camp where workers were forced by men with guns to pick tomatoes—and weeds, when there were no tomatoes. Later, I wrote about a woman judge who seemed to discriminate against welfare recipients and blacks. As a radio reporter in New York City, I roamed around 42nd Street investigating prostitution and pornography.

I was proud to have travelled on my own, to have advocated for social justice, to have made a difference. Maybe it was easier then than it would be later on; many of us, just out of college in the 1970s and bolstered by Lyndon Johnson's Great Society programs, were heady with a sense of mission. Perhaps, working on behalf of others came naturally; as a woman, that is what I had been brought up to do. There was a real sense of purpose, a drive to prove I could do things women *didn't* ordinarily do—to prove I could achieve equally with men.

By 1980, I had joined the Establishment. Outwardly, I was a hard-driving reporter, competing with men on their terms, and I was gaining recognition, skill, and power. Instead of feeling more competent, however, I was becoming less sure of myself. The outer world, which I had once explored with gusto, began to feel dangerous. There were, to be sure, real threats—after all, I *was* living in New York City and as a journalist I had survived more than a few close calls. A deeper problem was that progressing in the world of work, in that outer world, was beginning to threaten my inner sense of self.

Inside, I felt that the person attending press conferences and grappling with politicians, scientists, doctors, and lawyers wasn't really me. I knew myself as a shy person who had, as a child, spent hours at the piano, made doll clothes and held tea parties. I had become a journalist to help people and now I was making a name off of their woes. I was reporting on the world from two perspectives—the Establishment's, and my own. They valued power, speed, money, and machines. I valued, above all else, caring relationships and the enhancement of possibility for every individual. At work, I started to have trouble making decisions; achievement, there, was defined in terms that felt masculine to me. At home, I quit cooking and decorating, which I'd once enjoyed, because they seemed too feminine. I was stuck—unable to move ahead in any realm. Sometimes I felt like a piece of cardboard.

Then, Frank, a fellow reporter, was promoted ahead of me. Partly, he beat me out through luck—if luck means getting to cover a riot that breaks out in Miami while you happen to be there on vacation. But it wasn't only luck. When it looked as though a nuclear reactor in Pennsylvania might blow up, Frank volunteered for duty. I should have covered the story—my beats included health, the environment, and technology—but I opted out, worried about the possible effect of radioactivity on my unborn children. Another reason Frank got the promotion was that he covered business and economics—a clear path to upward mobility in our shop. Those fields felt foreign to an English and art major like me, and I wanted to give a voice to the people who were losing benefits as the Reagan administration dismantled social programs.

I felt trapped. I wanted equality and I wanted success. I had the skill, I had the opportunity, I had the drive. But I could no longer push forward—because it was no longer clear to me what forward meant. Yes, there was sexism; yes, there was sexual harassment; yes, there were equal pay problems. But I also approached the world differently from many of my male colleagues. I was interested in different stories; I didn't enjoy competing; I didn't like the detachment journalism requires of its practitioners; I was uncomfortable with the quest for power over others that so many of my colleagues seemed to enjoy.

Had I chosen the wrong field? Was the problem that I was a woman? Was it that my own strengths were devalued . . . or that I thought they were? How far would—and could—I bend to gain the respect of the men in charge? Would I ever reach a position in which I could influence how things were done? Or would I be forced to contradict my inner voice to the point where it was silenced? Could I find some compromise?

◆   ◇   ◆

Time for a breather. Fellowship. Sabbatical. School. I took a leave from my job for what I thought would be a year. I interviewed other journalists. What did I find?

One high-level reporter was concerned that if she continued to advance she would become a laughingstock, the butt of jokes. She believed, at some level, that she could not be both successful at work and well-liked as an attractive woman. While she continued to achieve, she played out this conflict in physical terms, through large weight gains and losses, in what she described as a near-obsession with her appearance.

Another journalist had accepted a promotion at the same time her first child was born; her husband took on most of the household and child-rearing responsibilities. She drove herself, convinced that she was "in a harness, uncreative," and tried constantly to mediate between her superiors and her underlings. This buffer role, she said, was one her own mother had played in her family in the 1950s. This journalist also shared something with her father—each night she arrived home angry and exhausted, just as her father had. "I didn't want to see my husband or my child," she said. "I just wanted to go into a room and shut myself off."

Yet another journalist had spent ten years scrambling from freelance job to freelance job. At thirty-two, she had been offered the job of her dreams—in New York. She had also managed to fall in love with a man who lived hundreds of miles away—in a conservative southern town where most women still didn't work. He wanted children, but the idea of having them terrified her—she was afraid having a child would make her "ordinary," like other women. All women, she believed, were devalued by men. She wanted to distinguish herself, to hold power, to run a news magazine. "To me," she said, "power is an aphrodisiac." On the other hand, she did not want to live without a man. "You can't cuddle up with your Rolodex at night," she said. Like most of the women I interviewed, she was, in her mid-thirties, at an impasse. But why?

Over the next four years, I interviewed more than forty successful career women in their mid-thirties. I wanted to understand the conflicts women were feeling and expressing. These conflicts went well beyond the problems of balancing career and family; I wondered if they might, somehow, be rooted in feminine identity itself. What was the basis of these conflicts? Where had they come from? How were they to be resolved?

For the women I interviewed, I had three main questions. First, why had they entered careers when most of their mothers had not? Second, what was it like to make the transition from a "traditional" background to a "man's" career? And finally, where did they see themselves going?

Answering those questions turned out to be more complicated than I ever could have imagined. The conflicts women expressed involved far more than psychology, sociology, law, organizational behavior, or history could explain. Rather, I found, these conflicts stemmed from the interplay of family, individual, society, and technology, going back generations.

◆　◇　◆

I believed, at first, that this would be a relatively simple project about the state of professional women. I expected to read a number of studies and illustrate them with a set of interviews. I soon found that the studies were limited, didn't ring true, or seemed outdated, so I designed my own study with guidance from fellow scholars at the Henry A. Murray Research Center at Radcliffe College. I used an open-ended questionnaire modelled on those used by such social psychologists as Sandra Tangri and Nancy Richardson. The objective was to try to explain, on the basis of a small set of in-depth interviews, the results of several large statistical studies.

I began quite formally by interviewing thirty women who had entered fields once reserved primarily for men—medicine, law, science, and corporate management. To select them, I drew from membership lists of women's professional organizations and a university alumni association; I also used a snowball sample, in which I asked people to suggest others to be interviewed. I then ascertained through a questionnaire potential subjects' ethnic, geographic, economic, and racial backgrounds, in order to insure as representative a mix as possible.

While not a scientific sample, the women I interviewed came from different backgrounds. Since, as late as 1980, some 97 percent of professional women were white, all but three of the women I interviewed were white. Some were Catholic, some Protestant, some Jewish. Some had parents who were rich, some who were poor; some identified their parents as upper, or middle, or working class. Some of the women were married, others were divorced, single, living with a significant other, or living with an insignificant other. At least one was gay; several were pregnant, some had children, others wanted them, still others did not. They were doctors, lawyers, scientists, architects, businesswomen, bankers. All were women who, unlike their mothers, had entered careers predominated by men.

None of the women I interviewed was famous—though several have since become well known in their fields. I wanted to tell the stories not of superwomen but of average professional women who had struggled and who could describe their struggles. Still, in some ways the women I interviewed turned out to be an unusual group: they were more psychologically insightful than I had expected, and quite articulate about their own feelings and emotions. Many saw themselves as role models, as "political"; most wanted to prove that "women could do things," as one doctor put it.

Sometimes their experiences sounded crazy or extreme: one woman, now a corporate lawyer, had spent a year as a subsistence farmer in Crete; a scientist had suddenly dropped her career to run off to Mexico with a man; several women described suicidal feelings. While some had dramatic stories to tell, the women I interviewed were, I believe, representative of the generation of women who came of age in the 1960s, a period of turmoil and flux and of heightened political activism. They were typical of women who set out to make major changes in themselves and in American society's deeply ingrained beliefs about women.

Women wanted to tell their stories. At my twentieth high school reunion, an old friend who had become a nutritionist told me, "I should be a chapter in your book." So did women I'd barely known at college, as well as perfect strangers. When I described my topic at wedding receptions, in my health club, in the classes I taught, woman after woman would say, "You should interview me. I'm just like that." (I have used some of their stories to illustrate my findings.) There was such a burning need to talk about the issues I wanted to raise that even women who first rebuffed me ended up asking me to listen. When I called the president of a women's professional organization to ask for its membership list she told me quite stuffily to write a letter to her board. When I wrote to explain my research, she called me to say that she—and all of her board members—wanted to be interviewed.

I interviewed women in their thirties because they had some experience to look back on and because I thought their potential for internal conflict was highest. Women who had put off having children for the sake of their careers were likely to hit both the limits of the biological clock and positions of real responsibility at work at the same time. As frontrunners born at the beginning of the baby boom, they were, I believed, different from women just a few years older than themselves, who had tended to marry in their early twenties and have families before entering the work force. But they were also different from women just a few years younger, who claimed not to know the struggle of breaking into "masculine" workplaces.

The women I interviewed came of age just after the modern feminist movement had begun to make inroads. They had more opportunities than previous generations, and they had the benefits of the birth control pill, a strong economy, liberalism, and increased legal rights. Still, they straddled two generations. Although they had broken new ground, they still carried within themselves the old values, notions of womanhood with which they had been raised.

I focused on women in fields that were predominantly male because I wanted to understand what it was like for women raised with those "traditional" feminine values—which I then understood to be nurturing or caring—to adjust to professions likely to be hierarchical, competitive, and concerned more with profits and power than with people. I also believed that women in these fields could, ultimately, reach positions of power and influence in our society. Their choices and philosophies would have enormous impact on the shape of society in the future.

I kept my sample small to allow in-depth interviews and analysis; hence, it was not possible to generalize about the experience of groups of women of differing backgrounds. I wanted to understand what drove a generation of women—despite the differences among them—to break personal, familial, and societal barriers that had previously held women back, so I chose to explore not their differences but their common experiences. Where possible, however, I have incorporated material from studies of professional women from varying ethnic, racial, and national backgrounds. Until recently, such studies have been limited in number and scope; those that do exist suggest added complexity in navigating within predominantly white male settings.

During the interviews, each of which lasted more than two hours and ran to about eighty pages when transcribed, I told women that they were free not to answer any questions that made them uncomfortable and that I was willing to talk "off the record." I also guaranteed anonymity, which inspired most of the women to reveal the intimate details of their lives with incredible frankness. To my surprise, though, not all women wanted to be anonymous; Annabel, the only woman assistant professor of history at a distinguished university, regaled me with stories about her colleagues and how she had fooled them into hiring her—then told me to be sure to use her name! I did not do so; throughout *Broken Patterns* I have changed the names of interviewees and some identifying characteristics to protect confidentiality. The women described here are, however, real, and not composite characters. (Because they spoke so personally, we were on a first name basis almost immediately, and I have used first names throughout.)

In the interviews, I delved deep, asking not just "What?" and "When?" but "Why?" Often, I asked about discrepancies or hesitations as I noticed them. As the interviews progressed, the women themselves offered memories from their childhoods and family histories. As they did so, I got some answers I had not expected.

Though I had tried for a geographic mix, for example, I would find that a woman who lived in the South had grown up in California, her parents in New York, and her grandparents in Eastern Europe. Class definition was equally problematic: one woman traced her wealthy ancestry to the Mayflower—but had a great-grandmother who had an illegitimate child and wound up selling hats in a millinery store. Another woman had a mother whose parents had been wealthy socialites and a father who worked as a travelling salesman. Other women had grandfathers who held blue-collar jobs—but fathers who rose to high-level jobs in corporations, universities, and professions. Some women described themselves as the offspring of marriages in which classes, races, and religions were mixed; sometimes their parents had left the farm for the city, and sometimes it was the other way around.

While I wanted to interview women from traditional 1950s households, that too was problematic—because "traditional" meant different things to different women. For most, it meant that their fathers had worked and their mothers had been full-time homemakers. "She was the kind of mother who stayed home and baked cookies," was a typical response. But some women described mothers who were divorced or who worked part-time as secretaries, sales clerks, or nurses. Two of the three black women I interviewed had working mothers. One woman not included in the study (because she worked in the predominantly female field of social work) described a social worker mother who became a judge. Yet even these daughters of working women considered their mothers "traditional"—because their mothers *believed* women belonged at home.

At first, the complications in these responses frustrated me no end. They were not the clear-cut answers I had hoped for; my study would not simply corroborate or illustrate the work of others. Again and again, I found, as psychologist Carol Gilligan once predicted I would, that it was the very points on which my interviews contradicted the conventional wisdom that led to my most important insights.[1]

My first such insight was that the women I interviewed chose careers mainly because they did not want to live the sorts of lives their mothers had led.

One professional woman described her mother as a "perfect middle class Catholic housewife" who gave no outward sign of the distress which led her to take her own life after the last of her four children left home for college. Already married with one child herself, the professional woman told me, "That's when I swore to myself that I'd always have a career." Some women saw their mothers as stifled by marriage and children; others believed their mothers had simply lost out on opportunities because of the Great Depression or the post-World War II trend back to domesticity. Regardless of the explanations, the women I spoke with wanted, above all else, to reverse the trend toward domesticity which they had felt, even as young children, swallowed up their mothers' opportunities and which threatened to swallow up their own as well.

This insight led to other questions. If these women simply did not want to be like their mothers, why was it so difficult for them to establish different sorts of lives? In part, it was because they themselves had changed more quickly than had the world around them. Even more important, I concluded, was that while the women I interviewed did not want to be like their mothers, in many respects, as women, they deeply identified with them.

That deep identification led to a central paradox: the more a daughter identified with a mother she saw as downtrodden, the more the daughter wanted to be different from her mother. That paradox created emotional push-pulls between the women I interviewed and their mothers—and within the women themselves. Those push-pulls would explain the tremendous drive of these women to succeed in the predominantly male world outside the home as well as their deep ambivalence about that success. It would also explain the feeling expressed by so many working mothers that no matter how much they did for their own families and children, it was never enough.

The push-pull paradox would also explain the difficult transition process through which the women I interviewed entered adulthood—a process that at the same time reflected and affected social change.

First, for the women I interviewed, came a period of rebellion—heightened by the turmoil of the 1960s—in which women lashed out against their mothers and fathers. In this rebellion, women also expressed anger at and vowed to change family and societal structures which had held back their mothers and which threatened to hold them back as well.

Then came deciding on careers—and starting them. In this early phase, many women suffered from anxiety and confusion. "I started medical school with my 'dukes' up," a doctor said. "I'd heard medical school changes people and I didn't want to change." In our interview, however, she wondered why not. "Heck," she said. "I didn't even like myself."

For a time, success became all-important. But soon, these women found they were on a collision course: success in the workplace often conflicted with the definitions of femininity they had internalized— based on their mothers' examples—as children. One businesswoman in her early thirties suffered from "constant anxiety." A journalist described feeling paralyzed by "a failure of imagination." A surgeon considered suicide.

Finally, in their mid-thirties—when career and family responsibilities collided head-on—the women I interviewed began to ask serious questions about the nature of womanhood. A central problem was how to succeed at work without losing themselves entirely.

A tax attorney in a major city opened her own practice after an unpleasant start at a corporate law firm. At the time of our interview, she was working eighty hours a week. She lived with a man ten years her junior and was putting him through law school, though she wondered if she shouldn't break up with him to marry a man who challenged her intellectually and to have children, as her mother advised. "I went to college to get my MRS degree," the attorney quipped. "I guess I flunked."

A computer engineer had given up almost all of her free time to devote herself to rising in the managerial ranks of a large computer company. At thirty-four, she missed the feel of finishing products and did not find managing others satisfying. She wished she had pursued her early dream of a career in anthropology, which she had given up for the sake of job security. She also wished she could quit work to stay home and have children with the man she was about to move in with, but she could not do that. At thirty, sure that she wanted a profession and no children, she had had her tubes tied.

A West Coast banker with a six-figure income and a seventy-hour work week was supporting her husband and twelve-year-old son but rarely saw them. She felt trapped in her marriage and trapped in her career. "All I ever wanted was to have a bunch of kids," she said. "I think American women have been sold a bill of goods."

Outwardly, these professional women were all highly successful. Inside they had deep questions about what success really meant. All were grappling—not just with balancing career and family—but with defining themselves in relation to their mothers and to women of the future and of the past. Many were considering more traditionally feminine paths, from working part-time to focusing on a branch of surgery oriented toward women. At the same time, they wondered if backing down even a bit would mean they had failed not only themselves but all other women.

◆　◇　◆

By the late 1980s, the proposed Equal Rights Amendment to the Constitution had failed, newly won abortion rights were under challenge, and the first female to run for vice president as a major party candidate had been discredited. Feminists who just a few years earlier had seemed to believe firmly that equality could best be established in the workplace were beginning to argue among themselves. A central issue was (as it still is) whether women were fundamentally different from men and whether the difference ought to be enhanced, rather than diminished.

Sometimes, I felt that my generation—encouraged by our mothers and older sisters to "go for it" through careers—had been sold down the river. Many of us had not married; we were sometimes accused of being too strong, too forceful, too late, or too unwilling to make the sorts of compromises our mothers had made. Younger women—called by the *New York Times* a "Post Feminist Generation"—said they could not understand why we would jeopardize marriages for the sake of careers. It was a period of discouragement, confusion, anger, and disappointment.

When I sent a proposal describing my interview findings to several publishing houses, the response was mixed. "What are these women going to do?" one editor asked. "What is going to happen next?" Who could know? I was stymied. One question continued to bother me. Why us? Why should our generation have been the one to try to break these patterns? If our mothers were so miserable, why hadn't *they* tried to break the patterns?

I turned to history to try to understand our mothers' experience and soon learned that we were by no means the first generation of women to enter "men's" careers. At least twice in the past, feminist movements—accompanied by movements of women into professions—had risen and fallen, most recently in the 1920s. I looked back at my interview notes. As I studied pages and pages of transcripts, I realized that hidden in them was evidence that while the women I interviewed did not want lives like their mothers', many admired grandmothers who had played strong roles both within their families and outside them early in the twentieth century.[2]

A surgeon described her father's mother as "a matriarch." An anthropologist whose mother had six children before she turned thirty spoke of one grandmother who had been a teacher and another who worked, even after marriage, as one of the earliest legal secretaries. A social researcher described an immigrant grandmother who got rich by starting her own clothing manufacture company. Other grandmothers ran farms, businesses, a restaurant.

A few women had grandmothers who did not work but described great-aunts or other family role models who did. One university professor, for instance, admired her grandmother's younger sister, who had become a psychiatrist before 1920. That generation, as their granddaughters saw them, had been feisty, independent, and strong; quite different from the mothers of the 1950s. As their granddaughters described them, their *grandmothers* seemed to have broken the patterns of *their* mothers—who lived during the Victorian era in the late nineteenth century.

In the family lore, there seemed to be substantial differences in the roles played by mothers and daughters. What accounted for these differences? Was there an every-other-generation pattern in women's roles? If so, how far back did it go? What might be driving it?

In search of answers, I conducted an additional ten interviews and began reading history. Although one black television producer knew that her great-grandfather had been a county sheriff, most of the women who could trace their family histories back more than two generations were white Anglo-Saxon Protestants who had access to letters and diaries of ancestors who had arrived in this country in the mid-1800s or earlier.

From historians, I learned that women increasingly worked outside the home from the colonial era on. It also seemed that the more women left the home for paying work, the more pervasive was the societal belief that they should not. However, the more women were restricted to a domestic role in one generation, the more their daughters wanted to break out of that role in the next. In generation after generation, women debated much the same question we debate today: can women best achieve freedom and equality by fulfilling a special spiritual and nurturing role— or by taking on roles and responsibilities similar to those of men?

Broken Patterns describes these historical and generational ebbs and flows in terms of the push-pulls women experience in relation to their mothers. Through a process of emotional separation and connection, it shows, women grow and change along the life cycle, struggling to develop as individuals different from their mothers in some ways, but like them in others.

Likewise, on a broad, societal scale, increasingly rapid social and technological change foster mobility, individuality, and independence. These trends are countered by and also heighten the desire for tradition, family, and intimacy. With modernization, the more women (and men) leave the home for paying work, the more we long for the safety of an idealized past in which women are seen as perfect nurturers, and men as strong protectors. When the idealization becomes too constraining for women in one generation, as opportunity expands, their daughters seek different roles in the next.

Broken Patterns describes this psychological and historical process starting with the American colonial era; it ends by asking what it might mean for the future.

◆　◇　◆

Chapter 2, "One Woman's Story," is an in-depth interview with a lawyer into which prevailing theories about women's career choices are woven. The chapter shows that while social scientists have many views on why women in the past chose careers, the women interviewed for *Broken Patterns* decided at early ages to enter careers largely based on what they knew of their mothers' and grandmothers' lives.

Chapter 3, "Historical Patterns: 1600–1900," places modern day women in broad historical context. It shows that in the colonial era, women played a wide range of roles, but that in the early nineteenth century, increasingly rapid technological change led to family break-up and to increased emotional need for the safety of home. Hence, as more men and women left home for paying work, an ideology of domesticity for women developed and deepened. At the same time, women's struggles for suffrage, property rights, education, and careers intensified, as did the debate over woman's proper place. In part because of a dynamic tension that exists between mothers and daughters, the more women were restricted to the home in one generation, the more their daughters wished to break free of the home in the next. By the end of the century, young women were entering colleges and careers in social work, law and medicine in growing numbers.

Chapter 4, "Generational Patterns: 1900–1950," describes how, in the early twentieth century, women continued to progress in education, the professions, and the struggle for women's rights. Some of these women were the grandmothers of the women I interviewed. By the mid–1920s, in the face of much societal and familial disruption and amidst debate and disagreement among women themselves, women's advances seemed to slow. Following the Great Depression and World War II, the next generation of women, the mothers of the women I interviewed, bought into a renewed belief that women belonged at home.

Chapter 5, "Push-Pulls: The 1950s," describes, through their daughters' eyes, the lives of women in the 1950s. It suggests that many present-day professional women decided on careers much earlier than has previously been believed—long before the most recent wave of feminism and the opening of opportunity—because they didn't want the sorts of lives their mothers led. Woven through the case studies is psychological theory which describes girls' identity development as a process of seeking both emotional connection to their mothers and independence from them.

Chapter 6, "Making the Break: The 1960s," is based largely on an interview with Molly Walden, a student radical-turned-corporate lawyer. It portrays the rebellion of women in the late 1960s as a simultaneous attempt to express anger at their mothers while expressing anger on their mothers' behalf. These contradictory impulses fueled young women's participation in the burgeoning civil rights, anti-war, and feminist movements of the time, and led them, as a generation, to attempt to break both their mothers' patterns and the societal patterns that had held their mothers back.

Chapter 7, "Success and Struggle: The 1970s," describes what it was like for the women I interviewed to enter careers once reserved for men. While many books focus on the external barriers women face as minorities in male-dominated workplaces, *Broken Patterns* centers on the psychological barriers with which women grappled as they sought success in professions. For these women, a central problem was how to prove they were not like their mothers by achieving in "masculine" terms—yet retain, or in some cases, develop, respect for themselves as females.

Chapter 8, "Impasse: The 1980s," shows that whereas early on, women asked how they could be different from their mothers and equal with men, when they reached their mid-thirties their central question changed. Now they were asking how they could be more *like* their mothers yet equal with men. The chapter also describes the parallel impasse reached in this country by the late 1980s. Having once encouraged women to achieve equality in terms defined largely by men (i.e., money and power), we as a nation had begun to ask how men and women could be different, yet equal.

Chapter 9, "Spirals: Present, Past, and Future," articulates *Broken Patterns'* underlying theme: that life and history are neither linear (as we might like) nor cyclic (which could leave us without hope) but spiral. It suggests that individual and generational pushes forward and pulls back can be creative processes through which we grow and change yet stay in touch with our past. But in generation after generation, daughters (and sons) have felt compelled to be unlike mothers depreciated in relation to men. These sons and daughters have, in turn, devalued women, perpetuating what has become a negative spiral.

Today, in light of vast changes in the world order, economic uncertainty, and lack of resources and time for parenting, we, too, are in danger of perpetuating this negative spiral. To keep this from happening, *Broken Patterns* concludes, professional women must take the lead in using the principles of separation and connection described throughout the book to develop new approaches to equality. Such approaches must take into account not just the differences between men and women, but also the differences that exist among women.

Thus, *Broken Patterns* has turned out to be a very different book from the one I expected to write. It is not simply a set of interviews; it is not a statistical study which sets up a hypothesis to be proved or disproved by empirical methods; it is not an advice book (all too often, it shows, women have been weakened by accepting the views of others). Rather, *Broken Patterns* is an exploratory essay that attempts to suggest a useful paradigm for thinking about a vexed and complicated history.

That paradigm suggests that a push-pull dynamic of separation and connection underlies patterns of individual and historical development. That development, as portrayed in *Broken Patterns,* is neither linear—deeming us failures if we do not achieve certain goals—nor cyclic, repetitive, or discouraging. Rather, advances and seeming retreats can all contribute to a personal and historical spiral process of growth.

Through this spiral process, which operates on many levels, we move toward the new, yet return psychically to reincorporate into our lives values and aspects of the past we care about in order to move forward once again. The principles of separation and reconnection, *Broken Patterns* concludes, can and should be used to explore the differences and similarities not just between men and women, but among women themselves. In this way, we can, should, and will find new ways of being, and of being equal, in the future.

2

ONE WOMAN'S STORY

I drove to Nancy Kelly's address expecting to meet a glass-and-steel woman in a split-level house. One of her colleagues had described her as "a lawyer, a litigator, one of those women men sometimes call 'too aggressive' at work." Nancy was Catholic, single, and in her early thirties. The colleague had said, "I don't know if she wants to get married; she may feel marriage would interfere with her career."

Nancy sounded like just the kind of woman I wanted to interview, someone who, unlike myself, would probably be from a very traditional background, and, as a corporate lawyer, a believer in the Establishment and its values. On the phone, Nancy had sounded smooth, professional, all business. I'd imagined her living room as sparsely furnished, with white sofas, chrome-edged glass coffee tables, picture windows, a Manhattan-style apartment designed for corporate entertaining. There would be beige wall-to-wall carpeting, low-slung chairs. She would be wearing expensive gabardine slacks, high heels, lipstick. Her hair, glamorous, would be up in a French twist; she would be in terrific shape. Since it was one in the afternoon, she would offer me a drink in a highball glass, but I'd have iced tea.

As I drove, I thought about what I'd ask her. Why had she chosen law, still considered a man's career when she entered it in the mid-1970s? I knew, of course, that Nancy and I were part of a major movement of women into careers, a movement which followed close on the heels of the 1960s student rebellions against the Vietnam War, the Establishment, and racial discrimination. Many women of our generation had been profoundly influenced by the burgeoning civil rights and feminist movements. But why did all of this happen when it did? And why to us?

I had already learned that these were questions experts debated among themselves. Some historians saw our movement into professions as part of a natural progression of women into the work force, a movement that had begun with the industrial revolution if not earlier. According to this view, in the nineteenth century women increasingly worked, not just as domestics, clerks, and teachers, but even as doctors and lawyers. In the twentieth century, a shift to light industry opened many jobs that did not require the physical strength of men, and after World War II, a growing service economy allowed more and more married women to work at part-time and unskilled jobs. By the 1950s, when Nancy and I were children, more women worked than ever before. With the added impetus of the civil rights and feminist movements of the 1960s, it seemed only natural in the 1970s for bright women to enter the nation's expanding professional ranks.

Another view was that as production moved from home to factory in the nineteenth century, men took more responsibility for wage-earning outside the home, and women for domestic, spiritual matters within it. This meant, to those who shared that view, that women worked for pay only if they had to; in times of economic stress or war, women might take what were considered nontraditional jobs; afterward, they would return to more "traditional" roles. While in the 1950s, more women worked than ever before, it was at less responsible jobs than women had held previously, and women were marrying younger and having more children than many women had a generation back. As late as 1964 social scientists predicted, based on those trends, that women's rate of increase in the labor force was likely to decline. This interpretation made the career choices of women like Nancy and me seem like radical and surprising departures.[1]

Still others described our entry into careers as in keeping with a cyclic pattern, driven in large part by economics or demographic changes.[2] It seemed to me, as I approached Nancy's house, that women didn't simply jump onto historical trends; while they were certainly affected by them, they also in large part created them. What part had we played in creating this one? And why?

As it turned out, Nancy lived in the first-floor apartment of a white frame two-family house on a country sort of street with no sidewalks. When I rang the bell, a stocky woman just my height—about five foot five—with short red hair answered the door. She wore a plaid cotton blouse with a button-down collar, a navy blue shetland cardigan sweater, a blue denim A-line skirt, and well-worn, well-polished brown penny loafers—without pennies. She smiled nervously, then showed me into a living room furnished with old things—an overstuffed chair, a comfy sofa with lace doilies on the arms, a glassed-in bookcase on which rested a number of framed family photographs.

Over tea, I asked Nancy how she'd happened to choose a career in corporate law, fully expecting her to describe a straightforward career path—college, government major, law school, clerkship, law firm. Instead, she explained that she'd grown up with no clear idea of what she wanted to do with her life. Her parents had wanted her to be a teacher, then get married. "That was the next best thing to becoming a nun," she quipped.

In her late teens, Nancy had rebelled—first by going to a non-Catholic college, then by joining a theater crowd. After graduation, she worked in theater management for a couple of years, then left because she didn't enjoy working with "crazy people" and wanted to earn a more stable living. She became the director of a community organization that turned out to be too conservative to suit her—she supported busing for desegregation and her constituents did not. Finally, she went to law school. "I wanted to do things that were 'important and serious,'" she said. "To bring class action suits that had tremendous social ramifications." She also wanted to make some money. Besides, a number of her friends were considering going to law school, and you could get in there with just a liberal arts degree.

As Nancy ticked off the rather incongruous reasons for her decision, she managed to sound quite lawyerlike. "Some of it was a fluke," she said. "I was interested in doing something more substantial. There was also an element of chance. And there was peer pressure." Then Nancy smiled and shrugged her shoulders. Maybe she was remembering the period in the early 1970s when it became trendy for women to go to law school when she joked, "Oh, yes, that seemed to be what was in that year."

As Nancy told it, all of this seemed to have "just happened." What about the deeper motivation? What would make a good Catholic girl, brought up conservatively, become part of a grand movement toward social change? Earlier in my research I had looked to studies done by sociologists and social psychologists—to little avail.

◆　◇　◆

Some studies found that a woman's religious background correlated strongly with her life plans. Jewish college women were the most likely to plan on graduate school, Catholic women slightly less likely, and Protestant women the least likely of all, studies showed. Because Nancy had been educated in Catholic schools, she would not have been expected to enter a field predominated by men; most women planning innovative careers voiced no religious preference and had parents who either practiced different religions or were agnostics or atheists.[3]

Some researchers explained these findings on the basis of religious groups' attitudes toward gender roles. In orthodox Jewish families, for instance, wives typically earn money and husbands deal with spiritual matters. In strict Catholic families, however, women have tended to be concerned with religion, and men with temporal affairs. Other researchers suggested that it is not the religion itself but rather each family's orthodoxy or conservativism within the religion that predicts its attitudes toward gender roles. Or perhaps girls whose parents do not insist on conformity in any realm are the likeliest to seek nontraditional careers.[4]

Another factor was nationality. In the 1950s, three fourths of the women mathematicians in America who went to graduate school were born either in Europe or Canada or had at least one immigrant parent, and half of women lawyers in a 1965 study were of immigrant origins. These women may have felt comfortable pursuing high levels of education because European women commonly did so. Or perhaps, as immigrants or daughters of immigrants, they already felt different and were *used* to not fitting in.[5] (Conversely, women from Native American, African-American, Puerto Rican, and Mexican backgrounds encountered almost insurmountable barriers to professional careers, such as poverty, language and cultural differences, lack of tradition in higher education, and prejudice.[6])

How about education? While certainly it had an impact, studies were limited, and the results were less than clear. One 1960s study showed that college faculty were almost as important as parents in helping students choose innovative careers, but another found that faculty prejudice discouraged many women from careers in science. In 1975, minority women scientists reported having been encouraged in their careers by some faculty members and discouraged by others. Nearly all considered the public education they had received "inadequate"; two of them, a Native American and a native Spanish speaker, said that in grade school they had been classified as mentally retarded.[7]

Among lawyers, assessing influences on career choice was no simpler; when sociologist Cynthia Fuchs Epstein asked a group of women why they had chosen legal careers, many said they could not remember.[8]

This was all rather discouraging. Why should it be so difficult to understand how women chose their careers? What I would come to understand was that despite the impact of economics, religion, education, role models, the media, and other societal forces, much of what we do and believe is shaped by less accessible, less tangible forces: the interplay of historical events and family memories going back generations. First and foremost, however, a woman is influenced by her relationship with her parents. The question is, how? Here, too, the study results were mixed.

In the 1940s and 1950s, many psychologists believed that women who wanted professional careers identified more with their fathers than with their mothers, and many psychologists considered professional women aberrational. In 1944, psychoanalyst Helene Deutsch went so far as to call women who competed professionally with men "deviates" who really wanted to *be* men. Such women suffered from a "masculinity complex," she wrote, and sacrificed the "warm, intuitive knowledge" of womanhood to the "cold, unproductive thinking" of manhood. In 1947, Ferdinand Lundberg, a journalist, and Marynia Farnham, a psychiatrist, wrote that "the shadow of the phallus" lay over feminists and that working outside the home turned women away from their true instincts—of passivity, dependence, and the desire to raise children.[9]

In the 1950s, one study found that women mathematicians felt closer to their fathers than their mothers; another, published in 1961, suggested that the most creative women mathematicians turned to the "symbolic activity" of their field because they felt alienated from their nonintellectual mothers and isolated from their professional fathers, who were not warm or affectionate. While these women were able to make use of cognitive resources generally attributed to both sexes, they also exhibited more eccentricity and early psychopathy than other women. "Overachievers" at Vassar College who were from ethnic minorities, socially unintegrated, or exhibited "personal adjustment problems" and were almost exclusively oriented toward professions, rated their fathers more favorably than their mothers and often had repressed hostility and guilt toward their mothers, who were talented but domineering.[10]

Among women who chose legal careers in the 1950s or earlier, 70 to 80 percent had mothers who were not professionals; high-achieving women in another study generally had mothers who were the admiring wives of brilliant men. These high-achieving women identified strongly with their fathers, perhaps because they found something lacking in their mothers' roles. A later study found that women who reached the top in business, science, or mathematics were often the only or eldest daughters in families with no sons, and had felt close to their fathers, who encouraged them in their careers.[11]

In the 1960s, however, studies started to show just the opposite— that women who wanted to pursue nontraditional professions identified more with their mothers than with their fathers, especially if their mothers worked, even part-time.[12] In 1966, psychologist Eleanor Maccoby wrote that a crucial factor in developing a girl's intelligence was a *mother* who encouraged her to fend for herself.[13] A few years later, social psychologist Sandra Tangri found that the college women most likely to say they wanted "innovative" professional careers—careers in which fewer than 30 percent of those working were women—had supportive fathers and mothers who worked.

Tangri's results, too, were based on a complex set of circumstances. Most women who said they were more interested in innovative careers than in marriage reported feeling close to their mothers, but believed they resembled their fathers more than their mothers. This was, perhaps, because their fathers tended not to esteem their wives, who ordinarily had little education, worked at low-status, low-paying jobs, and did all of the housework, Tangri suggested.

Daughters who hoped to combine career and marriage usually had better-educated mothers who sometimes held advanced or professional degrees or worked in traditionally feminine careers such as social work or teaching. Such daughters said they resembled their mothers more than their fathers, but often disagreed with their mothers. While their mothers did not encourage them to enter professions predominated by men, their fathers, who seemed to respect women, often did encourage them. Such daughters, Tangri suggested, were independent from their mothers yet saw their mothers as positive role models.

Women least likely to want innovative careers had mothers who did not work outside the home at all, Tangri found. Women with highly educated mothers who did not work expected to seek status and achievement through their husbands' and sons' accomplishments; women with less-educated mothers who did not work expected to marry; some sought traditional careers—those employing at least half women—at early ages.[14]

Most of the above studies were conducted among college students in the 1960s, so they speak mainly to the experience of white women. However, among a group of minority women scientists, doctors, and engineers, most said their parents did not understand their goals, but that at least one parent, family member, or teacher had provided encouragement. Black women attorneys, a third of whom had mothers who worked as teachers or social workers, and most of the rest in blue-collar jobs, commonly told a researcher that their mothers had encouraged them to be self-reliant and economically independent of men.[15]

Interesting as the studies were, none was definitive. Each had asked a different question; some were based on women in psychiatric treatment; most dealt with college women's hopes and dreams and not with their actual choices. Then, too, study results seemed to change according to the era: as it became more socially acceptable for women to work, researchers started to find that women who wanted careers often had working mothers. Had the studies changed? Researchers' attitudes? The mothers? Professional women themselves?

While the most recent studies seemed to show that women who worked had mothers who had worked, the professional women *I* knew had grown up in large families in the 1950s and were the daughters of full-time homemakers. I wondered why so many young women who did *not* have working mothers as role models surprised researchers and policymakers by putting off marriage and children to fight for equality in fields once reserved for men.[16]

In interviewing Nancy, I asked why. Was it the women's movement? The opening of opportunity? The desire to make money? The impact of class? Race? Religion? Did Nancy want to be like her father? Like her mother? To most of those questions, Nancy would answer "yes." But what emerged as I probed into her family background were still deeper, more personal reasons for her choices.

♦ ◇ ♦

Nancy told me with some pride that in her family, there were no role models for professional careers at all. Her grandparents had immigrated from Ireland; one grandfather was an engraver, the other drove a team of horses. "Heck," she said. "Both of my grandmothers were cleaning ladies." Nancy's mother had not worked after she was married—except for a few Christmas seasons when she wrapped packages in a department store. "She liked being out of the house," Nancy explained. Though Nancy's mother had once hoped to become a teacher, she couldn't: *her* mother, Nancy's grandmother, died young, and her father, Nancy's grandfather, had rheumatism, so Nancy's mother quit high school to support the family. She ran an adding machine in a store for a year or two, but stopped when she got married.

Asked why her mother didn't have a paying job after she married, Nancy first said, "Because she had five kids." But I pushed the point, asking, "But even after the time you all went to school?" Nancy reconsidered. "My father felt very strongly that his wife should not be working," she said.

Nancy described her father as a "very stern authoritarian figure," who held a series of jobs—first in a family plumbing supply business and later as a freight handler.

He had an incredible temper; there was a lot of yelling and screaming that would go on. He was the hard-working man who went out and earned a living for his family. He may not have always been

29

around very much, but that wasn't because he was down at the bar-room—it's because he was at his second or third job.

Nancy's mother seemed the polar opposite. "She was the social com-ponent in the family, the one who would laugh a lot," Nancy said. "She was gregarious, social. People loved her. They found her attractive, warm, supportive." As Nancy saw it, "She was a gem."

I have very clear memories of my oldest brother coming in from working in the department store at night and my mother cooking him dinner. She would do that from 5:00 at night to 9:30. One after another, she'd end up cooking meals for people as they came in and out. My mother spent so much time in the kitchen that we used to kid her about being a short order cook.

Nancy's mother also cared for a sister who was chronically ill and for people in the community.

There was an old lady who lived down the street from us who didn't have any relatives that lived nearby. Well, one of the things that we did as kids was to take her shopping and get her groceries. And my mother would go down and make sure that she was taken care of. She would do that two, three, four times a week. She had friends in nursing homes that she would visit. We have the kind of large, spread out family where there's always a poor relation who's sick, someone who needs to be cared for. There was always something for her to do.

Nancy described her mother as "a happy, self-satisfied person," and because many psychologists believed that daughters normally emulated such mothers, why hadn't Nancy followed in her mother's footsteps? Why had Nancy become an aggressive lawyer, a single woman driven to suc-ceed in a male-dominated profession? Could it have been the influence of her older brothers?

"I didn't deal with my brothers much. They did boys' things and I was supposed to be doing girls' things. My mother thought that I should dress differently," she said. "I never owned a pair of blue jeans until I went away to college."

"How did your brothers treat you?" I asked. She hesitated. "How did they treat me?" she repeated. Then she laughed. "They treated me like I was a girl. I wanted them to treat me like I was one of them."

So Nancy did see her brothers as role models and wanted their re-spect. How about her father's influence?

"I always did better at schoolwork than my brothers," she said, "and my father—both my parents—encouraged me to do well." Interestingly, while Nancy's father would not allow his wife to work, even though it meant he had to hold two jobs himself, he expected Nancy to hold an after-school job. Nancy believed this was because her father wanted to see his offspring break the working class barriers that bound him. "It's the classic story of third generation immigrants who got pushed to do something quite different than their own parents," she explained. While Nancy's mother was upset when Nancy went to a non-Catholic college, her father was "secretly tickled." He'd been to a wake in the well-to-do suburb where the college was located and "he liked the idea that a child of his could live there," Nancy said.

In choosing her career, then, Nancy had been influenced by the wish to be accepted by her brothers, to please her father, to seek upward mobility. How about her mother's influence? Had her mother encouraged her to do well in school? "Absolutely," Nancy said. This seemed strange, I was thinking, since Nancy believed her mother wanted her to play a stereotypically feminine role in most respects, which for many women, at the time, would have meant deemphasizing their intelligence.

Suddenly, before I could ask another question, Nancy sat bolt upright, as if she'd seen a light. She said, excited, forcefully, "Are you seeing this? The key is that I was educated so *I* could become a teacher. My *mother* had wanted very much to become a teacher and could not afford to go to school."

I *was* seeing what she meant, and it was exactly what more than a few women would tell me: their mothers wanted them to live out the dreams they had left behind. That still did not explain why Nancy had become a lawyer and not a teacher. When I pointed this out, Nancy responded almost angrily. She seemed irritated, as if the answer should be obvious. "It does not interest me to be locked away in a building with people I can't talk to who have nothing to do with the mainstream of life," she said, adamant.

Why was Nancy so angry? Evidently, I'd struck a nerve. Did she resent my suggestion that she could be anything like her mother? But then . . . she seemed to admire her mother. So I asked what her mother had wanted for her. She replied point-blank, "marriage and children." Then I asked what her mother thought about her career. Nancy hesitated. "The night before she was operated on for cancer," she said with a waver in her voice, "my mother turned to me and said, 'I wonder why you turned out this way.' I don't think she ever understood quite why I didn't turn out to be like her or like the daughters of her friends." With this, Nancy began to cry. I suggested we take a break, and Nancy quickly left the room.

As I waited for Nancy to return, I thought about what she had told

31

me. By choosing a legal career, Nancy had fulfilled a number of missions that teaching—or marriage—could not. It made her upwardly mobile, which allowed her to please her father; it put her in a good competitive position vis-à-vis her brothers, and it gave her power in society. Being a lawyer also allowed her to escape being locked up in a room all day with little children. Why, then, the anger? Why the tears?

Nancy returned to the living room five minutes later, notably more relaxed, more composed. She apologized for crying, then explained that she was going through the most difficult period of her life so far. "I worry sometimes that I'm thirty-three years old and not married," she said. "Sometimes I think I might like to have a husband and children." At other times, she was not so sure. Growing up, she said, her voice rising from a whisper, "I was so turned off by what I saw of my mother's life that all I can say is that I did not want to have that life."

What was going on here? Throughout the interview, Nancy had described her mother as a happy person, one whom she had liked and admired. Now she was telling me that she had been totally turned off by her mother's life? I felt annoyed and confused. It would be several years and some forty interviews before I would understand that both statements were true and that Nancy's anger and tears expressed the deep and powerful emotions many professional women feel in relation to their mothers. They chose their careers not simply because they did not want to be like their mothers or because they admired their fathers. They did so because they so strongly identified with their mothers as females that they wanted desperately to avoid the sorts of lives their mothers had led.

As much as Nancy had admired her mother, I would come to understand, she felt at an early age that her father held the power in the family, and that her mother had been stuck with children and restricted freedom. While Nancy's mother had seemed to enjoy her nurturing role, she gave her daughter, if subliminally, a second message: to have a career as she had not. As a consequence, the harder Nancy's mother tried to make Nancy conform to a stereotypical feminine role, the less Nancy wished to follow in her footsteps.

Like many women who chose lives quite different from their mothers', the psychologist Irene Stiver would later suggest in an interview, in her thirties, Nancy no doubt felt she had lost connection with her mother: living a life so different from her mother's had made it difficult for the two to share a closeness they both desired. Nancy may also have felt she had let her mother down both by not emulating her as a wife and mother and by not living out her mother's career dream. In her thirties, even though Nancy was extremely successful in her career, she was grappling with serious questions: How could she be a woman, different from her mother yet close to her, female and feminine? How could she also be equal with her brothers, with her father, with men?

At the end of our interview, Nancy admitted that she was thinking of leaving her job in corporate law. "I'd like to work in an environment where they take people's needs more into account," she said. That might mean going into public interest law or government work, she said, fields she hoped would allow her to fully express the caring qualities she had come to realize she did in fact share with her mother, who had died the year before. To this day, Nancy confessed, she volunteered in her old neighborhood, much as her mother had. She was even considering a move out of the suburbs and back to the working class neighborhood where she had grown up.

Nancy, then, had come almost full circle. Having wanted, early on, to be much unlike her mother, on reaching her thirties, she wanted to retrieve what she could of her relationship with her mother and of the elements of herself she felt she had left behind.

Again and again, I would hear of the dynamic and powerful relationship that exists between women and their mothers, a relationship that involves a struggle for both emotional connection and separation, a relationship that led Nancy and countless women like her along a complicated transition path. On that path, women resolved quite early to live lives different from their mothers'. In their late teens and early twenties, they rebelled; then, through careers, they sought to attain power over their own lives as their mothers had not. In their thirties, well on the way toward establishing their own separate identities, they expressed a renewed desire for emotional connection with their mothers and with their mothers' ways.

This wasn't the end of it. At the conclusion of our interview, as I was about to leave, I asked Nancy what was the greatest issue for her, at the moment. She hesitated. "This is going to sound silly," she said, "but what I'm really agonizing over is whether to have a maid." Could Nancy be serious? This was not the sort of thing women were supposed to be worrying about—when there were so many other questions—like, would she ever get married, would she ever have children, what would she do about her career? I looked at her quizzically, and she continued: "My mother never had a maid; and my grandmother would be turning over in her grave if I got a maid. I mean, she *was* a maid. But I can afford it—and I really need some help with the housework. I don't know what to do."

I jotted this down without comment, thanked Nancy for her time, and left. I drove away feeling, once again, irritated. Nothing was fitting, pat, into what I had expected to hear. Images of lace curtains and old photographs stayed with me, but it would be several years before I realized that Nancy had mentioned her grandmothers several times. Oddly, I thought, she had mentioned that one of her greatest satisfactions came from having coffee brought to her by an office helper who happened to be the grandson of the people her grandmother had worked for as a maid.

Later, as I read history and talked to more women, I began to understand that Nancy's images of herself as a woman were closely tied not just to her own struggles and to her mother's, but also to her grandmothers'. I came to believe that the same dynamic, that same push-pull tension that existed between Nancy and her mother had also existed between Nancy's mother and *her* mother before her. That push-pull dynamic would also explain, historically, why one generation of women left the home for paying work but their daughters wished to remain primarily within it. For generation after generation of women, in this country, as much as daughters identified with their mothers as females, the bottom line was that they did not want to live the sorts of lives their mothers had led.

3

Historical Patterns: 1600–1900

When I began my interviews, I really did believe that my generation was the first to enter professional careers—even though both of my grandmothers worked outside the home. My mother's mother, born in the late nineteenth century, taught kindergarten and ran a girls' summer camp in New Hampshire; I remember her standing at the front of the wooden recreation hall at dusk before 150 girls, chanting a prayer as she lit the sabbath candles. With my grandfather, who sold insurance and ran the boys' camp across the lake, she also owned and managed a nearby inn. My father's mother, who immigrated as a young child with her parents from Eastern Europe, was crucial to her husband, my grandfather, in running their dry goods store in upstate New York because only she could read and write English.

My grandmothers' sisters also worked for a living. On my mother's side, my great-Aunt Rachel went to law school in Cleveland in the 1920s; she married, had five children, and ran a legal practice and a real estate firm until she died in the 1970s. On my father's side, my great-Aunt Leila, the youngest of six children, shocked us at a family dinner when, in her seventies, she confessed that fifty years earlier, she had met her husband, my great-Uncle Sam, when she was hitchhiking to the movies one Saturday night in Brooklyn. After a seven-year courtship, Leila married Sam, a locksmith, and had one son; she also worked until retirement as a full-time secretary in state government.

Despite my own family history, for some reason, in the 1950s for me, as for many of the women I interviewed, a strange sort of generational amnesia had set in. Even though when we were growing up, more married women were working outside the home than ever before, the belief

35

that women belonged at home was so powerful that it blocked out the fact that many women—even those in our own families—had ever lived in any other way.

In fact, as this chapter will show, since before this nation was founded, women have achieved in a wide range of roles. Early on, Native American women held religious, economic, and political power; among the colonists, in the seventeenth and eighteenth centuries, women worked in agriculture and in household economies. Not a few owned shops, taverns, or printing presses and some even served as doctors or argued cases in court. In the early nineteenth century, women took part in the great religious, social, and political movements of the day, and as the century progressed, women began to take paying jobs—not only on farms and in factories, but in education and in the legal and medical professions as well.

This chapter describes the experience of these early working women, then shows how, in the nineteenth century, as women moved into new realms, Americans began to deny the broad capabilities of females. With industrialization and the rapid social change accompanying it, the chapter suggests, men and women alike idealized stereotypical roles, seeking psychological refuge in safe-seeming images of the all-nurturing mothers and fiercely protective fathers they must have wished for in childhood.[1]

These mythic stereotypes were incorporated into law, social custom, and scientific theory, which reinforced a developing ideology that maintained that men and women belonged in very different spheres. According to that ideology, which deepened from the 1830s on, men were meant to operate in the outer world of work and politics, and women in the inner realm, at home.

Whether women were well-served in the domestic role was hotly debated in the nineteenth century, as it has been in modern times. For some middle-class women of the nineteenth century, the homemaker role may well have been an improvement over the tough farm, factory, or frontier lives their mothers had led. For other women, no doubt, domestic life was constraining and debilitating. In any case, as the ideology of domesticity for women deepened in the nineteenth century, increasing educational opportunity and new technology, combined with growing belief in individual rights, highlighted the contradictions between women's capabilities and their prescribed roles.

In the late nineteenth century, based largely on the experience of their mothers, many daughters of the Victorian middle class, some of them the grandmothers of the women I interviewed, sought very different sorts of lives. A growing number entered colleges and careers. While the majority of educated working women became teachers and settlement house workers, others entered medicine and law. Then as now, professional women debated about their similarities with and differences from men, and about what those similarities and differences meant in a society based on premises of freedom and equality.

The Colonial Era

When the colonists arrived in North America, they were sometimes outraged to see Native American women chopping wood, building houses, and even taking part in trade—tasks usually reserved for men in Europe. Accustomed to a system of male-dominated, settled agriculture, the colonists evidently did not understand these Native American societies had gender systems of their own. In most tribes, women were responsible for tasks related to food gathering and men took charge of the hunt. In some tribes, women were responsible for constructing tepees or lodges, chose their own husbands, and took part in trade with whites. Cherokee women had the right to speak in village councils and some accompanied the men when their tribes went to war. The Iroquois were organized in matrilineal clans which traced their descent from a common female ancestor; women controlled the food supply and hence, the economic organization of the tribe. Older Iroquois women could nominate council elders and depose chiefs, and many served as shamans and chiefs themselves.

Christian missionaries spent a good deal of energy trying to convert Native Americans to a male-dominated, hierarchical way of life, and under colonization, Native American women lost some of their power.[2] But European women in the colonies, many historians believe, had more freedom than did their mothers in England, and more leeway in their lives than many American women would be allowed later on.

Among the colonists, men were considered the heads of households, but women could own property and divorce their husbands for nonsupport or physical abuse. While men, generally, were responsible for planting and reaping and women for making bread, butter, clothing, soap, and medicine, in the harsh subsistence economy of the time, men and women commonly worked together.[3] Colonial Englishmen were less concerned with abstract notions like "femininity" than with concrete roles like "wife" or "neighbor," so women were free to perform any tasks that helped their families and were acceptable to their husbands.[4]

In the North, farmers' wives commonly worked in the fields, and in the South, planters' wives tended their own herb gardens and acted as doctors for their families and slaves. Among the Puritans, women's legal identities were absorbed by their husbands' but women, considered "deputy husbands," could vote in town meetings in their husbands' absence.

37

New England women also commonly settled accounts, commanded field hands, negotiated with Native Americans, and filled orders in stores. In the Chesapeake colonies of Virginia, North Carolina, and Maryland, husbands helped with the spinning and weaving, named their wives as executors of their estates, and, in wills, sometimes left them with more land and property than the law required.[5]

At a time when most immigrants were male indentured servants under the age of sixteen, various colonies tried to insure stability and community by encouraging women to settle, sometimes granting them land of their own. In the 1600s, to entice men to marry and farm, Lord Baltimore of Maryland offered a planter 100 acres, a wife brought another 100 acres, and a child, 50 acres more. Female heads of families were often treated the same as men. Women who paid their own way to Pennsylvania could receive 75 acres—and more if they brought along servants and children. Salem, Massachusetts, briefly offered "maid lotts" to single women and South Carolina gave land to indentured servants who completed their terms of service.[6]

Other women simply took land to farm. In 1715, when a local sheriff challenged a group of women squatters near the Schohairie River in upstate New York, they armed themselves with brooms, rakes, and hoes, dragged him through barnyards, rode him out of town on a rail, and finally dumped him on a bridge.[7]

At this time, women were expected to help support themselves and their families, and colonial governments formally recognized the importance of women's contributions. In 1646, for example, the Massachusetts General Court assessed double damages of anyone convicted of destroying timber or coal, which were associated with men's work, but the court assessed triple damages for the destruction of fruit trees or linen or woolen garments, which were associated with women's work.[8]

In New England, so many single women worked at spinning that the term "spinster," which had originally meant "female spinner," became the legal term for "unmarried woman." Poor women were pushed to work in "manufactories" to keep them off the charity rolls; others worked as domestic servants or in shops. Unmarried daughters helped their fathers in stores or worked as servants or teachers; with skilled labor in short supply, colonial wives and daughters also worked in traditionally male domains as blacksmiths, silversmiths, shoemakers, tanners, printers, distillers, woodworkers, leatherworkers, and barbers. Widows typically took charge of large farms, businesses, and shops.[9]

In the late 1600s and early 1700s, women operated stores that sold groceries, pastries, dry goods, hardware, and liquor. Several dozen women owned print shops; six were the official printers for the colonial governments and sixteen published newspapers. In Boston, in 1690, women ran 40 percent of the taverns and at least thirty women had the rights to saw lumber and manufacture products.[10] In 1714 (when Boston had a population of 34,000), women held more than a third of the thirty-four licenses for inns and made up a third of the forty-one retailers of alcoholic beverages; in the 1760s in Philadelphia as many as 17 percent of the licenses for taverns went to women.[11]

In 1733 a group of New York businesswomen or "she-merchants," as they called themselves, organized to complain that they had been discriminated against. As taxpayers, they believed they ought to be invited to dine at the English Governor's Court, just as the "husbands" were. They wrote to a weekly journal, "We have the vanity to think we can be full as Entertaining, and make as brave a Defence in Case of an Invasion and perhaps not turn Taile so soon as some of them."[12]

Colonial women were by no means restricted to the trades and business. In an era when few men or women received formal training, there were at least thirty-five female "doctresses" in the colonies and, some suggest, more women than men acted as nurses, apothecaries, unlicensed physicians, and midwives. While men performed most of the surgery, women so dominated midwifery that in 1646, a Maine court prosecuted and fined a man for serving in that role.[13]

Also at this time, some women argued their own cases in court; a few exceptional women became entrepreneurs, lawyers, or statesmen. Margaret Brent, a wealthy Englishwoman who established her own plantation in Maryland, won most of the 137 lawsuits she argued; she was later appointed executrix of the estate of Governor Leonard Calvert and played a crucial role in resolving numerous political disputes. Mary Musgrove, the daughter of a Native American mother and an English father, mediated between the Creek tribe and the colonial government of James Oglethorpe in Georgia to maintain peace.[14]

In large part, women had to play broad roles simply to survive. Perhaps colonial women were valued because most settlers were male and there were too few women to go around. Or maybe it was that the settlers, most of whom were Protestants, believed in a family based on mutual respect and shared responsibility. In any case, while in theory colonial women played set roles in a hierarchical system, it appears that in practice they had more freedom in their daily lives than would women in some generations to come.[15]

This is not to say that the colonial era was a "golden age" for women. In seventeenth-century Maryland, women typically had an average of eight children apiece but half of those children died before reaching age 20.[16] Women tobacco workers in the Chesapeake region faced difficult labor conditions and often died of such diseases as malaria, influenza, and dysentery; indentured servants rarely lived into their forties. African women, taken from their homes in what are now Nigeria, Angola, and Biafra, were forced in the late 1600s to work as slaves in tobacco, rice, and indigo fields; many suffered rape and other sexual exploitation.[17]

By the 1700s, a market economy was developing and, historians suggest, Euro-American women's household contributions were coming to be seen as distinct from—and less valuable than—enterprises that brought in cash.[18] At this time, only 10 percent of white women worked for pay outside the home—most of them widows and spinsters. While in some letters and diaries, husbands and wives called each other "my good wife," "my sweet wife," or "my most sweet husband," other letters reveal that many women felt subordinate or inferior to men.[19]

Puritan court records show that at least 128 men were tried for abusing their wives. One Maine resident was tried for kicking and beating his wife with a club when she refused to feed a pig; an Ipswich man tried to poison his wife. Although two colonists were put to death for murdering their wives, men found guilty of lesser offenses against wives were usually simply fined, admonished, or placed under supervision.[20]

Most historians agree, however, that during the Revolutionary War, the Euro-American woman's role was elevated. In part, that was because home manufacturing took on a new importance as a way of reducing colonial dependence on British imports. Also, with men off fighting, women had to take on more of the farming and wage-earning tasks.[21] During the war, women wrote political tracts or served as spies; in 1780, Philadelphia women created a women's organization and raised substantial sums for the troops by going door to door.[22] Some twenty thousand women marched with the British and American armies, usually as cooks, nurses, doctors, laundresses, guides, seamstresses, and porters.

Molly Hays nursed her husband and others who collapsed on the battlefield; she was nicknamed "Molly Pitcher" by thirsty soldiers who called her when they needed water. Nancy Hart Morgan, who had a husband and eight children, lulled five Tories with homemade whisky; she shot some of them and captured the rest with their own weapons. Deborah Sampson Gannett, believed to have been a black woman with white Pilgrim ancestors, assumed a man's name and joined the American army as a soldier; after she was wounded, found out, and forced to resign, she took a different man's name and joined up again.[23]

During the war, after the governor of Virginia offered liberation, many slaves left their masters, thus enlarging the community of freed blacks in the North and upper South. At this time, Phyllis Wheatley, an African-born slave raised much like a daughter in a white household, became widely known in America and England for her poetry. Native American women, in general, fared worse. Most tribes supported the British in order to resist white settlement in the West, so Native American wives lost fighting husbands, brothers, and sons, and tribal territory as well.[24]

After the war, women who had contributed to the patriots' war effort were sometimes honored as heroines and received army pensions.[25] One British officer wrote to his general that even if the British were to defeat all the men in America, they would still have to contend with the women. At this time, many women expected to be treated equally with men. In a number of states, women could vote and hold political office and women increasingly decided for themselves whom—and whether—to marry.[26]

In the late 1700s, many white women postponed or avoided marriage by supporting themselves as teachers or factory workers.[27] Some single women went to work because so many bachelors had been lost to war or westward migration that marriage was not an option. Other women, encouraged by government leaders like Alexander Hamilton, who favored industrialization, worked in factories as a patriotic duty. Farmers could make good use of the money their daughters earned to purchase newly invented farm machinery and clothing, which were now cheaper to buy than to make at home. Many believed young women with some work experience would make better wives and mothers.

Farm families began to encourage their daughters to move to mill towns. In Lowell, Massachusetts, young women lived in supervised boardinghouses and worked to save money for their trousseaus, help pay off mortgages, or send their younger brothers to college. To many young women, these factory jobs offered economic independence, geographic mobility, regular hours, relatively high wages, companionship with other women, and adventure. Factory work, seen at that time as respectable, also left open the possibility of marriage—unlike teaching or domestic work, then the most common occupations for women, which often precluded it.[28]

Meanwhile, after the Revolutionary War, public and private schools were increasingly opened to girls. While these schools taught mainly "wifely" duties, many girls also studied grammar, rhetoric, history, geography, mathematics, and natural sciences. One fourth of this generation of native-born white women became teachers themselves at some point in their lives.[29] Others became missionaries, authors, and leaders of early nineteenth-century religious and/or reform movements. Judith Sargent Murray, the daughter of a prosperous Massachusetts merchant, was educated along with her brother who was preparing to attend Harvard College. In 1790 she called for "a new era of female history" in which

41

women would have an important role to play in the world beyond the home.[30]

Despite the record of these early American women, the founding fathers deemed females incapable of making decisions for the public good and granted them little voice in the new government. A generation later, factory work— in fact, any paying work—would be considered less than respectable for women. In the 1830s, Alexis de Tocqueville commented that "in no country has such constant care been taken as in America to trace two clearly distinct lines of action for the sexes."[31]

By the 1840s, when women had once run every kind of shop, most now operated stores that catered only to females. Medical schools had taken over midwifery; medicine and nursing were considered less than genteel and law was closed to women. The media preached the gospel of true womanhood: purity, piety, and domesticity.[32] "There has been no female lawyer and probably will be none," the *New York Daily Tribune* proclaimed in 1845.[33] A Boston newspaper editorialized that with women working, "the times are out of joint." And according to the *Boston Courier,* women who worked were assuming what had been, "from immemorial time," the prerogatives, attributes, and duties of the other sex.[34]

These attitudes would prevail throughout the nineteenth century in what came to be called the Cult of the Lady, the Cult of True Womanhood, or the Ideology of Domesticity—of which more than just remnants exist today.

The Ideology of Domesticity

Some historians trace the idea that women belong at home to the rise of cities, guilds, and mercantilism in Europe. According to Sara Evans, the image of "pretty gentlewoman" in the North and "the lady" in the South emerged along with the economic success of some eighteenth-century families. Jeanne Boydston points out that in 1800, with more than a third of the population under ten years old, America was "a nation of children"; as husbands became more involved in earning money, "Republican motherhood" was idealized as women's most significant role.[35]

It was in the 1830s, however, that American writers began to describe the world as a "brutal environment of untrammeled capitalism" from which man "retreated to the home" for "physical and spiritual refreshment" to be cared by woman . . . whose mission was to ensure an orderly, tranquil environment for her mate.[36]

As the nation industrialized, historians explain, reproduction and production, once centered in the home, were divided. The family increasingly came to be seen as a center for emotion and personal expression, and the workplace, for economic gain. Men were removed from contact with their children during long and exhausting days, so women assumed greater responsibility for child rearing, and soon women's role as mothers became paramount in their lives.

Whereas in colonial days, husbands and wives had shared much of the labor, by the 1830s, differences between men and women were increasingly emphasized. John Ruskin, an English writer, art critic, and social reformer of the time, described men's power as "active, progressive, defensive." The man, Ruskin wrote, "is eminently the doer, the creator, the discoverer, the defender. His intellect is for speculation and invention; his energy for adventure, for war and for conquest." A woman's power, Ruskin wrote, "is for rule, not for battle, and her intellect is not for invention or creation, but for sweet ordering, arrangement and decision. . . . By her office and place, she is protected from all danger and temptation."[37]

Women were asked to give up wealth, frivolity, and fashion to prepare themselves for the great calling of motherhood. "The mother was the obvious source of everything that would save or damn the child— the historical and spiritual destiny of America lay in her hands."[38]

Along with this enlarged view of motherhood came changes in attitudes toward sexuality. In the seventeenth and eighteenth centuries, sex manuals had suggested that women, like men, had needs and desires that should be fulfilled. By the mid-nineteenth century, however, a new literature on sexual behavior warned against too much sexual activity and advised limiting it to procreation.[39]

At this time, visiting Europeans were struck by the rigid divisions between married men and women, noting that at social gatherings women were compelled by public opinion to separate from men after dinner. In the American middle class, wives' daily lives were now largely circumscribed "within the narrow circle of domestic interests and duties beyond which they were forbidden to step."[40]

Why the Shift?

Some historians believe that in the early nineteenth century, the differing roles men and women already played were merely thrown into relief as factories replaced the home as the center for manufacturing. But according to historian Gerda Lerner, the adage that woman's place was in the home "took on a certain aggressiveness and shrillness . . . precisely when increasing numbers of poor women left their homes to become factory workers." Now, a new managerial middle class could afford to allow its wives to emulate the leisured European aristocracy. "Idleness," once a disgrace in the eyes of society, became "a status symbol."[41]

Alice Kessler-Harris writes that changing conditions in the workplace made paying work less appealing than it might once have seemed; in the 1830s, as factory owners began to pay off their startup debts, they cut wages, lengthened working hours, and speeded up production to the point where only women who *had* to work—the poor and immigrants—would.[42]

Taking a broader perspective, Carroll Smith-Rosenberg suggests that "against a backdrop of relentless uncertainty and change, bourgeois men and women sought to express their experiences, resist change, and assert order."[43]

According to historian Steven Mintz,

At a time when society had seemingly lost the stabilizing influences of many institutional and communal controls, people looked to the home as a bulwark against disruptive social change, as a source of order and morality, a counterbalance to the individualistic and commercial pressures buffeting modern life.

Seen as a sanctuary, "the family was invested with awesome psychological and ideological responsibilities."[44]

In a more psychoanalytic interpretation, historian Sarah Stage writes that "in a competitive industrial society which demanded aggressive optimism from its men, it became convenient, perhaps necessary, to externalize anxiety." By glorifying male strength and emphasizing female vulnerability and weakness, Stage explains, "men projected their own very real fears and anxieties onto women."[45] In many cases, women accepted them.

Overall, I would suggest, the ideology of domesticity and separation of spheres came as the result of two dynamic but contradictory trends that were exaggerated by industrialization and immigration. One trend was a natural push toward discovery, growth, and autonomy which can bring opportunity but which may be accompanied by instability and uncertainty; the countertrend was a natural pull toward tradition, stasis, and emotional or family connection. In the nineteenth century, rapidly increasing industrial and social change was countered, on many levels, by the idealization of a safe-seeming past and of oversimplified, set gender roles.

Indeed, one reason the ideology of domesticity may have felt comfortable to the Victorians was that it expressed a synthesis of several sets of older beliefs: the Aristotelian notion that women are "body," designed for childbearing, whereas men are "soul," responsible for reason and intellect; the physiological theories of the Middle Ages holding that women should not be sexually aroused because they were sexually more avid than men, hence dangerous; and the Protestant view of the home as a school for character and morals.[46]

The developing ideology also incorporated a new machine-age scientific theory known as the conservation of energy. According to that theory, roughly explained, human beings, like machines, were closed energy systems, in which one part drew energy from another. This meant that the brain and reproductive systems competed for energy. As a consequence, if men, considered creatures of reason, engaged in sex, they lost brain power. If women, designed for procreation, used their brains, they lost reproductive power.

All of the above, combined with growing anxiety over the instability of sex roles and belief in the efficiency of new industrial systems based on the separation of parts, mechanization, and specialization, contributed to an ideology that assigned men and women very separate spheres. Women were now believed morally and spiritually superior to men because of their life-giving natural powers—but at the same time, women were considered physically weaker than men, inferior in cognitive ability, and wholly unsuited to work outside the home.[47]

In the mid-nineteenth century, the ideology of domesticity deepened. Possibly to conquer their own fears, doctors, scientists, and writers idealized women as sickly, neurasthenic, depressed, incapable, and uninterested in sex, with nervous problems that meant they could not work outside the home and should not be educated. One doctor described women with chlorisis, an ailment that combined the symptoms of anemia and mild hysteria, as "delicate and sensitive, stricken by a disease from which they deeply suffer, but which often leaves their beauty untouched, or even heightens its attractions."[48]

In the *Blithedale Romance,* written in 1852, Nathaniel Hawthorne described a sickly heroine as a woman whose "impalpable grace lay so singularly, between disease and beauty." In *The Scarlet Letter,* written in 1850, he called women of this period less robust than their mothers and criticized healthy women as "of coarser fiber." According to modern historian Sarah Stage, as the "wan and wasted" woman became a perverse ideal of feminine beauty, healthy Victorian women drank vinegar and ate arsenic to achieve the pallor and blazing eyes of tuberculosis victims.[49]

Doctors often blamed women's many ailments on sex, and the womb, while revered, was also viewed as the center of disease. In 1879, Henry Maudsley wrote that "while woman preserves her sex, she will necessarily be feebler than man, and, having her special bodily mental characters, will have, to a certain extent, her own sphere of activity."[50] A woman's reproductive system came to be seen "as a sacred trust, one that she must constantly guard in the interest of the race."

At this time, Stage explains, "the uterus, considered the controlling organ in the female body, took on an importance which reduced women to simply a vessel, an organ bearer." In the words of one doctor of the time, it was as if "the almighty, in creating the female sex, had taken the uterus and built up a woman around it." Many Victorians believed that menstruation and pregnancy were "fountains of power" and that a woman could neither escape nor master her sexual system. That meant that normal exercise was pathological for women, and further reinforced the belief that women had to live lives "apart."[51]

Such beliefs continued in part because poor obstetrics, inadequate diet, and venereal disease led to all sorts of uterine ailments which did in fact weaken women. Poor working conditions for women also caused health problems. One nineteenth-century doctor wrote that overwork, routinized work, and certain body positions imposed by some work situations led to menstrual dysfunction, uterine disorders, and insanity.

Working women were nearly always undernourished; those who used sewing machines developed spinal problems, digestive disorders, and consumption. Saleswomen, forced to stand ten to twelve hours a day, suffered from varicose veins. Textile workers contracted brown lung disease, were scalped by machines and burned by flying cinders, and their hands were mangled by untended machinery. The death rate for female wage earners was more than twice that of non-wage earners, and a third higher than that of working men. As the numbers of working women increased, conditions deteriorated and the idea that work was dangerous for women became, for good reason, more prevalent.[52]

What is more, as the ideology of domesticity deepened, women who worked outside the home—most of whom were unmarried—came to be seen as a threat to the family and to Victorian moral values. In part, this was because, by 1869, so many men had died in the Civil War or moved West that a quarter million more unmarried women than men lived on the Eastern seaboard. Since one-third of all women over twenty-one were not married, a congressional witness testified in 1883, they would probably remain single and have to work for a living.[53] These working women, who were paid less than men, created a labor surplus which, it was argued, depressed wages for all workers. Low wages would discourage men from marrying; this, in turn, would, theoretically, leave even more women single, poor, and forced into prostitution or other crime. In this era of Victorian sensibility, there were also concerns about the morality of men and women working together and about living conditions in tenements and boarding houses where some 16 percent of women were "adrift."[54]

To keep women out of the Eastern workforce, one editor encouraged single women to move west as teachers or domestics. A union representative testified that to preserve jobs for men, the males in his shop were asked to either marry their single female coworkers or find them husbands. Another proposal was to tax single men and use the proceeds to support single women.[55]

Yet another factor in the deepening ideology of domesticity in the nineteenth century was immigration. Between 1840 and 1860, 4.2 million foreigners—six times as many as in the preceding twenty years—entered the country.[56] This, combined with a reading of new Darwinian theories which brought up concerns of native-born white Americans about the purity of their race, further heightened and romanticized the belief that motherhood—especially in the white middle class—was women's most moral and important function.

Other "scientific" beliefs based on Darwinism were used to buttress that view. In 1873, Dr. Edward C. Clarke wrote that the "mental divergence of the sexes" is a positive sign of civilization. "Differentiation is Nature's method of ascent," he wrote. "We should cultivate the difference of the sexes, not try to hide or abolish it." Exposing women to education was dangerous, he believed, because it would overstimulate their relatively undeveloped brains. The neurologist George Beard observed that intellectual exertion was difficult for the civilized woman because she had evolved to the point at which she "uses her brain but little and in trivial matters, and her muscles scarcely at all." Another physician asked, "Why should we spoil a good mother by making an ordinary grammarian?"[57]

The overall picture, then, is that in the face of great change, increasing individualization and atomization, Americans idealized women's family role. "Sons found themselves in a world neither they nor their fathers understood . . . bourgeois daughters, who no longer worked side-by-side with men on the family farm or in the artisan shop, developed a gender-specific sense of time and space, of permissible and forbidden behavior."[58]

By the 1850s, the multifunctional traditional family had shrunk. Nuclear and isolated, Carroll Smith-Rosenberg explains, it had lost all but its most intimate sexual and emotional functions. This new family, considered the basic unit of society, was viewed as a miniature state with just one head—the husband—who represented it in the world outside.

This view was firmly articulated during the 1866 congressional debate on suffrage, when one senator argued that women should not be allowed to vote. "When God married our first parents in the garden," he said, they were made "bone of one bone and flesh of one flesh . . . and the whole theory of government and society proceeds upon the assumption that their interests are one." Freedom for woman, he asserted, would "put her . . . in an adversary position to man." This would "convert all the now harmonious elements of society into a state of war, and make every home a hell on earth." During the same debate, Senator Peter Frelinghuysen of New Jersey insisted that women had "a higher and holier" function than to engage in the turmoil of public life. "Their mission is at home," he said, "by their blandishments and their love to assuage the passions of men."[59]

At this time, in the mid-nineteenth century, most married women had no legal existence apart from their husbands; in most states, women could not vote, sue, sign contracts, own businesses, or execute wills on their own. Women who publicly addressed mixed audiences were often greeted with shock and hostility, and women who worked for wages earned one third to one half of what men did.[60]

In the South, slave women endured sexual abuse at the hands of their white masters. White males' guilt, Evans suggests, was a factor in their insistence on white women's purity and rigid separation from the public sphere. Early on, black women, who worked alongside men, had placed no stigma on fieldwork, but as the ideology of domesticity developed, they began to bitterly resent the fact that they were not considered "women" by the dominant culture and they, too, "endeavored to attain modesty, sexual purity, innocence and a submissive manner." (Once slavery ended, many black women workers refused to work in the fields, and many white Southerners expressed surprise that it became a matter of pride for black men to support their wives and families.)[61]

Among Native Americans, as early as the 1820s, leaders in at least one tribe had begun to insist that women adhere to white norms of domesticity and allowed only males to vote on tribal matters.[62] At this time, most women, in all walks of life, viewed suffering, self-sacrifice, and self-control as their major avenue of transcendence.[63]

Yet, despite the predominant ideology, or perhaps because of it, especially in the North and West, women led industrial strikes, petitioned for property rights, and taught school. They fought for health reform, and attacked the double standard of sexual morality and the victimization of prostitutes. Mothers joined together to discuss child rearing, and large numbers of women entered Christian benevolent associations to reform through religion. Women worked in the antislavery movement, out of which developed a fledgling movement for women's rights.[64]

In fact, over the course of the nineteenth century, women left the home in ever increasing numbers. While some of these women struggled against their prescribed roles, others explained their work outside the home as in keeping with, even enhancing, the societal ideology that commanded women's presence within it.[65]

Differing Views

Many early women reformers, whom sociologist Alice Rossi has dubbed the "Moral Crusader Feminists," not only accepted the nineteenth-century Protestant belief that women were more moral and nurturing than men, but used that belief to justify their activities outside the home. Historian Nancy Cott suggests that many women in the early 1800s became involved in religious movements of the day because this allowed them to operate in the spiritual realm but also assert themselves by becoming part of a community beyond the home, based on an authority higher than their husbands'—a heavenly one. In the crusade against illicit sexuality, Smith-Rosenberg writes, Victorian matrons could legitimately express anti-male sentiments and receive emotional redress for the passivity imposed on them.[66]

Also in the early 1800s, women worked outside the home on behalf of abolition and women's property rights, many of them adhering to a philosophy which Alice Rossi calls "enlightenment rationalism." That philosophy, which underlies the beliefs set forth in the U.S. Constitution, draws on the ideas set forth by the eighteenth-century English philosopher John Locke who viewed individual rights as basic to a democratic society. Enlightenment rationalists believed that the ideology of domesticity prevented women from living full lives by denying them the rights and privileges enjoyed by men.[67]

A third, broad-ranging public stance was taken by feminists who, based on socialist philosophy, advocated emancipation from the conventions and inequities they believed were imposed by industrial capitalism.[68]

Throughout the nineteenth century and well into the twentieth, women would draw on and debate these differing views. A central issue in these debates was whether women were best served in an elevated family role or in one that allowed them the same rights and responsibilities as men.

One early proponent of an elevated family role for women was Catharine Beecher, an early nineteenth-century educator who believed that women should be educated as expert homemakers. By dominating in the home, Beecher believed, women could bring up their sons to dominate outside it. Women would be saviors of society because "the mother writes the character of the future man." In Beecher's view, the wife was "the heart, whose energies may turn for good or for evil the destinies of a nation." If women were virtuous and intelligent, she believed, men would "surely be the same."[69]

The transcendentalist writer and philosopher Margaret Fuller, however, wrote that women should be autonomous and recognized in the economic, political, and social realms as individuals in their own right. Women's minds and bodies should be "fully developed" so that women would be "fit" for any calling. "Women should be sea captains if they will," she wrote, and men should "remove arbitrary barriers" so that individual talents, not gender, would lead to a new social order.[70] Still other women saw sexual freedom as tantamount to women's equality and power.

In the 1850s and 1860s these different views led to serious divisions within the abolition and suffrage movements. As the century progressed, these philosophies and values and others continued to divide women within and among themselves.

Women Leave the Home

As the ideology of domesticity deepened, in the 1840s and 1850s, middle-class women began to enter colleges and medical schools. Some became teachers, missionaries, or writers; Harriot K. Hunt, Mary Gove Nichols, and Elizabeth Blackwell pioneered as women physicians and health reformers. Hunt, credited as the first woman to lecture publicly on physiology to women, was opposed by many who considered any discussion of the human body by women to be "indelicate." In 1846, she set up a clinic specializing in women's diseases in New York City, arguing that women should be treated by women. Along with other women doctors, she embraced preventive medicine as women's special province.[71] Dorothea Dix, a New England woman, launched a crusade to save the mentally ill by having them institutionalized rather than confining them to jails.[72]

During the Civil War, women took jobs in service, office, and retail trades, and the proportion of women teachers increased dramatically—a trend that had begun earlier, when men began to choose higher-paying factory jobs. The federal government also opened jobs to women; in 1862, the Treasury Department hired women to cut currency, and in the Post Office eight of twenty-five new employees were women.[73]

Also during the Civil War, women in both North and South formed some twenty thousand aid societies to supply the armies with food, clothing, supplies, and money. Nursing was legitimized as a profession, and Dr. Blackwell founded a central relief association that trained nurses to do volunteer work in hospitals. Under her auspices and others', some 3,200 women became nurses or administrators.[74]

Dorothea Dix, now superintendent of nurses in an army regiment, hired only nurses who were "over thirty, plain and thickwaisted," because she was worried that younger, more attractive women would be too tempting to the soldiers. Mary Bickerdyke and Clara Barton founded their own organizations of nurses; Barton, who organized first-aid facilities and collected supplies, often short-circuited military routine to get supplies to the front; in 1864 she became head nurse with Butler's Army of the James and won a reputation as "Angel of the Battlefield." In the Confederate Army, Sally Tomkins ran a hospital and was commissioned a captain; Ella Newson supervised a military hospital in Kentucky.[75]

During the war, in the North, women's rights leaders collected 400,000 signatures on a petition to encourage Congress to abolish slavery. Hundreds of younger women went south as missionaries, largely to bring Victorian values to freed slaves in territories captured by the Union Army. As during the Revolutionary War, white women ran farms, plantations, and businesses.[76] In various states, women took the places of men in colleges that in peacetime would not have accepted them.

After the Civil War, women increasingly entered colleges and professional schools. Elmira, Smith, and Vassar were founded in the East to offer women curricula comparable to those of men's schools. By 1870, Wisconsin, Michigan, Missouri, Iowa, Kansas, Indiana, Minnesota, and California had opened coed state universities; they admitted women largely because male enrollments were dropping as a result of an economic depression and complaints about curricula.[77]

That year, eleven thousand women students accounted for 21 percent of all college students; by 1880, the 40,000 women enrolled made up 32 percent of the total.[78] Most women college graduates entered such growing "female" professions as teaching and nursing; others joined the settlement house, women's college club, and reform organizations that were proliferating in the cities. A small number began to pave the way in law and medicine as professional schools opened to them.

One medical college, founded in 1857, which trained "hydropatic" physicians in a water-cure process, recruited women students by advertising in the pages of a feminist journal and offering scholarships.[79] In 1864, the New England Female Medical College became the first to award an M.D. to an African-American woman, Rebecca Lee; three years later, the Women's Medical College of Pennsylvania—established in 1850 as the first medical school for women—awarded the second.[80]

In the late 1800s, because most "orthodox" medical colleges admitted only men, women doctors increasingly started their own schools. By 1895, there were nineteen medical schools that admitted only women. While early on women were deemed too delicate to study alongside men, as standards in women's medical colleges rose, men began to argue that there was no *need* for men's schools to admit women.[81]

Still, while a few women's medical colleges offered women educations comparable to those offered at the best men's schools, most women's medical schools were sectarian or marginal. Aimed mainly at earning profits, they shortened their courses and made it easy to enter and graduate. One could, quite legally, get a medical diploma and open an office after taking just two five-month courses of lectures and passing only five of nine oral exams, and many doctors graduated without ever seeing a patient or a disease.[82]

By 1880, in this country, there were some 2,500 women surgeons and physicians, who accounted for 2.8 percent of the nation's total. In 1893, 42 percent of Tufts Medical School graduates were women, as were 19 percent of the doctors in Boston. By 1900, women physicians numbered 7,000 and made up between 4 and 5 percent of the profession nationally—almost the same percentage as in 1960.[83]

After the Civil War, women also began to enter the legal profession. In most states, one could become a lawyer by reading law in a law office and passing an exam. Some women worked as teachers during the day and studied law at night; others became lawyers by working in their husbands' law offices. Still others entered law schools which were beginning to develop at this time.

While elite law schools such as Harvard and Yale remained closed to women well into the twentieth century, in 1869, the law schools at Washington University in St. Louis and the University of Iowa admitted their first women. The following year, Union College of Law (Northwestern) graduated its first woman lawyer and both the University of Michigan and Boston University admitted their first women law students. In 1872, Charlotte Ray, the first black woman to receive a law degree, graduated from Howard University Law School. By the end of the century, women could attend Hastings College of Law in San Francisco, and law schools at the University of Pennsylvania and New York University, among others.[84]

While in the nineteenth century most employed women worked in agriculture, as domestics, or as teachers, by 1881 there were 75 women lawyers in the country, and by 1891, more than 208. The number of women in law was far smaller than that of women in medicine, historians say, largely because law was deemed less in keeping with women's special spiritual, healing role than was medicine.[85]

Some historians describe the entry of women into these professions as a natural progression, made possible by growing educational opportunity and technological developments such as gas stoves and indoor plumbing, new transportation networks, and the rise of cities, which opened new work possibilities and freed young women from many of the household chores their mothers performed. For most women, however, entering these fields was by no means a simple process.

Some early professional women had the support of their families, but many faced opposition from their parents, educational institutions, the courts, and society at large. Mary Church's father, a black entrepreneur in Chicago, ordered her not to become a teacher but she did so anyway—and went on to become a leading suffragist. Elizabeth Mosher's mother declared that she would rather see her daughter shut up in a lunatic asylum than have her attend medical school. Bertha Van Hoosen became an obstetrician and surgeon even though her mother cried at the mention of medical school and her father refused to pay for it.[86] When Elizabeth Blackwell entered Geneva Medical College in 1847, "A hush fell upon the class as if each member had been stricken with paralysis. A deathlike stillness prevailed during the lecture, and only the newly arrived student took notes."[87]

More than twenty years later, in 1869, when Dean Ann Preston of the Women's Medical College of Pennsylvania and her thirty-five female students attended a teaching clinic at the Pennsylvania Hospital, men jeered, whispered, stamped their feet, threw stones and tinfoil, and spat tobacco juice. The following year, the medical faculty at the University of Michigan strongly opposed the presence of women medical students; they argued for separate classes, and male students referred to their female colleagues as "hen-medics." At this time, many women went abroad for training because most good medical schools would not admit them.[88]

The legal profession was hardly more welcoming. In its December 1872 term, in deciding a lawsuit brought by Myra Bradwell, the U.S. Supreme Court refused to overturn an Illinois law which prohibited women from practicing law. The "paramount destiny of women is to fulfill the benign offices of wife and mother," one justice wrote. "This is the law of the Creator." Seven years later, Charlotte Ray was forced to close her law office in Washington, D.C., for lack of business. It took a lawsuit brought by two California women, Laura Force de Gordon and Clara Foltz, to open the Hastings College of Law to women; Emma Gillett and Ellen Spencer went so far as to found the Washington College of Law which admitted men but was aimed at the legal education of women.[89]

What motivated these women to buck the tide in order to pursue professions?

Some women who entered medicine between 1840 and 1870 came from reform families or from families with "unorthodox" social and political ideas. Others saw medicine as a way to combine a religious calling with community reform; still others were "stubborn nonbelievers" who loved science or were fascinated by the study of human nature. There

were those who had had a childhood or adolescent encounter with ill-
ness—their own or that of a close friend or relative.[90]

Most early women doctors came from middle- or upper middle-class
families; not infrequently, a father or uncle was a doctor. (Later in the
century, a daughter occasionally followed in her physician mother's footsteps.) Early African-American doctors usually came from socially privileged families; a few came from families that encouraged their daughters
to become educated to avoid domestic service. Eliza Greer, a former
slave, worked her way through medical school. Susan LaFlesche Picotte,
who, in 1889, became the first Native American to earn an M.D., was
the daughter of influential Omaha parents who supported bringing white
education to their Nebraska reservation.[91]

Several early professional women confessed to "the power of sheer
ambitions." One doctor wanted "social status," "growth and advancement," and to be her "own boss." In an article for *Lippincott's* in 1888,
lawyer Belva Lockwood, the first woman to practice before the Supreme
Court, wrote that she "possessed all the ambition of a man."[92]

Whatever the individual circumstances, some historians suggest that
as a group, many nineteenth-century feminists chose education and careers in rebellion against the constraints imposed on women by Victorian
family life.[93]

In the late nineteenth century, daughters of domestic ladies "resisted
the lady-like decorum of their mothers," writes historian Peter Filene.
"Maternal teachings to be a lady carried unconvincing authority when
uttered from a sickbed." Without realizing why, the girls ran outside to
jump off rooftops or play baseball or watch their fathers at work in law
offices, banks, or stores.[94] Now, young single women could attend school,
earn independent income, and travel unchaperoned; many were so afraid
of the constraints of marriage that they experienced a "marriage
trauma." Their letters express fears about losing their liberty, and link
marriage with death, loss of self, and the dangers of childbirth.[95]

Not surprisingly, many of these "new" women never married; with
a record 13 percent of women remaining single, the late-century generation was what one historian calls "the least married group of women in
United States history." Encouraged by a growing literature written by
some of the more radical members of their mothers' generation, many
entered professions or joined the movements for temperance, social purity, and women's equality largely in response to the doctrine of separation of spheres that had kept their mothers at home.[96]

Jane Addams, the renowned settlement house leader, for instance,
wrote that she had become a social worker in part because growing up
she had felt "simply smothered and sickened with advantages." It was

"like eating a sweet dessert the first thing in the morning," she wrote, and she had felt that she was "helplessly sinking into a nervous depression."[97]

Elizabeth Blackwell confessed in her autobiography that she became a doctor in part to keep herself "permanently distracted from the temptation to marry."[98] Asked why she had become a suffragist, author Mary Austin wrote: "It was seeing what my mother had to go through that started me." Another suffragist wrote, "It was being sacrificed to the boys in the family that got me going." And another: "my father was the old fashioned kind."[99] Lorine Pruette, an economist and writer, had seen her mother abused; by the time she was six, she "knew that men could do something terrible to women. . . and flamed with the injustice of it."[100]

In *These Modern Women,* a collection compiled from a series of articles written for the *Nation* magazine in the 1920s, most women said they decided to enter professions because of what they had seen of their mothers' lives.

Crystal Eastman, a lawyer, described her mother as powerful, yet a frustrated schoolteacher; Kate L. Gregg wrote that she had resolved to get a Ph.D. based on the experience of her mother, who, married to a man who was perennially drunk, threatened to shoot herself if she was alone when her sixth child was born.

By the time writer and suffragist Inez Hayes Irwin was fourteen, she was appalled by the "monotony and the soullessness" of the lives of women who had too many children too soon. Their lives, she wrote, were symbolized by the mid-Sunday dinner.

> That plethoric meal—the huge roast, the blood pouring out of it as the man of the house carved; the many vegetables, all steaming, the heavy pudding. And when the meal was finished—the table a shambles that positively made me shudder—the smooth replete retreat of the men to their cushioned chairs, their Sunday papers, their vacuous nap, while the women removed all vestiges of the horror.[101]

These professional women, like thousands of others in the late nineteenth century, struggled to break free of the constraints that limited their Victorian mothers. Then as now, there was much debate as to how best to do so.

Early professional women—who practiced at the height of the Victorian era—often struggled with the question of whether they ought to emphasize their similarities with or differences from men. Historian Regina Morantz-Sanchez explains that by the middle of the nineteenth century, women appeared especially suited to medicine because it combined the alleged authority of science with what seemed to be an inherently feminine dedication to the alleviation of suffering. Dr. Ella Flagg Young observed that "every woman is born a doctor. Men have to study to become one." Dr. Elizabeth Blackwell wrote that the "spiritual power of maternity" made women morally superior to men and that "the true physician," male or female, "must possess the essential qualities of maternity."

Nevertheless, the combination of what Morantz-Sanchez calls "sympathy and science" contained within it an inherent conflict: because most women doctors saw themselves as having a special relationship to motherhood and family life, women doctors usually limited themselves to "feminine" specialties and prevention rather than pursue research and acute care. This tendency, as medicine became increasingly hospital-based and specialized, ultimately circumscribed women's influence and curtailed their roles.[102]

While emphasizing women's "special calling" may have made it seem more socially acceptable for women to enter medicine than other professions, it also risked perpetuating what Morantz-Sanchez calls "an exaggerated concept of womanhood" and forced women doctors to walk a tightrope in exhibiting a "manly strength of character" without seeming "masculine."[103] Not surprisingly, this led women to question what to wear, and how to act.

Emily Dunning Barringer, New York's first woman ambulance surgeon, as an intern at Gouverneur Hospital in 1902, agonized for days over what to wear; she settled on a suit that would "attract as little attention as possible." Dr. Sara Josephine Baker, the first head of the Bureau of Child Hygiene, said she was grateful to the Gibson Girl for introducing shirtwaists and tailored suits because they provided "protective coloring." Years after medical school, Dr. Ida Wilson described in her memoirs a "Miss Belau" who entered the second year medical class at Ohio, as "a full German blond, hair of gold and very fair," who was "quite loudly dressed" in vivid scarlet . . . and "sleeveless of course." As "the men could not keep their thoughts or eyes on the doings of the class" the writer "never palled around with Miss Belau."[104]

Many nineteenth-century professional women also struggled with the question of whether to marry—and if they did, whether they could or should continue to work. Two-thirds of the female physicians in the nineteenth century never married. Some appeared "asexual," and said they had no interest in marriage. But Dr. Anna Wessel Williams, who remained single, wrote that she had to work hard to develop the quality of "detachment" from "all disturbing longings," a quality she believed essential to the good physician. She did wish to marry. "Of course I want it with the RIGHT one," she wrote in her diary. "But . . . how can I be sure? Is there ever a single right one?" Many early women doctors established deep emotional relationships with other women; others gave up much or all of their early professional promise when they married.[105]

Still, the marriage rate for women doctors in the nineteenth century was surprisingly high; between one-fifth and one-third of women physicians married, and the majority of those who married continued to practice. While the sixty-five black women physicians practicing in the late nineteenth century were sensitive to the prevailing social attitude that higher education and professional training threatened femininity, limited economic opportunity for black males made black women physicians highly attractive marriage partners. By 1900 the marriage rate of women physicians was twice that of all employed women and four times the rate among professional women. Many female physicians married men who were also doctors.[106]

Not surprisingly, "the question of marriage . . . which complicates everything else in the life of women," could not fail to complicate their professional lives. As Dr. Mary Putman Jacobi explained in 1880, "it does so . . . whether the marriage exists or does not exist, that is, as much for unmarried as for married women. . . . Many married women will lose all interest in medicine as soon as they have children, as many now fail to develop the full needed interest precisely because they have no other, and are dispirited by isolation from family ties."[107]

Women lawyers of the period wrestled with similar issues. Although the earliest professional women entered their fields saying they wanted to further women's causes, by the 1880s, there was lively debate among lawyers as to whether women should pursue their profession *because* of their gender—that is, work to prove women's capacities or to help their sisters—or, instead, forget their gender in order to pursue their profession.[108]

For members of a correspondence club made up of graduates of the University of Michigan Law School, a symbolic yet highly controversial question was whether to wear bonnets in court at a time when men commonly removed their hats indoors as a sign of respect. While some members of the club believed that women should leave on their bonnets so as not to make male lawyers and judges feel uncomfortable, one member adamantly disagreed. She urged her female colleagues to remove their hats "on principle," just as men did.[109]

In 1887, attorney Lelia Robinson advised club members to "simply be lawyers" and recognize no distinction from men. "Do not take sex into practice," she wrote. "Do not be a 'lady lawyer.'" Another "sister-in-law," as the members of the correspondence club called themselves, wrote that having children had prevented her from opening a practice; her correspondents advised her to stop having sex and to get a bedchamber of her own. Also in these letters, written at a time when women were deemed by far the weaker sex, club members questioned whether they had the physical strength and stamina to practice law.[110]

The debate about the degree to which women were—or should be—different from men and how women could best achieve equality was also reflected in the feminist and suffrage movements of the time.

Like their counterparts earlier in the century, many feminists in the 1890s believed that women were best suited to the family role—or to its extension in the settlement house and social reform efforts. In 1898, however, Charlotte Perkins Gilman, a radical feminist, suggested serious changes in women's roles. While some women were well-suited to housekeeping and child care, she wrote, others would do better in business or professions. To make careers more possible for women, Gilman proposed the creation of central kitchens, public nurseries, and a corps of expert housekeepers. If most women were liberated from domestic chores, she wrote, marriage would evolve into a partnership of equals, individual human beings could maximize their diverse abilities, and society would be free of the crippling effects of a dual system of labor. The result would be "a world of men and women humanly related, as well as sexually related, working together as they were meant to do, for the common good of all."[111]

Another arena of feminist debate was suffrage. In the 1890s, many feminists believed that joining forces to win the vote was the best way to achieve equality with men. But other women opposed the female vote on various grounds. Some suffrage opponents believed that feminists should, instead, put their efforts into the trade union movement to help working women. Ellen Key, who favored free sexual expression for women, spoke out against suffrage and the feminist insistence on women's right to work on grounds that love and motherhood were the two spheres most suited to female nature. Many proponents of social purity and temperance, as well as members of women's educational organizations, opposed female suffrage on grounds that women, divided by class, race, and special interests, would vote with their husbands' parties rather than as a separate and united bloc.[112]

The debate on suffrage led to serious racial and ethnic divisions among women. Frances Ellen Watkins Harper, a black activist, argued that any man or woman who could pass moral and educational tests should be able to vote, and Mary Church Terrell, a black suffragist, appealed to white women to join with black women to become a unified political force. Many white women suffragists, however, opposed allowing black women in their ranks; some advocated the women's vote as a way to ensure white supremacy in the South, where white women outnumbered black ones two to one. Others favored the women's vote on the grounds that it would help dilute the influence of an ever-growing number of ignorant immigrant men.[113]

Throughout the nineteenth century, then, there were dynamic struggles within and among individual women, and societally, about women's roles. These struggles both reflected and affected the ways in which women lived their lives, and the opportunities that opened to them. The struggles also reflected and affected a pattern that would continue well into the next century. That is, the more women left the home for paying work, the more pervasive the societal belief that they should not. But the more women's roles were constrained in one generation, the more their daughters sought to break free of those roles in the next.

4

GENERATIONAL PATTERNS: 1900–1950

By the turn of the twentieth century, women were working for birth control, suffrage, and temperance, and against prostitution. Some advocated the sterilization of criminals; others supported prison reform, physical education, sex education, vocational education, pure food and drug laws, good nutrition, free libraries, parks and recreation, or peace.[1] Middle-class women flocked to settlement houses to help the poor; they demanded an end to child labor and to corrupt political machines. Others were beginning to take paying jobs.

While in the nineteenth century, most working women had been immigrants or blacks employed on farms or as domestic servants, by 1910, 60 percent of working women were native-born whites. As the economy shifted from farm to factory, working women with little education were hired as stenographers or clerks in offices and stores. Better-educated women increasingly became teachers, social workers, nurses, and professors. By 1910, one in twenty physicians and osteopaths was a woman, Portia Law School in Boston had been founded just for women, and in Washington, D.C., the Washington College of Law and Howard University regularly admitted women. A woman lawyer had defended a man accused of murder, businesswomen had formed their own bank, society women were starting tea rooms, and suburbanites volunteered as motorcycle police.[2]

Through the next decade, women continued to work for temperance, birth control, and the vote. Some suffragists went so far as to chain themselves to fences or starve themselves in prison to draw attention to their cause. Encouraged by women activists, state legislatures enacted minimum-wage and factory safety laws to protect women workers.

Women entered politics and leaders of a growing women's movement proclaimed a new era of feminine equality.

In 1917, Margaret Dreier Robins told the Women's Trade Union League that this was "the first hour in history for the women of the world." At last, after centuries of disabilities and discrimination, she proclaimed, women were "coming into the labor and festival of life on equal terms with men."[3]

During World War I, women doctors and lawyers served on government advisory committees and in the Public Health Service. Both black and white women raised funds for the war effort;[4] the number of women in iron and steel factories doubled and some 100,000 worked in the munitions industries. Others held jobs as streetcar conductors, elevator operators, furnace stokers, and bricklayer helpers. Some worked overseas as nurses or ambulance drivers.[5]

In late 1919, the Smith College weekly editorialized that "We cannot believe it is fixed in the nature of things that a woman must choose between home and her work, when a man may have both." That year, one in five women over the age of fifteen was employed. Whereas in 1890, just over 3 percent of married women worked for pay—and generally it was considered shameful—by 1920 the figure had nearly tripled to 9 percent.[6] By 1920, women had won the vote. "We are no longer petitioners," the feminist leader Carrie Chapman Catt told participants at a victory celebration for suffrage. "We are not wards of the nation, but free and equal citizens."[7]

That year, a thousand times as many women enrolled in private colleges as had in 1900. Women made up half the undergraduates, 40 percent of the graduate students, and nearly 6 percent of law and medical students, and they earned 15 percent of the Ph.D.s. Half of the women who worked held white-collar or professional jobs and many professional institutions accepted qualified women applicants; in 1920, women made up 1.4 percent of the nation's lawyers, 6 percent of the doctors, and some 30 percent of the nation's college presidents, professors, and instructors.[8]

By the 1920s, women were becoming bankers, investors and hotel managers. A female architect and contractor designed "tidy, easy-care dwellings to fit the requirements of busy career women," some six million of whom were members of women's business organizations. In those years, as many women entered professional careers as men, and women engaged in professional life rose from nearly 12 percent to more than 14 percent. While most professional women worked in such "female" fields as teaching and social work, in 1923, more than a thousand women enrolled in medical school and two thousand went to law school.[9] There were now sixty-five black women doctors, and at least two black women attorneys.[10]

In the 1920s, women entered nearly every aspect of government and there was a woman in nearly every level of office in state and local government. Two women were appointed to the U.S. Senate, and two won gubernatorial elections. One, the anti-suffragist Miriam "Ma" Ferguson, ran for governor of Texas when her husband was impeached; the other, Nellie Tayloe Ross of Wyoming, ran after her husband died, and established a record of economy and efficiency.[11] Over the course of the decade, while faculty appointments for men doubled, faculty appointments for women more than tripled.[12]

Middle-class women hoping for jobs "besieged the offices of publishers and advertisers," one journalist wrote. So many others opened tearooms that "there threatened to be more purveyors than consumers of chicken patties and cinnamon toast; they sold antiques and real estate in little shops" and "even worked as clerks in department stores in hopes of becoming buyers or managers." Small-town girls borrowed money from their fathers to seek their fortunes in New York or Chicago; maiden aunts and unmarried daughters left "the shelter of the family roof to install themselves in kitchenette apartments of their own."[13] In the political sphere, social reformers continued to win health and welfare legislation designed to protect working women, families, and the poor. In the social sphere, an entire generation of young people rebelled against nineteenth century attitudes.

On college campuses, radicalism and sexuality were stylish. Engagement in premarital sex increased, and men and women talked openly and joked about sex, using language that traditionalists considered slangy, coarse, and profane. Young people danced the shimmy, the toddle, the collegiate, the Charleston, the black bottom, and the tango. In 1920 a female seminary in the Midwest dismissed four girls for smoking, and the following year, Stanford University nearly expelled a women's editor for even suggesting that women be allowed to smoke. "We do all the things that our mothers, fathers, aunts and uncles do not sanction, and do them knowingly," a student wrote in the *Ohio State Lantern* in 1922.[14]

In part, these young women took their cues from working-class women whose movement toward independence and autonomy had begun before the turn of the century. As early as 1900, a fifth of wage-earning women were living apart from their families. Many, from poor backgrounds, had left home for economic reasons or to escape family problems; a few sought to pursue their ambitions, romance, or adventure for a few years before marriage. While, early on, these single, working-class women were portrayed as "adrift," in the 1910s, bohemian and intellectual women began to emulate their unconventional behavior, taking on, as flappers, the manners and mores of cabaret singers and chorus girls. In the 1920s, growing numbers of young, middle-class women—some of them college graduates—followed suit.[15]

They congregated in New York City, took apartments, worked for a living, and attempted to be truly self-sufficient. Believing that women's emancipation depended on sexual emancipation, they claimed, like men, the right to enjoy sexual affairs without marriage. They wore a new, consciously sexy look: short skirts, bare arms, bright red lipstick, and tweezed eyebrows. "They threw out their corsets, bound their breasts to make themselves look flat and wore comfortable clothing so they could move more freely and be athletic."[16]

According to 1920s traditionalists, these changes "were all outward signs of escape from convention. . . . In the process of discovering life for themselves, the young were consciously and knowingly rejecting the conventions in manners and morals. . . . They now called hypocrisies those same behaviors and beliefs that had stabilized the prewar world."[17]

While most working class women of this ilk withdrew into their families once they found mates, many college-educated women sought new lifestyles and ideologies; some, as socialists and anarchists, challenged the American political and social systems, and advocated birth control and alternatives to traditional marriage such as communal kitchens and childrearing.[18]

By the mid-1920s, alternatives to Victorian marriage were being proposed in mainstream society. In 1926, a family court judge named Ben Lindsay suggested a new family model called "companionate marriage." In order to free women from sexual constraints, unwanted pregnancy, and their husbands' domination, Lindsay wrote, husbands and wives should consider themselves equal partners in relationships based on love, fidelity, sexual compatibility, and a deep commitment to child-bearing and democratic child-rearing. The success of such marriages, according to Lindsay, depended on legalized birth control, divorce by mutual consent for childless couples (usually without alimony), and state-administered education on sexuality and the responsibilities of marriage and parenthood.[19]

By 1930, women made up 40 percent of the professional workforce—double the percentage of women in other sorts of jobs. (The 40 percent includes women in such traditionally feminine fields as teaching, nursing, and social work.) Nearly 12 percent of the nation's wives worked outside the home and almost a third of working women were married.

According to a 1925 study, if you counted women who were divorced, widowed, or separated along with married women, that figure became nearly half.[20] "At luncheon tables," wrote the journalist Frederick Lewis Allen in 1930, "no topic was so furiously discussed . . . from one end of the country to the other as the question whether the married woman should take a job and whether the mother had a right to." Women who were "encumbered with children and could not seek jobs consoled themselves with the thought that home-making and child-rearing were really 'professions' after all."[21]

Crystal Eastman, a radical lawyer of the 1920s, described the modern woman of her day, as

> not satisfied with love, marriage, and a purely domestic career. She wants work of her own. She wants some means of self-expression, perhaps, some way of satisfying her personal ambitions. But she wants a husband, home, and children, too. How to reconcile these two desires in real life, that is the question.[22]

These women, and others like them, were the grandmothers of the women I interviewed—and were quite different from their own Victorian mothers.

Grandmothers

One of Alison Hartley's paternal great-grandmothers was a minister's wife who stayed at home with her thirteen children. "She had so many children that she ran out of names." So she simply called one daughter June 14—"after the date she was born on." But Alison's great-grandmother "shoo'd (Alison's grandmother) out of the kitchen." That grandmother—June 14th's sister—worked as a high school math teacher until she married. She then became a writer and continued her career, even after her only child, Alison's father, was born.

Alison also had a step-grandmother, a doctor, who was one of five children of a socially prominent doctor and a minister's daughter. The step-grandmother, who went to medical school in the 1910s, married and had two children, then maintained a part-time practice. "She once told me that if she had to do it over again, she wouldn't bother with marriage," Alison said.

Linda Appleby, a government official, described her father's grandmother as the daughter of a Civil War general who was "a traditional Victorian lady," so overshadowed that she does not even appear in the family lore. But her daughter, Linda's grandmother, was the powerhouse in her family. "I never knew my grandfather," Linda explained.

He was a lawyer, or maybe an engineer. My grandmother dominated him. She was the businesswoman. She ran a girls' camp in (a northeastern state). Once a summer she would dress up very fancy with a parasol and take a canoe out into the middle of the lake and tip it over. She was probably awesome to those girls but this was the one moment when she would let down.

Jackie Gerard's grandmother was from the South.

She had a governess, a comfortable background, though she never finished high school. My grandfather died when my mother was thirteen so my grandmother had to take over his tobacco farm. It was eight thousand acres. It had been run by tenant farmers and it was a sinkhole for money. It also turned out he had been carrying a lot of clients in his insurance business, so there was no money there, either. But my grandmother passed the insurance licensing exams, then she ran both the farm and the business at a profit. She continued to lead a typical upper-middle class existence. They had servants and my mother went to boarding school.

Carolyn Woodward, a television producer, described her grandmother as

a brilliant woman, a genius unable to exploit her worth—not so much because she was black but because she was a woman born in the late 1800s. She had a doctorate, or at least a master's degree. She spoke three languages; she had been to Europe three or four times. She had this knowledge and what did she do with it? She tutored young white kids; she was a nanny or something. My grandmother felt she had a place in life, she fought against the tide.

Though Carolyn's grandmother stayed with her husband for twenty-five years until he died, "she didn't want to be bothered with a man."

Carolyn's paternal grandmother was also strong and independent. Educated in a music conservatory, she played the piano, the violin, the cello, and the clarinet. As a young woman, she left her husband and went back to New Orleans.

He was not a nice man; he was a womanizer. But my grandmother didn't get bitter; she liked men. She had my father, my uncle, other children who died. [Although she was black] she passed for white, as she couldn't feed her children otherwise. She worked as a musician in dance halls, churches. Her second husband was the grandfather I knew and loved. He owned a bar; they bought property. He wasn't educated; he was a rough man. I think she had a couple of men in her life; I never asked. My grandmother was very philosophical; she was able to gain by her experience. She would say, "It's fate." She had an abundance of friends and was full of life.

Suzanne Lewis, a newspaper reporter, explained that her grandmother immigrated from Austria as a teenager. Suzanne's grandfather was

the baby, the eighth or ninth child of a huge Russian Jewish family. They were really poor. But he had grown up to be a rabbi, to study the Talmud, and was babied thoroughly by the whole family. When the Czar's army drafted him, the family decided this would not do for their grown-up little scholar, so they shipped him off to America, where he married my grandmother. Since my grandfather thought factory work was beneath him . . . he spent his days communing with other Talmudic scholars about the great mysteries and so forth of life, and the family was supported largely by my grandmother, who ran a restaurant above their flat in Brooklyn.

Eileen Carlson's grandmother, the daughter of pioneers, worked as a secretary in the 1920s. Rebecca Fine's grandmother, also an immigrant from Austria, started and ran a clothing manufacturing business. Jody Richards's grandmother became a lawyer and property owner in the Midwest and, with Jody's grandfather, a softspoken man, raised five children.

These grandmothers were members of a generation which moved out of the traditional women's roles called for in agricultural Europe and Victorian America to enter what many historians call "the modern age."[23] Growing up at a time when the nation was changing from agricultural to industrial, rural to urban, traditional to modern, they lived through a vast immigration from Europe, migration from the farm, and upheavals in social class. As a generation, they married later, had fewer children, and divorced more frequently than had their mothers.

By the mid–1920s, however, when the changes wrought by this generation were at their height, the tide began to turn. Men and women started to marry younger and to have more children than had their counterparts at the turn of the century.[24] Magazines published "Confessions of ex-feminists" and portrayed working women as a threat to the family. Career women wrote of dissipated energy, frustration, and anger. The proportion of women entering college and graduate and professional schools began to decline, and fewer women were choosing to work in the settlement house and feminist movements. Unlike an earlier generation of feminists, many of whom had viewed education and careers as ways

66

of escaping Victorian marriage, "new style" feminists believed that to develop fully, women needed husbands and children.[25]

By 1930, a new generation was tiring of "a modernism which leaves you washed out and cynical at thirty." People read sentimental novels about the 1890s and looked "with less scornful eyes" upon Victorian furniture. Women wore their hair longer; frills, ruffles, and flounces came back into style and "corset manufacturers were once more learning to smile."[26]

Marjorie Nicholson, who received her B.A. in 1914 from the University of Michigan, believed that hers was the only generation of women that ever really found itself. "We came late enough to escape the self-consciousness and belligerence of the pioneers," she wrote in 1938, "but early enough to take education and training for granted." In the 1910s and early 1920s, "positions were everywhere open to us . . . the millennium had come; it did not occur to us that life could be different." But within a decade, "shades of the prison house began to close, not upon the growing boy, but upon the emancipated girls."[27] Within another decade, the daughters of her generation, the mothers of the women I interviewed, were back in the home.

Two Trends

Conventional wisdom has it that women lost opportunities for education and careers during the Great Depression of the 1930s and that the pressures of World War II led people, in the 1940s and 1950s, to marry younger and to have more children, at earlier ages, than did the previous generation. Both of those explanations are true, but I would suggest that underlying those explanations are deep, dynamic trends and countertrends integral to the process of societal change.

On the one hand, technological innovation, modernization in the professions, universal suffrage, and the great social and political movements of the early twentieth century led to increasing independence and autonomy for women and men. On the other hand, those very developments, combined with massive immigration, social disruption, war, and disorder in cities and in families also contributed to a counterpull, to a growing desire for order and tradition, and for simpler, safer-seeming, and highly differentiated gender roles. Paradoxically, the renewed emphasis on women's domestic role at mid-century was rooted in the very forces that might have been expected to propel women from that role.

The rise of technology in the early twentieth century certainly seemed likely to free women from many of the burdens of household work. Factories had already largely replaced home manufacturing, and now, most households regularly used canned and packaged food and ready-to-wear clothing. Many homes had electricity and running water, and high-volume, mass-marketing systems allowed both rural and urban households to buy irons, stoves, vacuum cleaners, washing machines, and refrigerators, all of which should have cut the time needed for household chores. Improvements in health care meant that women no longer needed to have many children to ensure that enough would survive for farm work and increased access to birth control allowed women to limit the size of their families.

By the 1920s, half of America's population lived in cities or suburbs and there was an automobile for every six people in the nation.[28] Sophisticated transportation systems provided women access to new jobs in offices and industry, and educated women met to share ideas being developed in the new fields of anthropology, psychology, and sociology. At the same time, however, modernization—especially birth control, the growth of social science, advertising and retail trade, new labor-saving devices, and increasing professionalism—all reinforced women's domestic role.

Although birth control was legalized in many states and became more accessible in the 1920s, it did not lead to later marriage and longer working lives for women, as might have been expected. Instead, women began to marry younger—partly because birth control allowed them to enjoy sex without having children right away. Whereas once women had seen paying work as a way to escape marriage, marriage now seemed more palatable. Single women took jobs in order to save for it, and married women worked to contribute to the family income.[29]

While in the early twentieth century white, native-born Americans did have fewer children than their parents, smaller family size did not diminish women's roles as mothers. Rather, the new field of social science focused tremendous attention on the importance of the mother to every single child. The family came to be seen not as a miniature state or economic center but as a center for children's healthy and normal adjustment.[30] Simultaneously, in the 1920s, the drop in the fertility rate of native-born, educated white women renewed fears that non-whites and immigrants would take over the nation. Colleges, under fire because their women graduates tended to have fewer children than did other women, began to emphasize women's "wifely" and "mothering" skills instead of careers.[31]

At this time, the growth of advertising and retail trade opened many jobs to women, but also encouraged a view of women as a huge group of consumers whose major role was to buy products for home, husbands, and children. In 1932, an advertisement from *American Magazine* includes a photograph of a glamorous woman in black and white who is draped, like a statue. The photo is headlined: "Women lovely women vote"; it is captioned "To thousands of women of this type—charming, educated, well-to-do, prominent in the social and civic life of her city, we put this question: what toothpaste do you use?" (The caption goes on to respond: "To our delight, the majority answered Listerine.")[32]

What is more, new "labor-saving" devices like vacuum cleaners and washing machines actually increased the amount of time middle-class women spent keeping house by creating higher standards for cleanliness. If housewives saved time by using appliances or packaged commodities, they often reallocated it to child care, shopping, or household management. Whereas a generation back, their mothers might have had household help, now middle-class women increasingly did their own work—in part because immigrant women, who once might have become maids, could now earn more money as factory workers.[33]

To counter the devaluation of the housewife, practitioners of the developing field of home economics sought to banish the idea that women are "born homemakers" who know instinctively how to keep house. They portrayed housework as a vital profession with managerial, business, and spiritual elements and a "product" of "happy, healthy, useful human beings." The U.S. Department of Agriculture made the Bureau of Home Economics a government agency, and the Bureau's leaders became public spokeswomen on the central feminist question of whether women could successfully combine careers and household management.[34]

Meanwhile, modernization in the professions was making it more difficult for women to pursue "non-traditional" careers. In part, this was because of a backlash against working women which, some historians suggest, was the strongest in fields in which women had made the greatest numerical gains—that is, in medicine before 1910 and in academe after 1920.[35] Much of the difficulty, however, came as a result of changing institutional structures, which widened the gulf between male and female professionals.

For example, with increasing professionalism came the rise of large institutions and a need for links with capitalists to fund buildings—links that most women did not have.[36] Also, in the 1910s and 1920s, members of the legal and medical establishments felt threatened by the increasing numbers and prestige of a wealthy business class and, under fire for laxity, tightened their standards and shut down many of the substandard schools that had opened, usually for profit, after the Civil War.[37] Unfortunately, it was those schools, particularly in the Midwest, that had most welcomed women. In law and medicine, fear of being overtaken by an influx of Eastern European immigrants, especially Jews, led to "exclusivity and discrimination" at the very core of the professionalizing process.[38]

As medicine became more sophisticated, much of general practice, which most women had pursued, was replaced by specialties which required hospital training. In 1920, however, only 40 of the nation's 4,782 general hospitals accepted women interns. For African-American women interns, who numbered fewer than 70 in 1920, the situation was even bleaker; they were expected to train at black hospitals, which were limited in number, often had inferior programs, and preferred to admit black men. As a result, most women doctors, by choice or necessity, ended up treating mainly women, the poor, and immigrants and were left with almost no voice in the professional power structure.[39]

In law, newly developing corporate firms tended to hire associates from prestigious law schools, which, like most bar associations and county law societies, excluded women, who were still deemed "too emotional and too lacking in objectivity to function effectively in professional life." Women trial lawyers were stigmatized, so most female attorneys confined themselves to issues concerning women and children and had little impact on the profession itself. Although thousands of women—many of them well-to-do—trained in law, a large number evidently never practiced.[40]

Women were more easily accepted by graduate schools than by law and medical schools—and made much headway in entering new social science fields like anthropology and sociology. Women academics had a difficult time advancing, however, in part because they tended to pursue broad social issues and practical problems, which brought in less grant money than did statistical analyses of narrow topics that tended to interest men. Although women made up nearly 40 percent of graduate students in 1928, they received only 4.6 percent of the fellowships.[41] Even women who received fellowships rarely reached regular faculty rank. Most women scientists ended up either working as assistants in men's laboratories or teaching in undergraduate women's colleges—cut off from collaboration in mainstream research and unable to develop protégés.[42]

While a few women scientists became superstars by outperforming men, more commonly, women scientists achieved success by avoiding competition with men—by specializing in such "traditionally female" areas as nutrition or home economics, by moving to exotic regions or urban slums, or by working on the problems of the disadvantaged such as birth control, lead poisoning, or the quality of milk in infant formula. Alice Hamilton, for example, who later became the first female professor at Harvard Medical School, left a position in bacteriology to investigate conditions in factories that used hazardous materials—thus establishing the new field of industrial health. Ordinarily, however, in medicine, as in other fields, advancement took place through personally conducted mentor relationships between leading men and their protégés, so that women who made it into faculty's lower ranks, but were without supportive male mentors, usually did not rise.[43]

One reason women were not enthusiastically received in most professions was that it was often assumed that they would leave their careers when they wed; some married professional women were forced out of their jobs by anti-nepotism rules that prevented husbands and wives from being employed within the same department of a university.[44] But by 1910, more than a million married women worked outside the home, and professional women, 12 percent of whom were married, were more likely than other women to continue to work.

The going was not easy. In 1915, one author wrote that without child care and domestic help "single women [were] forging farther and farther ahead" while many a married woman was "finding herself between the upper and nether millstone."[45] By 1930, 25 percent of professional women were married, and it was increasingly acceptable for married women to work. That year, a third of women medical graduates were married and of them, more than 86 percent were still in practice.[46] The author Virginia Collier wrote in 1926: "The question is no longer, should women combine marriage with careers, but how do they manage it and how does it work?" In a study of 100 professional women, Collier found that 90 percent had at least one domestic servant—a luxury available to just 5 percent of families at the time.[47] Elaine Showalter and Rosalind Rosenberg document the divorces, marital difficulties, and even the breakdowns of many early professional women.[48]

All of these problems were heightened because many highly successful, professional women identified more with the standards of their professions than with other women.

While many professional women joined such organizations as the National Medical Women's Association, others refused to believe in the existence of sexism or discrimination, and blamed themselves if they failed to advance. Some successful career women acknowledged that discrimination existed but denied having experienced it. For example, to secure one woman's appointment to the Harvard Medical School faculty, her supporters had to promise that she would never use the faculty club, request faculty football tickets, or "embarrass the faculty by marching in the commencement procession and sitting on the platform." Yet the same professor would later write, "I must admit that though I have seen the difficulties women doctors have to overcome, I have never suffered from them myself."[49]

Also, by the mid-1920s, many professional women felt little solidarity with a feminist movement that had, partly because of its own success, reached a serious impasse.[50] In the 1910s, feminists, professional women, and others involved in various social reform movements had managed to join forces to win the vote, and in the early 1920s, women reformers were successful in lobbying for the passage of major health and social welfare legislation. By 1925, however, the economy had begun to decline, reform sentiment was beginning to die, and it had become evident that there was no solid women's vote.

The Democratic committeewoman Emily Newell Blair said at the time that she knew of no woman who had any influence or political power simply because she was a woman. Nor did she know of any woman who had a following of other women, or of a politician who was afraid of the women's vote "on any question under the sun."[51] In part, that was because then, as now, women were divided by class, race, and ideology—as well as on issues of war, peace, and temperance.

Among working women, considerable tension and conflict existed at all levels. In some factories white women commonly refused to share dressing rooms or bathrooms with black women; black women received lower wages and were often relegated to jobs that white women refused to perform. Within the trade union movement, white leaders, Bell Hooks writes, tended to focus on rights for white women workers.[52] As in the past, female activists divided among themselves.

A major bone of contention concerned "protective legislation" versus "equal rights." The League of Women Voters argued that working women—especially those in blue-collar jobs—needed special protection from long working hours and heavy physical labor because trade unions did not adequately represent them. But the National Women's Party (NWP), made up largely of professional women, instead favored an Equal Rights Amendment to guarantee women equal pay and equal responsibility with men.

The NWP argued that protective legislation would merely protect jobs for men by keeping capable women out of them, and would harm professional women by allowing employers to take the physical differences between men and women into account in assigning jobs and promotions. The League held that the NWP was elitist and that while its proposed Equal Rights Amendment might correct a few instances of discrimination, "it would wipe out years of progress. For the sake of giving an individual woman the right to drive a taxi in Ohio, feminists were willing to junk the rights of almost all female industrial workers to decent working conditions."[53]

Passions ran so strong that in 1926, the debate led to what one historian has described as a "wild floor fight" in the Women's Bureau in

Washington.[54] The debate on the Equal Rights Amendment continued into the 1930s. A House subcommittee endorsed it in 1936, the Senate Judiciary Committee reported it to the floor two years later, and the Republican party officially supported it in 1940, as did both parties and President Harry Truman in the 1940s.[55] The Equal Rights Amendment was brought up again in the 1970s, but as of this writing, still had not passed. Women remained divided as to how they could be equal with yet different from men.

Given this and other disagreements among women in the 1920s, there was not enough support to maintain some of the reform legislation that had already been passed. In 1929, the Sheppard-Towner Health Care Act, which provided maternal and infant care, was rescinded. This, Sheila Rothman writes, ended an important era of female expertise in health care and left the provision of health services to the private sector, which employed fewer women than had the federal health care system.[56]

Well before the Great Depression of the 1930s, the impetus toward careers for women had weakened, despite the gains of women in many fields. Even though more women were working for pay than ever before, careers no longer seemed novel, different, or romantic to young women, and feminism seemed petty, divisive, and unnecessary. Young women took from the gains of their mothers' generation what seemed relevant: personal autonomy and self-fulfillment, combined with a new view of woman as a "wife companion," who could be liberated in marriage, yet not have a career.[57]

As William O'Neill explains, it became quite possible to "fall away from the old feminist standards," to "abandon paid employment and public service and lapse into familism while at the same time remaining thoroughly up to date."[58]

Then came the Great Depression, and with it the belief that working women were taking jobs away from men. Even though women held mostly low-skill or pink-collar jobs at which men had never worked, as men's jobs in heavy industry diminished, women workers were seen as expendable.[59] "There are approximately 10,000,000 people out of work in the U.S. today," Norman Cousins wrote in 1939. "There are also 10,000,000 or more women, married and single, who are jobholders. Simply fire the women, who shouldn't be working anyway, and hire the men. Presto! No unemployment. No relief roles. No depression."[60]

Employers evidently agreed. In 1932, the federal government had decreed that the spouses of government workers should be the first to be laid off. Three quarters of the nation's school systems refused to hire married teachers; railroads fired women who got married; Texas laid off women in transportation jobs if their husbands earned more than $50 a month; and in 1939, twenty-six state legislatures considered bills barring married women from state jobs entirely.[61]

Under the New Deal, men began to regard publicly funded jobs in such female-dominated areas as schoolteaching, social work, librarianship, and nursing as more secure than jobs in private industry, and employers hired male applicants wherever possible. By 1940, men held more than 15 percent of all library jobs, compared with under 9 percent a decade before, and the proportion of men employed in social work had risen from one fifth to one third. Although some 30 percent of women now worked outside the home, most were clustered in low-paying occupations such as light manufacturing, service, and clerical work.[62]

High unemployment during the depression also played on fears about the future of the family and led to increased emphasis on women's maternal role. When fathers lost their incomes they often became irritable, explosive, tense, or unstable; sons and daughters tended to lose respect for them and mothers became more central as both authority and affectional figures.[63] In light of a relatively high birthrate for immigrants, blacks, Jews, and the poor, many native-born white Americans worried, as in the past, that they would lose their power as a majority.

In response, the government increasingly funded marital clinics, home economics education, birth control, maternal and infant hygiene, and visiting housekeepers. Colleges that had once encouraged women to enter professions now told women that they should not work unless they had to.[64] Women's magazines published articles with titles like "You May Have My Job: A Feminist Discovers Her Home" and "The Return of the Lady."[65] Experts accused working mothers of deserting their families and blamed them for teenagers' truancy, incorrigibility, robbery, and tantrums,[66] and public opinion polls showed that 80 percent of the population believed women should not work if their husbands could support them.[67]

As jobs and money grew scarcer, families that ten years earlier might have sent their daughters to college reserved their money to educate their sons. When mothers worked, older daughters often gave up their educational aspirations to care for the family.[68] Even women who did go to college were more likely than their mothers to drop out before graduation. Although during the Great Depression many Americans delayed marriage and childbearing, middle-class women from families that experienced financial deprivation were more likely to marry younger and to have more children sooner than had their mothers. According to sociologist Glen Elder, the reasons may have been largely psychological or emotional.

In his study of depression era families in Oakland, California, Elder found that boys from middle-class families that lost income and status tended to overcompensate by becoming more aggressive, more achievement-oriented, and more anxious to prove themselves than other boys. Girls from such families tended to be more oriented to home and family, perhaps because these daughters took on household duties at young ages when their mothers went out to work, or because they did not get along well with their unemployed fathers and married young in order to leave home.

In ambiguous situations, such as when a family's social status is clouded by financial loss, Elder explains, girls tend to become more sensitive to the needs of others and hence, even more family-oriented than they might otherwise be. Boys from such families, Elder suggests, tend to believe they have lost more in status than they really have; they tend to become independent of their parents at younger ages than they might have normally and to feel a greater need for recognition, first in school, and later, in careers, than boys from families less affected by economic loss.[69]

During World War II, the situation for working women seemed to be looking up as some six million American women—some of them the mothers of the women I interviewed—joined the labor force.[70] Companies provided on-site day care, shopping and banking facilities, transportation to work, and hot lunches. Entrepreneurs "harangued women to work on street corners" or bribed high school principals to send them workers; *Fortune Magazine* suggested drafting women to work in industry if they didn't volunteer. The Rensselaer Polytechnic Institute accepted its first woman engineering student; the Curtis Wright Company sent 800 women to engineering school; and Monsanto, DuPont, and Standard Oil took on their first women chemists. The federal government hired women attorneys, Wall Street brokerage houses recruited women analysts and statisticians, and the U.S. Army commissioned its first women doctors.[71]

By the end of the war, nearly 20 million women were in the labor force—they accounted for 35 percent of all workers, compared with 25 percent five years earlier—and for the first time, more wives than single women were employed.[72] Yet, with the possibility of draft deferments for married men early in the war years, and, later, the imminence of their departure for foreign battlefields, couples had rushed into marriage; between 1940 and 1945, the birthrate climbed from 19.4 to 24.5 per thousand population. When the servicemen returned, despite women's wartime employment record, the predominant belief was that wives belonged at home.[73]

After the war, millions of people were laid off, almost two-thirds of them women. The most dramatic decline in women's employment was in the manufacturing sector, where most of the highest paying war jobs had been, but even highly educated women doctors and judges lost their jobs. While some skilled women workers protested, younger women tended to accept the cuts; those women who did return to industry often accepted lower-paying, less-secure jobs than they had held before, usually in service and clerical areas. Black women workers, who had made the greatest gains of any group through their first-time forays into factory jobs, were hit especially hard; at the end of the 1940s, their income was half that of white women. Women who in an earlier generation might have gone to medical or law school instead became social workers and nurses; for most women, family remained paramount.[74]

These trends were reinforced by public policy developed to help returning veterans. The Servicemen's Readjustment Act (better known as the "G.I. Bill" of rights) paid for veterans' education but not for the education of their spouses; highway and housing grants promoted the growth of suburbs, which led to the increasing isolation of women as housewives.[75]

In the late 1940s nearly a third of all women worked outside the home—10.2 million of them married. But only about a quarter of Americans believed women should have an equal chance with men for any job, and fewer than half thought that even women who had to support themselves should have an equal chance.[76] Most Americans seemed to believe that women were and should remain homemakers.

Historians suggest that despite the record of working women during World War II, conservative attitudes never really changed. During the war, working women had been paid only 55 percent of what men earned—a drop from the 1939 figure of approximately 62 percent—and little child care was actually available. In addition, female war workers were constantly reminded that they were women in "men's" jobs. In 1943, for example, an ad in *Fortune Magazine* described a woman operating a steel-cutting machine as "a skillful seamstress" cutting "a tailor-made suit" to Axis size with "scissors of oxyacetylene, cloth of bullet-proof steel, and pattern shaped to our enemy's downfall."[77]

Historian Elaine May argues that women's wartime independence gave rise to fears of female sexuality; she links the "domestic containment" of women in the 1950s to America's cold war policy of containing Communism—and describes both as responses to the horrors of World War II and the nuclear threat.[78] Joseph Adelson has called the deep desire for home and family of this generation "an expression of the wish to undo the psychic disruptions of the Depression and war, to achieve the serenity that had eluded the lives of their parents."[79]

According to feminist Betty Friedan, "After the loneliness of war and the unspeakableness of the bomb, against the frightening uncertainty, the cold immensity of the changing world, women as well as men sought the comforting reality of home and children."[80]

Overall, I would suggest, the belief in women's domestic role deepened as technological and social change increasingly challenged that very role. Early in the twentieth century, new technologies opened careers to women but also made marriage seem more inviting. Modernization led to greater selectivity in professions but also encouraged discrimination against women. Increasing opportunity raised difficult questions about how men and women could be different, yet equal. Later in the century, immigration, economic depression, and war led many women to work for pay out of necessity, but the uncertainty, disruption, and loss of the times inspired a yearning for idealized roles.

All of the above had a profound impact on the mothers of the women I interviewed, who grew up in a period of major societal disruption. But on a very individual level, those mothers—themselves the daughters of powerful working women of the 1920s—retreated to the home largely because they did not want to live the sorts of lives their mothers had led.

Mothers

Barbara Fielding's mother grew up in a wealthy family, but lost her father when he died of a heart attack in his early forties.

> He owned some orange groves in Florida, which he left to my grandmother. She sold them in the land boom of 1924 for $100,000 to buy some property where she could raise my mother and my uncles. During the Depression, my grandmother had to sell the property, but she could only get $25,000 for it, so my mother couldn't afford to go to college.

Clara Zolen, a business executive, described her mother as the daughter of German immigrants. "My mother didn't get that far because she grew up between the two wars," Clara said. "There was a lot of anti-German sentiment and in school there was tracking on the basis of language." Then, during the depression, Clara's grandfather, who was a patent attorney, "lost everything."

> My mother lost her piano, her dog. She was protected but lonely, until late in her teens when she was shoved out on her own. My mother had to work; she had to drop out of college. She became an army nurse. After she got married, she worked nights and weekends

as a part-time nurse to help make ends meet. Her mother may have worked as a housekeeper for rich people, but I'm not sure when or where. My mother didn't get along that well with *her* mother.

Flora Dawson's mother never finished college.

She married young, during World War II, in 1943. She didn't want to be like her mother—who was a southern belle type of person. My grandmother played tennis, did social things. Since her mother was not that concerned about her, my mother saw her mother as a negative example.

Flora's parents weren't always happy—her father had affairs and never made much money and her mother "ran him down." But Flora thinks her mother was content with her lot.

She liked having children; she liked taking care of us. She did a lot of social stuff, volunteer work. She put energy and time into her children, to put them on the right path to life, to help them achieve academic success. She was reacting to her mother, who wasn't nurturing.

Before Sally Jeffers was born, her mother worked for seven years as the executive secretary for the head of a major television station. "Her boss begged her to stay on when she got pregnant with me. He even offered to let her have a room at work so she could take care of me. But she refused," Sally said. "She believed that she ought to stay at home." Sally's mother was "a very talented woman who spent her time doing pottery, weaving, needlepoint, painting."

I think she did that because *her* mother lost two husbands between 1910 and 1920. One died of tuberculosis and the other had a heart attack when he was thirty-six. So my grandmother worked really hard all her life to raise my mother and her sister—she had all kinds of jobs. My mother never had a traditional upbringing—and I think she wanted her children to have that. Also, my father's mother also lost her husband young—so she packed up the five kids and moved back East. She ran a boarding house during the Depression. So neither of my parents had traditional families, and they wanted them.

Alison Hartley's step-mother, whose own mother was a doctor, "specifically decided not to work." Even though she was offered the job of assistant dean at an exclusive women's college where she did volunteer work, she turned it down. "She liked doing the job. It was interesting," Alison said.

But she decided to hold back and to be a housewife. She thought it was appropriate for a lady to stay at home. It was a class issue. Anyone who worked at anything but a professional career did it because they had to. And she didn't want it to be thought that she was of the class of women who worked.

In these stories, the impact of class, economics, and social pressure is clear. While every story is different, each in its own way illustrates the effects of social forces on families, and on the lives of women. One by one, each woman I spoke with explained her mother's life choices in relation to *her* mother's life.

The anthropologist Beatrice Whiting hypothesizes that men and women whose mothers worked in an era when most women did not may have wished for families like those they believed others had. Judith Lewis Herman, M.D., and Helen Block Lewis, Ph.D., suggest that in a sexist society in which women are denigrated, mothers and daughters grow up as natural adversaries.[81] Perhaps the mothers of the 1950s were simply caught in prevailing social trends. Many no doubt saw their immigrant mothers as overworked and underpaid, were emotionally bound to family roles when their mothers went to work, or, as immigrant daughters, looked to their peers as role models.[82]

I would suggest that given the disruption and difficulties in their parents' lives and in their own—immigration, family breakup, educational setbacks, war, early paternal death—the mothers of the women I interviewed did not want to emulate their mothers. Rather, as their daughters described them, the mothers seem to have adopted the simple, safe, and stereotypical gender roles idealized during the Victorian era, their grandmothers' time. Wishing, perhaps, for the safety and care of the all-nurturing, full-time mothers they had not had, they intended to be such mothers for their own children.

In the absence of strong, protective fathers, the mothers of the women I interviewed typically married men who attempted to fulfill masculine roles reminiscent of those idealized in their grandfathers' day. These men, the fathers of the women I spoke with, also tended to have powerful working mothers and weak or unsuccessful fathers.

Patricia, a pediatrician, described her paternal grandmother as the supervisor of girls in a factory. "She had to be responsible," because her husband was an alcoholic who couldn't hold a steady job. "My father remembers being angry with him," Patricia said. Susan's paternal grandfather died young, so that by the age of fourteen, her father was driving a truck to help support the family. Flora's father was the son of a small-town banker who lost his shirt in the depression and constantly moved his family around the country.

The fathers of the women I interviewed were not unlike the men sociologist Glen Elder described, men who had grown up as the sons of working mothers in deprived, female-dominant families during the Great Depression. Such sons, Elder found, felt hostile toward their fathers, insecure, less tied to their families, and more driven toward workplace success than many other men. Some of them and others returned from World War II harboring tremendous doubts about themselves and their world. Where, asks historian Elaine May, could a man "still feel powerful and prove his manhood without risking the loss of security?" In a home, she answers, "where he held the authority with a wife who would remain subordinate."[83]

The women I interviewed described their fathers as wanting wives who would be quite different from their own mothers. They wanted wives, I suggest, who would stay home to provide an idealized sort of mothering for them and for their children, the sort of mothering they perhaps felt they had missed in their own childhoods.

In return, these men, the fathers of the women I interviewed, struggled to compete in the burgeoning corporate world of the 1950s, to provide for their wives and families as their own fathers had not, to prove themselves where their fathers had not—to fulfill impossible stereotypes of the heroic men their fathers were not. They resembled a group of alienated Harvard men studied in the 1950s, who, with the encouragement of their disappointed mothers, idealized their grandfathers, the seemingly powerful men of the Victorian era.[84] Finding it difficult to live up to the mythic images of men of the past, I would suggest, the fathers of the women I interviewed never felt successful enough. Often, as you will see, they took their frustrations out on their wives.

All across the country—in row houses, suburban tracts, and mansions alike—men tried to live up to the stereotypical image of strong provider. Women, the mothers of the women I interviewed, tried hard to fulfill the traditional view of woman as sweet nurturer and gentle helpmate. In the rapidly changing world of the 1950s, however, those old ideals did not fit. And while the mothers of the women I interviewed were constrained by society's standards and their own internalized stereotypes of the perfect woman, they also carried within them images of their own powerful working mothers. It was those contradictory images of womanhood that they passed on to their daughters—images that motivated their daughters to want very different sorts of lives.

5

PUSH-PULLS: THE 1950s

Alison Hartley's mother quit college at nineteen to get married and had five children by the time she was twenty-nine. She got pregnant yet again, went through an illegal abortion, then had her tubes tied. The next year, when Alison was thirteen, her mother committed suicide. "My father told me it was because once she'd become infertile, she felt she had no role as a woman," said Alison, a writer and social scientist. "But I have always wondered about that. I have a diary she left me and in one of the entries she had written, 'Is this really all there is?'"

Rhonda Parker's mother was the only woman in her pharmacy school class but married just after graduation and never pursued a career. With Rhonda's father often away on assignment as a newspaper reporter, "she told me constantly that a woman's role is to take care of her husband and family," said Rhonda, a reporter. "When I said I didn't want to do that, she told me, 'Rhonda, shut up.' But I am convinced to this day that being deprived of her work killed my mother. And [depressed throughout her life] she died a long slow death."

Eunice Roland, a banker, had a mother who, as a girl, wanted to be a farmer. Against the wishes of her well-to-do parents, Eunice's mother went to the state agricultural school. After a year, "the school told her, 'women can't be farmers.' So, it being World War II, my mother went to Europe and drove an ambulance." There, she met Eunice's father, and after the war, she came back to this country and married him. Within a few years, she had three children and a nervous breakdown.

Carolyn Woodward's mother was "a black woman who grew up at a time when they were lynching black people." She graduated from college at sixteen and a much older man wanted to marry her. Her mother, Carolyn's grandmother, said, "Here's your chance for money and power; do it." She did it, but her husband abused her. The marriage ended—and so did three others.

◆   ◇   ◆

As I conducted the interviews for *Broken Patterns,* I was often shocked at the vehemence and anger with which most told their mothers' stories. But, then again, their mothers were the women Betty Friedan wrote about, women of the 1950s, the women who married younger and had more children at an earlier age than women in any other western nation.

"By the end of the fifties," Friedan wrote, "the average age of women at marriage had dropped to twenty and was still dropping, into the teens"; in fact, fourteen million girls were engaged by the time they turned seventeen, and half of all women married before they reached twenty. Whereas in 1920, nearly half of college students had been women, in 1958, only 35 percent were. A generation earlier women had fought for higher education, but they now went to college to find husbands. They often quit before they graduated or just after—because they were afraid too much education would scare men away.[1]

The few who did manage to earn Ph.D.s or professional degrees commonly left their careers when they got married. Some quit because they could not advance; others because their husbands' careers, and kids, demanded it. Whereas in 1930 women earned 40 percent of the bachelor's and master's degrees and just over 15 percent of the Ph.D.s, in 1960, women received just a third of the lower level degrees and a tenth of the Ph.D.s. By 1965, only one in eleven Ph.D.s was awarded to a woman.[2]

Even though in the 1950s more women were working than ever before, it was, increasingly, at jobs that required minimal training and carried little prestige. The percentage of bank tellers who were women rose from 45 percent in 1950 to 69 percent in 1960; the percentage of hucksters and peddlars—such as those who sold products door-to-door—who were women increased from 14 percent to 59 percent, and the percentage of women adult education teachers in technical and private schools increased from 26 percent to 61 percent.[3]

In contrast, the proportion of college presidents, professors, and instructors who were women plummeted from nearly a third in 1930 to under a fifth in 1950. In the 1950s alone, women judges and lawyers just managed to hold onto 3.5 percent of the jobs, but the proportion of women clergy, dentists, engineers, chemists, and physicists all dropped—with the proportion of women in mathematics diminishing the most, by more than 10 percent.

For nonwhite women, the numbers were so small that they were rarely analyzed. Nationwide, in 1960, the census counted just 490 black women physicians, 176 black women lawyers and judges, and about 370 black women social scientists. (As late as 1970, there was no breakdown on minority women in medicine, but among scientists and engineers, there were 837 Asian-American women, 249 black women, three Native Americans, and 34 "other minority women" in a total science and engineering labor force of 244,921.)[4]

Overall, between 1930 and 1960, while in Sweden, Great Britain, France, the former Soviet Union and Israel the proportion of professional women at least doubled, in the United States, it went down. Whereas in 1940, women had held 45 percent of the professional and technical jobs, as late as 1966, women held only 38 percent of them. In those jobs, according to sociologist Cynthia Fuchs Epstein, no matter what women worked at, "like sediment in a wine bottle," they seemed to settle to the bottom.[5]

This, many women said, was how they wanted it. They did not want careers, they told researchers. They did not want to be Miss or Mrs. America; an outstanding film, stage, or television star; or one of the ten best-dressed women in America. They did not even want to be known for volunteer work or political participation. What they did want "was to marry a prominent man and have several highly accomplished children."[6] What they wanted, or believed they wanted, or said they wanted, or had to want, was to be at home.

◆　◇　◆

Growing up in the 1950s, it certainly seemed like we were being primed to follow in our mothers' footsteps, to grow up to become the tranquil flowers of domesticity women were supposed to be. Countless studies showed that we were encouraged to be passive, subjective, emotional, and dependent. Discouraged from playing team sports and trained to empathize with others, we were deemed unsuited for competitive professions. Girls who *wanted* careers were usually guided into "appropriate" fields like teaching and social work, expected to work for a few years at most, then get married. Although many women of color grew up expecting to work, those aspiring to professional careers were also encouraged to enter fields then considered feminine.[7]

Alison Hartley wanted to be a veterinarian but her parents thought she should study art. When she went to discuss her career dream with the local vet, he discouraged her too. "Do you want to spend the rest of your life with your arm stuck up the back of a cow?" he asked. Jennifer Howe's mother told her she could have a career or marriage, but not both. Abby Nathan's sister was a runner. "Before a race," Abby said, "my mother would tell her it was O.K. to lose." In my own junior high school, the mathematics department divided my class in two and put the smartest boys in an advanced class; they grouped all the girls and two less talented boys in another section.

Even so, Alison became a social scientist, Jennifer, a scientist, and Abby, a doctor. I became a journalist, and one of my female classmates got a Ph.D. in math. We were just five of thousands of women who surprised researchers, parents, and teachers alike by choosing careers once reserved for men.[8] Why?

In my interviews, woman after woman told me about her mother's hopes and dreams, hopes and dreams that ended with marriage in the late 1940s and early 1950s. Several women described mothers who were alcoholic, many described mothers who were depressed, passive, and inept; two had mothers who had killed themselves. Even women who viewed their mothers as emotionally healthy knew, often when they were very young, that they didn't want to emulate them.

Eleanor Valera decided when she was nine years old to be a journalist. "It's not a particularly long and drawn out story," she explained over coffee in the cafeteria of the large city newspaper where she worked as an editor. "I really was one of those kids who at the age of nine mimeographed a newspaper and took it around the neighborhood." While Eleanor could not explain just why she chose journalism, she was "quite sure" that she wanted a career "because what happened to my mother had a really strong influence on me."

> Here was a really bright woman. She had been a straight-A student at college, she had been trained as a social worker and she had a career in retailing in New York where she was making a lot of money by the standards of the day. She was really on her way. Then she got married. They moved to a midwestern town and she couldn't get a job that was worthy of her. She got pregnant right away. She had me and then she had twins and then she had a fourth child three years after that. She's a bright woman who spent her life doing the children thing and being a wife to a husband who was really very demanding and not at all sensitive to the needs that she had.

Eleanor's father grew up in a lower-middle-class Jewish family in New York. He had wanted to be a certified public accountant.

> But there was World War II and he didn't want to waste time CPA-ing, so he got a college degree at a public university and quickly got a job in a discount store. He was working at something his heart

wasn't in. Although he didn't often say that aloud, it's really come clear in recent years. And it changes you to work 30 years in these kinds of stores. I think he could have been a very different kind of person if he'd picked a different kind of career.

Unfortunately, Eleanor's father took his frustrations out on his family. "He had a tough childhood and a tough life. But he is also a brutal, domineering person," she said. Although he reads a lot, and he and Eleanor now talk about books, when Eleanor was growing up "he had very little concern for my mother and very little concern for us."

> All of us were pretty terrorized by him as kids. It was the sort of thing where he walked in the door at night and all of us had to say, "Hello, Daddy." We had to greet him politely, but within two minutes he might start screaming at us if he was in a bad mood that day.
>
> It wasn't as though we were physically abused, although he did spank us until we were twelve or so. Emotionally, though, we were put through the wringer. My mother's whole attitude was to try to smooth things over and pretend everything was O.K. I remember saying, "It's not fair. You know he's yelling at me for something I didn't do; it's not fair." And she'd say, "It's just easier to let it go. *You* know you're right."

Eleanor could never understand her mother's passivity or insistence that Eleanor get a teaching degree, then get married. But for Eleanor, "The whole passivity thing built in me a real anger. A lot of what I do now is to avoid ever being in a situation where someone can treat me like that. I don't ever want to be under somebody's heel."

While Eleanor's mother went through the motions of being the proper 1950s housewife—never complaining, but never joyful, Eleanor said—and expected her daughter to do the same, other mothers were more up front about their own frustrations. Not a few actively encouraged their daughters to have careers.[9]

Dorothy Johnston, a government lawyer who grew up in California, described her mother as "an avid reader, which my father was not. She could have done well, she was bright." When Dorothy was eight or nine she wanted to be famous and her mother was all for it. "I thought I would write a book; at one point I wanted to be the first woman Supreme Court justice," Dorothy said. "My mother used to say to me, 'You should go to law school.' I remember her telling me not to waste my brains."

Carolyn Woodward, a fast-talking television producer, sat behind a desk piled high with papers and videocassettes. Growing up in the Midwest, she said, her friends were always thinking about marriage: "The idea of marrying a doctor, a lawyer, pervaded the air." But Carolyn's mother, who had experienced considerable discrimination as a black woman, and who would have preferred not to have to work, did not tell her daughter to marry a doctor or a lawyer.

> She told me not to marry a man who would beat me up. My mother told me, "Go in on your own two feet, so you can support yourself." She said, "Carolyn, don't have a lot of children. Make sure you can support them. Marry somebody who will treat you right."

Suzanne Lewis, a newspaper reporter who grew up on the West Coast, described her mother as "overconcerned with appearances, looks." Even so,

> the first thing you have to know is that my mother, well, both my parents, wanted their daughters to contribute something. They were not pushing us to be little housewives. There was a great emphasis on things intellectual, on things political and on things journalistic. When I came home from school, as often as not I got questions about what I'd read in the paper that day. At breakfast we read the paper and at dinner we talked about it. And during the week we weren't allowed to watch television; the emphasis was on homework and every Friday night we either went to temple or to the library.

When she was in the fourth grade, Suzanne's parents wanted her to be a doctor. "They subscribed to a science magazine for children and bought me microscopes for my birthday, when other girls were getting dolls," she said. But Suzanne knew she did not want to go into medicine: "I told them that I didn't like blood. So it wouldn't do." In fact, she said, there were long stretches of time when nobody was quite sure what would become of her, "but it was just assumed I would do something with my life."

Other mothers were less overt in advising their daughters. Jennifer Howe's mother seemed happy enough in her marriage to a machinist— but as a Campfire Girl leader, she took Jennifer's troop to the science museum where her daughter learned she could have a life of discovery. Only much later, when Jennifer was thinking of getting married, did her mother tell her, "I hope he's not going to make you have children."

A lawyer told another researcher that her mother had always wanted to be a nurse. At the time her mother graduated, however, there were very few black nurses. "It was very difficult for her and she didn't go on," the lawyer said. "But she taught me to."[10]

Despite the popular image of the middle-class family of the 1950s as a pleasant haven in which daughters learned to be happy homemakers, in many families, a very different message was being delivered. That message was that women could and should do more. It was a message sent in different ways, depending on the particulars of each family constellation, on the relationship between each woman's parents, and on their relationship with their daughters.

It did not seem to matter if a family was rich or poor, white or black, Jewish, Protestant, or Catholic. It did not even seem to matter if a mother claimed to be happy or sad, or even if she had a paying job. What did matter was that daughters, seeing how their mothers were treated by husbands and by society, resolved at early ages to fight for power and equality in their own lives, as, they believed, their mothers had not.

This was not expected. In the 1950s, it was as though earlier generations of feminists—the grandmothers of these women, the working women of the seventeenth, eighteenth, and nineteenth centuries—had never lived. After decades of societal turbulence and change, in the 1950s, women were encouraged by their families, educators, and policymakers to be full-time mothers, and their daughters were expected to follow suit. Psychologists looked at stereotypical ideals of white, middle-class men and women, called those who fit them "normal," and developed theories explaining that for biological and psychological reasons, boys grew up to be like their fathers—achieving, aggressive, and rational—and girls like their mothers—in an ideal world, nurturant, passive, and emotional.

Some of those theories were based on the belief that because only women are capable of bearing and nursing children, they were biologically destined for the maternal role, and *only* for that role. Recent studies do show that before and after birth, and even into adulthood, hormones account for some gender differences in behavior. For example, boys tend to be more involved in "rough-and-tumble" play and girls in nurturing, as shown by their play with dolls.

Scientists say, however, that hormones do not in themselves determine behavior but rather, may predispose children to learn certain behaviors more readily than other behaviors. Action and experience also affect the production of hormones. For instance, stress can temporarily lower testosterone values, and travel, nutrition, and living with other females can affect women's menstrual cycles. A study showing that professional women had higher levels of the male hormone androgen than did clerical workers or homemakers might mean that the professional women were biologically predisposed to expend high levels of physical energy and to develop skills transferable to professional life. It might also mean that social reinforcement had led these women toward professional careers, which in turn stimulated their endocrine systems to increase their androgen production.

And because male and female hormones occur in both sexes—albeit in different quantities—there may be as much variation in play and nurturing behavior within one gender as between the genders. Hence, the attitudes of society, educators, and families have a profound effect on the ways in which men and women develop their conceptions of themselves. The most powerful of these forces is, perhaps, a child's early experience in relation to his or her parents.[11]

When the women I interviewed were children, the prevalent—and essentially Freudian—view was that both male and female infants were born feeling one and the same with their mothers. As boys developed, it was widely believed, they came to recognize that they were anatomically different from their mothers, and separate from them. Craving to be close to their mothers, yet fearful of their fathers' anger should they fulfill these desires, boys repressed their desire for attachment to their mothers and competed with their fathers by emulating them. In the process, boys, theoretically, grew up to become independent and autonomous individuals, eventually replacing their mothers with wives.

Girls, on the other hand, theoretically never experienced themselves as physically different from their mothers and had difficulty in emotionally detaching from them. In order to do so, they rejected their mothers, competed with them for their fathers' attentions, and somehow, eventually, as adults, attached themselves to men and had children in order to complete their identities.

A related view was that women never fully separated from their mothers, and as a result remained throughout their lives more dependent, more nurturant, and more involved with the needs of others than were men. For these reasons, it was believed, women were less interested in or capable of succeeding in competitive careers than men. Women were often considered less psychologically developed than men, because they failed to become fully autonomous.

In the late 1970s and early 1980s, psychologists began to suggest that women are not less developed than men but are simply different from them. According to one view, boys, as a rule, grow up independent and more concerned with the outer world than with emotions and feelings, but girls remain emotionally involved with both parents. Sociologist Nancy Chodorow suggests that girls grow up to replicate "the triangle of childhood—preoccupied, alternatively, with men and children." Women's ongoing ties to both parents make women more empathic and intuitive than men throughout their lives, she writes. Psychologist Carol Gilligan and others emphasize that such traits should be considered women's special strengths.[12]

Other researchers criticize all of these models as overly stereotypical in that they do not take into account the varying family constellations within differing racial and ethnic groups.[13] Also, overgeneralizing about the differences between the sexes presents the danger of perpetuating and exaggerating those differences. Still, there is, I believe, a continuum, determined by individual chemistry, family situation, and experience, along which males and females exhibit certain traits to greater or lesser degrees.

The theory underlying *Broken Patterns* is that females—and possibly males—develop their identities largely through a process of emotionally separating from and connecting with their mothers (and sometimes with their fathers). This process may become more complicated depending on the particulars of a woman's family constellation and life experience; at present, there is little research on this where boys are concerned.[14] According to psychologist Irene Stiver, the natural developmental process for girls is a push-pull struggle in which they seek to become individuals in their own right, different from their mothers, yet emotionally close to them. This theory best explains why the women I spoke with knew at early ages that they wanted careers and why, as young adults, they entered fields that were largely reserved for men.[15]

Growing up, the women I spoke with wanted to be different from their mothers. Some had mothers who told them to avoid certain traps; others saw their mothers mistreated by their husbands. It was not simply that these women did not want to be like their mothers, or that they wanted to reject them. Instead—and this paradox is central—the drive to be unlike their mothers was heightened precisely because as females, they knew they were much like them.

◆　◇　◆

Take Becky Wilson. When I interviewed her in her downtown apartment, I was struck at first by how dark it was, with small rooms off one long corridor. At the same time, the living room—cluttered with an old couch, too many chairs, a footstool draped with a half-finished afghan and lots of photographs—felt cheery. Becky's story, too, had a somber side, but she herself seemed lighthearted enough as we shared a pot of coffee. An athletically-built blonde wearing a navy-blue suit, she laughed often and made fun on her own situation and her qualms.

When I asked what her mother did when Becky was growing up, Becky said, without missing a beat, almost before I finished asking the question, "She ate." I realized Becky was only half joking when she went on to explain, "When she was happy, she ate. When she was sad, she ate." I asked what else her mother did. "Cocktail parties," Becky said immediately. "Mother was good at cocktail parties." Becky's light tone started to darken as she continued. "My mother got fifty pounds overweight in response to feeling that my father thought she was unattractive."

Becky's mother grew up in a wealthy, white, Anglo-Saxon, Protestant family that did not think she was smart enough to go to college. "And neither did her school. So she went on a secret interview to a prestigious women's college and told them nobody wanted her to go to college; the college admitted her on the spot," Becky said. After graduating from college, Becky's mother married a man from a poor background. He became a doctor, and then a university president. While Becky's father was pursuing his career, her mother had four children, three boys and Becky.

Unfortunately, Becky's father harbored an intensely negative attitude toward women.

> He still sees all women as people to go to bed with. He talks about women in sexual terms. His reaction to women always involves the shape of their boobs or their legs. He talks about what they'd look like in a nightgown; he thinks it's funny. Every time he sees a woman he thinks of making love to her. He tries to rub it in that my mother is not the right shape.

It was easy, then, to understand why as a child, Becky did not particularly want to be like her mother, why she should tell me proudly, "I was a tomboy, a trailblazer." Growing up among faculty children near the university, she played only with boys. That did not explain why she chose to have a career; in Becky's family, women did not work except, perhaps, for "mad money." She worked hard at school, she explained, because "I needed to do impressive things for my parents." I couldn't help substituting *father* for parents, because while her father denigrated her mother, he would sometimes tell Becky that professional women were "more interesting." As Becky reported, "'For a woman,' he'd say, 'it's pretty good to be a doctor.'"

Becky's desires to avoid being like her mother and to please her father do not tell the whole story: Becky also told me that she had always sympathized with her mother, and emulated her in some ways. She shared her mother's interest in art and her love of food, and when Becky graduated from college, she married almost immediately, as her mother had.

At that time, Becky fully expected simply to "do crafts," and for several years, she lived with her graduate student husband and his parents. When her husband was hired to teach college in the South, she accompanied him. Eventually, she "got bored playing tennis with the faculty wives" and decided to have a career. She considered social work and teaching—both traditionally feminine careers—but rejected them as "uninteresting." She chose law, she said, because "I thought back over what I had liked best in my life, and it was draft counselling [during the Vietnam War] in college."

It may be that Becky simply opposed the war, or that using the law to help her fellow students avoid serving was, in part, a way of rebelling against male authority. It seemed to me, however, that the clue to Becky's career choice lay still farther back. In explaining why her father so denigrated women, Becky said,

I think he was insecure because he has never felt successful enough. He was striving for the admiration of his stepbrother, who was eighteen years older and worked as a lawyer on Park Avenue. His insecurity extends to me. When I got the job in the law firm I'm working for now, my father said it was only because one of the partners knew my uncle.

Choosing a legal career, Becky must have hoped, would compel her father to respect and admire her. But it would also allow her to surpass him, to have the sort of control over him and over her own life that her mother never had.

While Becky's family was well-to-do, Janet Peters, an architect, described her background as lower middle class. Slender, with black hair to her shoulders and small gold hoops in her ears, she wore a calf-length beige dress and a subtly-printed silk scarf. "Chic," I thought when we met for lunch at a trendy café. Over salad and Perrier, Janet seemed glad—even anxious—to talk, though the interview turned out to be less straightforward than others I had done, perhaps because Janet's life had taken a lot of twists and turns.

The first in her family to go to college, Janet initially hoped to study insects, then, encouraged by her advisors, switched to interior design when she "started having trouble with the science." After college, unhappily married and selling drapes at Sears Roebuck, she took a secretarial job days to put herself through architecture school at night.

Where did she get her drive? At first, she said she wanted to compete in a "masculine" field because she had an older brother whom she "really admired." As Janet explained,

91

My brother was always interested in different things; he pursued them; he was in the band; he played basketball; he was a wheeler dealer. He always managed to get by. I would do anything for him. For a quarter, I'd clean his room, give him a rubdown after basketball practice, run errands; I'd spit shine his shoes. He always got straight A's. My mother paid us for A's, we paid her a dollar for B's. I was always in debt. He always made money.

But while Janet admired her brother, she also envied him.

Everybody would ask my brother what he was doing but they didn't ask me. When I would tell them, they would change the subject. He was a real person to them. No matter how well I did at something, I was never as real as my brother was.

In part because she no longer wanted to live in her brother's shadow, she decided to leave interior design almost as soon as she entered the field.

I did a joint project with some architecture students and that was my first experience with being relegated to doing the furnishings. I think the resentment began to build right then and it just burst when I finally got a job in a professional office. If you're working in an architect's firm, architects are more respected than interior designers. And I guess I had fought this thing with my brother all my life, and I was darned if I was going to live my whole life as an underling.

While studies of earlier career women showed that many grew up as only daughters or as the elder of two daughters in families with no sons, many of the women I spoke with grew up in the typically large families of the 1950s; like Janet, they spoke of trying to emulate and compete with brothers, who were often treated as special by both parents. As we talked, though, it became clear that Janet's disdain for a secondary role stemmed not only from her relationship with her brother, but more importantly, from her mother's experience.

Janet's mother was divorced from Janet's father, an optometrist, when Janet was five. She got married again three years later to a man who managed shoe factories. He was transferred often. He and Janet's family moved to Arkansas, then to other small towns in the South and Midwest. "I didn't like my stepfather," Janet said. "I didn't like him at all. He hit my mother." When her stepfather died, Janet was still in high school. "It was a mixed blessing," she said, "because he left my mother with nothing. We had to move because we couldn't afford the house. My mother hated moving; it was a nice house." That's when Janet vowed that "no one would ever treat me that way. I never want to be in a position where I am that dependent on somebody else."

Did Janet's decision to become an architect—after all she could have become a scientist or a doctor like her brother—stem in some way from her concern over the loss of that house and a wish to retrieve it for her mother? Janet did tell me that switching out of science and into design felt natural because her mother always kept books about interior decorating on the coffee table. But Janet decided on architecture because, she said, she feared that if she chose a traditionally feminine career such as interior design, she would wind up as her mother had, as a woman with no control over her own destiny.

> I've always looked at my mother as really struggling. And I've always wanted to prove that where my mother failed, I could succeed. She's had children in the house for 37 years. She's tired and disappointed and she was unhappy all her life. I don't want to grow old that way. I want more graciousness than she had.

Abby Nathan, an internist, grew up in a Jewish middle-class family, in which "people thought boys were more important." In the Jewish tradition, Abby's grandmother chose a name starting with "S," the first initial of a relative who had passed away, for her first grandchild. "Before I was born," Abby explained, "my grandmother had a name all picked out for a boy. It was Samuel. When I was born, she said to save the name. Then my sister was born; they saved it again. Finally, when I was seven they had a boy and he got the name."

Abby's mother evidently bought into the idea that females were not worth much; she spent most of her time "lying around the house doing nothing." Although she was in a couple of organizations, she was not very active, Abby said. As a result, Abby always thought her mother was "a failure." So, evidently, did Abby's father. While Abby's mother claimed to be happy in her marriage, Abby's father was not. Nor was he happy with his job as a salesman for an engineering company. "He didn't make much money. He used to come home and yell at my mother. The dishes weren't done; he'd be angry," she said.

Although deeply disappointed in her mother, Abby sympathized with her. Yet as angry as Abby was at her father, she desperately wanted his approval: one reason she chose a medical career was that her father had wanted one.

> He'd wanted to be a doctor but couldn't afford medical school. He never said much about that but he would "operate" on eggs on Sunday

mornings; he would do pretend operations on us, cut open our stomachs and pull out all sorts of unlikely things.

Afraid of becoming like her mother, Abby attempted to ally with her father by becoming a physician. This allowed Abby to surpass her mother yet be in a position to take care of her. It also allowed her to surpass her father, possibly to please him, and above all to enjoy the sort of power in her own life and in the world that neither of her parents ever had.

◆　　◇　　◆

In the studies discussed in an earlier chapter, there was much debate as to whether professional women wanted to be like their mothers or like their fathers. For the women I interviewed, who most often saw their mothers as nurturant but unfulfilled, it was not an either-or question. While they may have liked and admired their mothers, they did not want to be treated as their mothers had been treated. Whether they liked their fathers or not, they saw them as powerful; often, they tried to please their fathers by emulating them. Such women may have been competing with their mothers for their fathers' attentions, as good Freudians might suggest. Yet at the same time, they were "standing in" for their mothers, fighting the battles their mothers had failed to fight for themselves.

My interviews, then, showed that for women who saw their mothers as downtrodden in relation to men—and most, though not all, of the women I spoke with viewed their mothers that way—what might otherwise have been a relatively simple push-pull process of identity development became more complicated. The worse a mother was treated, the more her daughter wished to avoid being like her and to surpass her. Yet at the same time, on a psychological level, such a daughter wished to protect her mother, to fight on her behalf, and in some cases, to take her place.

This was true even in families in which mothers had some power. Marjorie Babson, a social scientist, described her mother as a professional woman and feminist living in an egalitarian marriage. Yet even Marjorie admitted that a major motivation in her own choice of careers was not to get stuck in the same trap as her mother had.

Marjorie's parents grew up in Alabama and all of her relatives lived in the deep South. The family was very religious. To them, she said, "the soul mattered more than what you did." Her mother's father was a farmer. "He was also the chairman of the board of education and ran a little gas station," she said. Marjorie's maternal grandmother took care of the house and her six children. Marjorie's mother was the only daughter and she "felt extremely put down by being a girl." In her family, "being a girl was nothing." Marjorie's mother did all the farm work and all the housework. "She made straight A's and her parents said 'fine.' The boys brought home C's; her parents said, 'Fine, great,'" Marjorie said. As a result, Marjorie's mother grew up ready for the women's movement. "She had a lot of fury about women's lot," Marjorie said.

Marjorie's mother got her master's in child development when Marjorie was in the third grade, and when she started working, she made more money than Marjorie's father. A minister on a college campus, he told Marjorie and her older brother (who became a minister) to "do what you love." Marjorie's mother, however, was definitely working mainly because she had to earn a living. "I bring home the bacon" was her attitude. There were problems because Marjorie's mother provided most of the family's income. "There was a time when it was difficult for my dad to adjust," Marjorie said. "But soon, he started doing a lot more housework, cooking, cleaning; that was normal. He did half the housework; it was taken for granted."

But Marjorie's mother seemed split. "The work and home parts of her were separate," Marjorie said. "I always saw my mother as very capable and it was hard for me to get a sense that she wasn't secure. But she wasn't. She always thought she wasn't working hard enough." Even though she had a job, because she didn't have a doctorate "she was always in a one-down position at work," Marjorie said. "She worked hard, but there were limits to what she could achieve." She told Marjorie story after story about the politics in her office.

"My mother felt put down by being a woman," Marjorie said. "I was interested in her stories. Her situation took such a toll on her. She came home and told Dad; he told her to tell them off. Work was hard for my mother; the battles never stopped." As a result, Marjorie, who greatly admired her mother, chose a social science field similar to her mother's, and like her mother, she married a man who works at what he loves—art. Unlike her mother, she made sure to get a Ph.D.

Other women with working mothers described similar experiences. After Janet Peters's stepfather died, her mother went to business college, then got a job as a secretary for the president of an insurance firm. "She was doing all of the boss's work but she was paid as a secretary," Janet said. "I thought it was unfair." Anna Bart's mother was also a secretary; she worked for a doctor to support the family because her husband lacked the confidence or wherewithal to succeed as an insurance agent. Anna's mother didn't make much money and never advanced but she encouraged Anna to go to medical school. Clara Zolen, a businesswoman, used to hear her mother, a part-time nurse, complain about the physical labor. "So I knew I didn't want that. She used to yap a lot about the doctors, too, so I didn't want that, either," Clara said.

A group of black women attorneys interviewed in the 1970s expressed similar sentiments; while they had grown up expecting to work for a living, most said they had decided against traditionally feminine careers based on their mothers' experiences in teaching, social work, and blue-collar occupations.[16]

While studies in the 1950s and 1960s showed that many women who sought "innovative" careers saw their working mothers or their fathers as role models, the women I interviewed were different. In their stories they described a range of experiences: some women had mothers whom they liked and admired; others had mothers whom they said they did not want to emulate at all. In some ways, all identified with their mothers, yet all believed that their mothers had missed out. From what they saw of their mothers' lives, constrained as they were by the sex-role stereotypes of the 1950s, these daughters resolved to do things differently. They vowed, many well before the feminist movement of the 1960s and 1970s, not to be trapped by the family and societal patterns that had engulfed their mothers and that threatened to engulf them as well.

Breaking those patterns involved challenging old images of women—images held in society, in families, and in women's own psyches. It meant asking questions about the now familiar polarization of roles, about divisions between men and women, about achieving and nurturing, about autonomy and intimacy. The central questions, though, were how women could be different from their mothers yet close to them, and how, later in their lives, they could achieve on their own, yet remain emotionally connected with others.

In trying to answer those questions, each woman I interviewed would go through a lengthy transition process, a series of crisis points that culminated in a grander crisis when she reached her mid-thirties, when it was time for her to become a mother herself. For each of these women, the transition began when she left home for college and embarked on her quest for a new feminine identity.

6

Making the Break: The 1960s

When my parents drove me up to start college at Cornell University in the fall of 1966, three young men stood at the edge of the parking lot, directing traffic. They directed us right out of the parking lot for the women's dormitory—and right into the parking lot for what turned out to be their fraternity house—"Theta Zoo," I later learned to call it. There was no hint, that sunny day, of the often chaotic challenges to "the system" that would take place over the next five years or so—the civil rights marches, the protests against the Vietnam War, the bomb scares, the building takeovers—challenges that would escalate at Cornell until 1969, when the National Guard was called in. That fall day offered no signs of the changes in women's lives that would be catalyzed by those events, and others, in the broader society.

Until the mid-1960s, the social life at Cornell, as at many colleges, was dominated by fraternities and football, and the typical college woman had diffuse, idyllic plans for marriage and life in the suburbs.

Abby Nathan, now a doctor, expected at seventeen "to be a psychiatric social worker or something like that." She'd work for a few years to get some experience—"just in case."

Monica Edwards, a business consultant, thought she would do volunteer work as her mother had. Whereas her mother was in several organizations, Monica would join only one: "And I would be the president."

Becky Wilson thought she'd get married, have babies, and do crafts.

Even Jennifer Howe, now a scientist, who had known from the time she was seven years old that she wanted to make a life of discovery, and

Sandy Smith, now a surgeon, said that at seventeen they thought they would teach high school science.

At this time, almost half of female high school students in one study expected to be homemakers for their entire lives; half expected to work at certain times and to be homemakers at others; fewer than 4 percent expected lifetime careers.[1] Many of the brightest women college seniors had no plans for future work or study because they were about to get married. Those who did have plans had switched out of professional and research fields into "practical" fields far below their abilities. Many young women seemed increasingly uncommitted to anything beyond early marriage, motherhood, and a suburban house.[2]

At Queens College in New York City, 95 percent of Cynthia Fuchs Epstein's women students (most of them from middle- or lower-middle-class backgrounds) opted for one of the most traditional women's paths: teaching public school before marriage. While most black women college students expected to work after marriage, it was usually as teachers; most minority women scientists questioned in a 1975 study said that they entered college expecting to teach grade school or high school.[3]

At Barnard College, women from upper-middle-class backgrounds had "scattered" interests and lived their lives in fragmented ways. If they read a great deal, it was about many topics in a superficial manner. They were rarely expert in anything because, like most American women, they rarely found themselves in situations in which they could become deeply involved in interests of their own. They viewed themselves neither as future career women nor as homemakers. "Rejection of both alternatives indicates they have no clear visualization of the future, and thus do not prepare themselves for what is to come," Epstein wrote. As a result, their talents seemed to "die on the vine."[4]

This was to be expected, many psychologists believed. In 1942, Clara Thompson had described adolescence as a period in which boys opened up, but in which girls shut down.[5] As late as 1968, most psychologists still believed that soon after adolescence, normal young women would forsake earlier goals for marriage and children. Some young women might go through "a psychosocial moratorium," in which they felt relatively free from "the tyranny of inner space" (simply put—the womb); they could "venture into 'outer space' with a bearing and a curiosity which often appeared hermaphroditic if not downright 'masculine.'" But, in Erik Erikson's view, the moratorium would be short-lived—because, essentially for biological reasons, woman's identity was complete only "when attractiveness and experience" allowed her to join a man and have children.[6]

In the 1960s, many women entered college with more liberal attitudes than those of their fathers or boyfriends, but their views "came around" by graduation. They often became more "traditionally feminine" as they proceeded through college—in large part because they were afraid academic or career success would jeopardize their relationships with men.[7]

Some psychologists found these reactions normal—believing that women were by nature passive. Others explained that in growing up, women were caught in a sort of emotional web. Needing approval and nurturance from others, they theoretically grew up less interested than men in competing and were, perhaps, less capable of achieving on their own.[8] Still others believed that women were reluctant to achieve on their own because a sexist society and their families restricted them and the possibilities open to them. Or perhaps the research done until recently simply ignored the reality of women's development.[9]

Based on my own research, I have come to believe that in generations past, the tendency of young women to hold themselves back expressed societal and parental restrictions internalized from childhood on until they became individual, emotional restrictions. With no external forum in which to fight those restrictions, and knowing they would be considered aberrational if they did so, many women held those restrictions inside, and stopped themselves from achieving as they entered adulthood.

For young women in the late 1960s, something happened to turn all of that around. Events unfolding at the time provided a forum in which they could express the conflicts and anger they felt inside. For some women, rebellion took a political form; for others it did not. But all of the women I interviewed saw the upheavals they experienced in the 1960s as crucial turning points in their lives, points at which the personal and the political merged to catalyze changes in their inner and outer worlds.

For Suzanne Lewis, now a respected national journalist, college was "really a revolution," and, at the time, a job had seemed "irrelevant." Though she had once wanted to be a reporter, when she was twenty, "newspapers were part of the establishment and a career was really the farthest thing from my mind. I did not have any long-term goals. I didn't know what I was going to do. It was a very exciting time to be alive." But, she said, tensing, "it had grave consequences in my personal life. It was the source of a great rift with my parents that still hasn't healed."

At this point, Suzanne threw back her head and shoulders and continued theatrically: "I would write them and say, 'You capitalist pigs, how can you enslave us.' Back and forth, terrible clichés." She relaxed, then went on. "And at the bottom it would say, 'and by the way, could you send a hundred dollars for tuition?'" She smiled. "I think my parents were as generous as anybody could have expected under the circumstances. I was not a pleasant person. I was very much an absolutist."

Andrea Digby, now a professor, grew up in a town in a desert, where her father ran a fruit shop. She had always expected to become a secretary like her mother but did so well in high school that her teachers encouraged her to go to college. As we sat in Andrea's small office—cluttered with papers, a Native American rights poster on one wall—she told me that in college she had spent twenty hours each week in community action. Her parents did not approve: they felt she was neglecting her studies.

At first, Andrea said she did not blame them. "My university had pass/fail grades, and it was hard to know if I was doing well." Then she sounded hurt. "They threatened not to pay tuition if I kept up the community work." Then she seemed angry. "They wrote to a professor, who showed the letter to me. In the letter my parents referred to me as an 'overemotional and uncontrollable' person. They wrote that they never knew if I would settle down."

Andrea's parents never spoke to her of the correspondence with the professor nor did she ever ask them about it; she continued with her community work and they continued to pay tuition. But since she was bringing the incident up in an interview ten years later, it seemed clear that her defiance of her parents was an important—and highly emotional—point in her life.

In college, Clara Zolen was interested in engineering and "should have majored" in math. "I was stupid not to," she said. She was interested in politics, however, and "scientists were not political." They were not women either. "It was a sex-role thing. I was always the only woman in math class," Clara said. Feeling that as a woman she did not fit in, she did not complete the math major, even though she only needed one more course. Instead, she majored in social science. After graduation, she became a community organizer, and still later, a business executive.

Robyn Sparks had always wanted to be a doctor. But in college, she said,

> I couldn't deal with science. I wasn't oriented to spending the time and the science didn't come easy to me. I majored in German. I had first taken it because of wanting to be a doctor; I liked the head of the department; I could see nothing else to do. I thought of sociology, but that wasn't it. I didn't know anything else I wanted.

Even though she knew she was dramatically affecting the course of her life, she told herself the decision did not matter. "I figured, what difference does it make?" she said. Then Robyn began to work against the Vietnam War, became active in student politics, and when she graduated from college, went to work for a congressman committed to broad social change. She also lived with a man against her parents' wishes and eventually entered law school.

Nancy Kelly refused to go to a Catholic college and instead won a scholarship to a prestigious private university. Her mother was very upset. "Her religion meant a tremendous amount to her and she was convinced that my religious practice would be jeopardized," Nancy said. Knowing her mother cared greatly about how Nancy dressed, in college, Nancy always wore blue jeans. Instead of studying, she spent most of her time working in the student theater. "My parents hated the theater thing," she said. As Nancy explained her actions, "From the time I went away to college 'til my mid to late twenties I was in the process of rejecting my family background totally." Why wasn't she involved in 1960s politics? "Because I was already getting enough parental disapproval for what I was doing with theater," she explained.

While Nancy rebelled in part by leaving the church, Sandy Smith rebelled by entering it: she became a nun. Her parents were not practicing Catholics, she said, and "they were very much opposed." As Sandy explained her thinking at nineteen,

> It was the 1960s. You either went into the Peace Corps or the convent or you went off to Eastern Slobovia and took care of somebody. I had been working in Latin America and it seemed to me that you could do more if you had a group behind you than if you were working by yourself. The idea of living with a group of people who thought similarly and would be able to support me was appealing.

Among a group of black lawyers studied in New York City, many said they had chosen their careers as a result of their social activism which had been "ignited" by the civil rights movement when they were in college; 75 percent of them had experience organizing community groups. One attorney said that she had stopped talking to white people, for a time, and began working with an organization concerned with black poverty. She later became a lawyer because she believed that "you could effect greater change through the courts . . . and that as a lawyer you could help people."[10]

In my own experience, the late 1960s was a wild time, a time in which young men and women alike challenged the status quo: their parents, the roles of men and women, the family, and the society that had formed us. At graduation, many of us wore black armbands and civilian clothes instead of caps and gowns to protest America's involvement in the

Vietnam War; the ceremony was interrupted three times by demonstrations. At one point, the leader of the procession hit one of my government instructors over the head with a mace to stop him from disrupting the ceremony. Later, a group of black students walked out. Then, antiwar activists created a commotion.

In the previous four years, we had seen the end of parietals, and the liberalization of attitudes about sex and politics. One spring, three separate bomb scares disrupted a single hour-long seminar in English literature—Conrad and Hardy, I believe it was. I will never forget the time the university president gave a talk to explain why Cornell maintained investments in South Africa: as he spoke, bongo drums began to beat in the background. Then, two muscular black male students walked onto the stage, took him by the elbows and herded him into the wings. Soon after that, on parents' weekend, several students from my comparative literature course—Existentialism and Revolution—became part of a group which took over the student union building. When the group emerged days later, at least one member was carrying a rifle and wearing a shoulder-to-waist belt filled with bullets. The following year, standing in the graduation processional, students passed marijuana joints back and forth as the university muckety-mucks passed through.

Cornell was by no means an isolated case. In 1968, Columbia University was disrupted by protests over the building of a gym, which would demolish housing in a run-down neighborhood adjoining the university. In 1971, National Guard soldiers shot and killed four student protesters at Kent State. At Brandeis, a women with whom I had gone to grade school ended up in a bank robbery in which a man was killed—in the name of equality for poor people, for "the revolution." In 1970, the majority of college students in one national study said they believed that American society was so "sick" that it could not be repaired from within.[11]

◆   ◇   ◆

Some historians trace the tactics and philosophy of the feminist, student, and antiwar movements to the civil rights movement, beginning in the late 1940s, when many blacks began to leave farms for the industrial North. For the first time, an economy of plenty rather than scarcity created the possibility of economic equality, which gave minorities something real for which to fight.[12]

Historian Sara Evans suggests that in the late 1950s and early 1960s, youths' reaction to the emptiness of a materialist culture led to the beatnik challenge of the bourgeoisie and to the free speech movement at Berkeley; the Vietnam War, she writes, threatened individuals' beliefs in America's goodness.[13]

Doug McAdam sees the rise of 1960s activism as a result of the post-war baby boom combined with an economic boom, which made well-to-do youths experience themselves as at the center of everything—in a "decidedly schizophrenic" era in which politicians promoted cold war "brinksmanship" abroad, but liberal idealism at home.[14]

Sociologist Todd Gitlin explains the turmoil and violence of the 1960s as a reaction to the 1950s: a time of affluence under which lay the terror—with the Great Depression, the explosion of the atomic bomb, and the Holocaust all recent memories—that it could all be lost.[15]

To some, the 1960s was a "revolutionary" period in which more humane organizations were replacing "corporate manipulation" and the "welfare-warfare state." To others, it was a "counter-revolutionary" time in which rebellious youths lashed out against technological and managerial changes that would consign them to the "dustbin of history."[16]

Overall, I would suggest, the social and cultural movements of the 1960s were a generation's attempt to express and resolve a dynamic societal tension that had begun much earlier. Since the early nineteenth century, rapid social and technological change had led to increased belief in individualism and equality for all. Simultaneously, rapid change and the turmoil and family breakup caused by war, economic crisis, and immigration led, also, to a yearning for the seeming safety of homogeneous communities, close family ties, and set gender roles.

That dynamic societal tension was exhibited, in the 1950s, in a sharp dichotomy between the nation's egalitarian ideals and its actual practices abroad, domestically, and within the family. Internationally, for instance, in the 1950s American policy ignored the Third World poverty. Domestically, Americans tolerated widespread racial discrimination. In many families, women were treated as second class citizens. The result, in the 1960s, was the sort of youth rebellion that arises, one analyst wrote, "whenever social and historical circumstances combine to cause the younger generation to lose confidence in the older one."[17]

How did such a loss of confidence lead to rebellion? Some psychologists explained youthful activism as a reaction against permissive parenting; others saw it as a reaction against parents who had not been responsive enough.[18] Psychologist Kenneth Keniston found, however, that many of the activist young men he studied in the 1960s were responding to mixed messages delivered by parents who instilled altruistic values in their offspring but did not live out those values themselves. Sons of such parents grew up intolerant of hypocrisy, Keniston reported; at adolescence, when youth are characteristically unable to deal well with ambiguity, they simultaneously rebelled against their parents and expressed their parents' underlying humanism.[19]

Nearly all of the analysis of 1960s activists were conducted by men studying men—perhaps because, at the time, most social scientists and the most visible rebels were men. What of the young women? Certainly the times had an effect; anyone growing up in the 1950s and early 1960s would have been aware of the sit-ins in the South, the Free Speech movement, and the Vietnam War.

Family background was also important. White women active in the civil rights movement and in radical or feminist politics in the 1960s and early 1970s often came from religious backgrounds or had powerful mothers who had been feminists, socialists, or communists in the 1930s, 1940s, and 1950s. Some of these 1960s activists became leaders of the women's liberation cause after encountering sexism within other political organizations.[20]

A group of black women lawyers interviewed in 1978 were, generally, the eldest or youngest children from small middle- or working-class families. Usually one or both of their parents had migrated North from the South or from the West Indies, had some college training, and worked in professional or white-collar occupations. The lawyers themselves had integrated the schools and colleges they had attended; their experience of alienation within predominantly white educational settings—as well as their knowledge of the black experience—had increased their determination to correct massive societal inequities.[21]

As for the women I interviewed, most from white, mainstream backgrounds, the politics of the time and the growing movement for women's rights certainly struck a responsive chord. Politically active or not, every woman I spoke with challenged the status quo. In her own, sometimes quiet way, each lashed out against the family and societal restrictions that had crippled her mother and other women in the past. On a very personal level, each woman's rebellion was an expression of anger at her mother and of a firm resolve not to be like her. Yet at the same time, it was an acting out of her mother's anger and of her oft-unspoken wishes.

◆　◇　◆

As I waited to interview Molly Walden in her law firm, the furnishings in the reception area spoke loud and clear. "Money," they said. From the salmon-colored velvet sofa, I took in the panoramic view of skyscrapers against ocean and thought about how far the women of my generation had come since college. Within minutes, a blond-haired woman, obviously pregnant under her navy blue maternity dress, entered the reception area. She wore low-heeled navy blue shoes and one of those female bow ties; she handed a file folder to the receptionist with a few words, then turned to me, held out her hand, and introduced herself. She led me to her office, which also had a spectacular view.

Her chestnut desk was clear, except for a gold-framed picture of a thin, dark-haired man in his thirties. I sat on a rust-colored chair opposite her, and as we spoke, almost immediately I learned that beneath Molly's well-polished exterior lurked quite a quirky individual. I asked how Molly happened to decide on a law career, and she got right into it.

In college Molly had majored in philosophy; then she went to graduate school. "But I dropped out of the Ph.D. program because the employment situation looked bad and I wasn't sure I wanted to spend the rest of my life in libraries thinking about esoteric things," she said. "I got a master's degree so I could teach English, then I went to Europe to visit my grandmother, who lived there." Nothing unusual here, I thought. Then the surprises started.

In Europe, Molly landed a teaching job in a girls' boarding school but after six months was fired "for not being disciplinarian enough." So she went travelling.

I picked tomatoes in Crete, went through an anarchistic phase. I lived in a communal agricultural situation. Some people were there with the idea of going back to the Amazonian jungles; I met a guy I was interested in. I liked the agricultural life; it was primitive, water from a well; it was also cheap. I made six dollars a day and my rent was nine dollars a month; I spent three months there, through the winter. Then I got sick of it. Actually, the relationship came apart. We had told everyone we were married, and I had to leave because it would be dangerous for me to be living there alone and unmarried.

Molly was telling her story in short sentences which sometimes seemed disjointed; she moved from point to point with little embellishment. Her tone was matter-of-fact, but I wondered later if her lack of expression masked some underlying conflict. Her story continued: "When I got back to this country, I ran into an old friend who got me a job working with a political candidate. After the candidate lost, I got a job as an assistant to a manager at a television station." She worked there one year, met a law student, married him, and moved with him to another city.

I was in a new town; I knew nobody and my husband was away all day, having big opportunities. I was just looking around, staying at home, refinishing furniture. That was when I knew I could not be

105

like my mother. Law school was the easy way out. I had been writing
program notes; I had played with the idea of becoming a movie re-
viewer and was building a clip file. Things got easier once I got into
law school; I felt more secure.

Despite its seeming disjuncture, Molly's story made sense to me; my
own experience was not dissimilar. I, too, had gone through a period of
turmoil after college, before becoming a journalist. But by the time I
entered graduate school, in the mid-1970s, it was as though the 1960s—
the politics, experimentation with drugs and sex, communal living arrangements, the challenges to the status quo—had never happened. By
the mid-1980s, we had already completed a dress-for-success phase and
"femininity" was back: you could wear color in the office, now, and even
cry if you felt like it—especially if it worked as a tactic. In television
news, as in most professions, you would never reveal that you had ever
had radical inclinations, or even political—let alone feminist—convic-
tions. So as Molly spoke, I hid my surprise at her candor and asked the
rest of my questions.

As a college freshman, what had she expected her future would be
like?

I wanted to be a journalist. I wanted to be one of the women on TV
or the first woman president of the United States. My mother told
me I should go on television or be the first woman lots of things. An
astronaut. My father wanted me to be a doctor; he thought it was
important to be your own boss.

Then Molly said, in what seemed like a non sequitur, "That's why I didn't
take any science courses." I thought, "Huh?"

Molly explained that when she got to college, she became very rebellious: "My mother told me no one would marry me, because I was so
fresh. She would say that when she was angry with me." Although Molly
had been close to her father when she was growing up, when she got
to college, their relationship deteriorated. "I was involved in marches,
petitions, draft advice," she said. This upset her father because "his experience in the McCarthy era, not that he was that active or persecuted,
made him wary."

That's why I didn't take any science courses. I was very rebellious
and then, later on, I had too much pride to turn around. I was a
radical and he was a conservative. So I majored in philosophy in
order not to be a professional. I was going to further the cause of
the revolution.

106

While Molly saw much of her rebellion as against her father, as she spoke, I could see that it had just as much—if not more—to do with her mother.

Molly's mother had grown up in an agricultural village in Switzerland. Her grandfather, a schoolteacher, died when her grandmother was just thirty-six; Molly's grandmother lived off his pension. Molly's grandmother, ninety at the time of our interview, had always been "strong-willed and hard to get along with." Molly's grandmother raised three children—Molly's uncle, who is in real estate; her aunt, who is married to a farmer; and Molly's own mother.

Before marriage, Molly's mother had trained as a nurse. She worked in a library at a research institute for a while, then became a governess for wealthy people in Italy, in the north of France, in the war zone. "When the Nazis came in, she always seemed to be the last one out on the last train out," Molly said with pride. "My mother met my father in this country when he was in medical school. She was independent; she had rejected the religion of her mother; her father died when she was young. She was an expatriot; she came to the U.S. and married."

"You admired her, then?" I asked.

"Yes. She was smart and rebellious and I think she was happy with her life," said Molly. "Though I did wonder how she could not be unhappy or disappointed."

"Why was that?" I asked.

My mother spent her time shopping, shopping; cleaning; doing traditional things, sewing, knitting. She would see a dress in the window, make up a pattern. I don't have the patience. I start things like that and don't finish them. Also, it struck me that my mother was smarter than my father; she could see through problems faster; my father tries one thing, then he tries the next. He is not analytical.

"What was he like?" I asked.

"He was somewhat anti-establishment," Molly said. "He believed you should be independent."

"Was he egalitarian, then, at home?" I asked.

Not at all, Molly said: "My father did no housework. He was the worst. He still refuses to boil water." What's more, both parents were passive. "Each of them would wait for the other to make decisions, something I find frustrating to this day," she said.

Molly's parents sounded much like the parents of the young radical men Keniston had described, who were forward-thinking humanists who professed egalitarian, democratic values. Yet, her parents adhered to stereotypical gender roles. Molly's father, who prided himself on being a "non-conformist," insisted that his wife do all of the cooking. Her mother, once adventurous, had left her home in an agricultural village to live a more exciting life, but in the America of the 1950s, she spent her time "shopping, shopping, shopping, cooking, cleaning."

As Molly described her parents, they sounded contradictory, even hypocritical; to her they seemed "passive" and she sensed "a frustration." Some of that frustration was conveyed directly: while her parents themselves observed strict gender roles, they not so subtly told their daughter not to. Molly's mother wanted her to have a prominent career. Molly's father, a doctor, wanted Molly to follow in his footsteps. Often, he took her sailing. "My father had a twenty-seven-foot boat," Molly said. "It was like we were the men going off to sea, leaving 'the women,' my mother and sister, behind."

Perhaps because of the conflicting messages she was receiving from her parents, Molly's relationship with them was "constantly fluctuating." Sometimes she would agree with one parent, sometimes with the other. "My mother would accuse my father of looking like a slob and I'd agree with her," Molly said. "But at other times, I'd take my father's part and admire him for being 'anti-establishment.'"

Given the mixed messages about women's roles that Molly received when she was growing up, it is no surprise that she had to struggle, when she left home, to establish just who she was. Consider the bind she was in. To please her mother, Molly should not be a housewife, but if she rejected her mother's role, it was something of a slap in the face. Meanwhile, becoming a doctor would have allowed her to be different from her mother, but at the same time, by doing exactly what her father wanted, she would be right back in her mother's shoes. The result was inner turmoil, outwardly expressed.

As Molly explained her rebellion, it was against her father: she did not take any science courses precisely because he wanted her to be a doctor. Yet while telling her father to "shove it," she was also telling her mother, if indirectly, the same thing. She would not do what her mother did: serve her father. What did she risk by her attitude? A complete loss of connection with both parents. Fearful of breaking all ties, she lashed out against the system instead. She called herself a radical anarchist: she said she believed in complete individual freedom with no rules at all.

After Molly graduated from college, she tried out all sorts of different roles. At times, she seemed to be acting much as her mother had when she was young—leaving home, taking up with men—only in a more exaggerated way.

At the same time that she was seeking an identity apart from her mother's, she was repeating her mother's pattern by doing exactly what the man in her life suggested she do.

How did she break free? The year she married and spent refinishing furniture was "the very worst" of her life, Molly said. "That's when I knew I could not be like my mother." The experience of staying at home while her husband was off "having big opportunities" is what finally catalyzed her decision to go to law school.

Psychologists used to describe adolescence as a period in which young men broke away from their parents to become autonomous, but young women did not. (Paradoxically, young women who asserted their independence were often considered aberrational but those who fulfilled societal norms of docility and dependence were sometimes seen as backward.) Now, however, psychologists are beginning to explain adolescence as a period in which young men and women alike begin a process of negotiation with their parents. At the same time as they leave their families of origin and begin to establish themselves in the world outside the home, youths seek to maintain emotional connection with their parents, to find a balance between autonomy and intimacy both in relation to their parents and within themselves.[22]

Psychologist Carol Gilligan has called female adolescence "a crisis of connection," a "watershed" in which girls must find ways of making "connection in the face of difference." The central problem, she explains, is that "for girls to remain responsive to themselves, they must resist the conventions of feminine goodness; to remain responsive to others, they must resist the values placed on self-sufficiency and independence."[23] In psychologist Irene Stiver's view, adolescence is a period in which women, particularly, begin to define themselves as separate from their mothers, yet as they move away, struggle not to lose connection with them.[24]

This struggle for connection and separation would explain why, like Molly, most of the women I interviewed seemed, in their late teens, to be fighting their parents, trying to break away from them—yet at the same time to be repeating their mothers' patterns. For example, when Suzanne wrote those letters calling her parents "capitalist pigs," she seemed to be lashing out against them. At the same time, she was following in her mother's footsteps: Suzanne's mother had defied her own father when *she* was an adolescent simply by going to college.

Abby Nathan wanted to break away from a mother who had never seemed to rebel against her own family: Abby's maternal grandmother even lived with Abby's family. When Abby's father came home at night, he would yell at Abby's mother for not keeping house well enough. While Abby sympathized with him, she was also angry at him. In college, Abby said, "I got involved with feminism because I thought my mother was such a failure. I wanted to hear that women could be strong." It would seem that in becoming a feminist, Abby was trying to break away from her mother. At the same time, feminism allowed her to remain close to her mother, and to stand up for her symbolically by joining with other women to fight for change.

Peggy Talbot, a lawyer, described her mother as "passive-aggressive." Resentful of her husband's career success and of his affairs with other women, Peggy's mother refused to get a job herself or to confront her husband. Until Peggy entered college, Peggy accepted her parents' idea that she should become a music teacher, and in high school she even conducted a choir and had her own music students. But in college, Peggy dropped her musical ambitions. As she explained the change,

> It was the effect of the women's movement and politics. I perceived my interest in music as a dream my parents had. I had gotten 800 SATs in math and was wondering why I hadn't considered a career in engineering or math or something like that. In a burst of rebellion, I dropped the music; then I broadened my activities to more political things.

By dropping the music career her mother wanted for her, Peggy was at the same time rejecting her mother's way of life yet expressing her mother's frustrations and anger about women's lot.

While these women described their rebellion as being against their parents, a large part of the struggle was against being caught in their mothers' roles. This sometimes meant lashing out against their fathers, who, many believed, had oppressed their mothers. It also involved attempting to break free from their mothers and fighting the battles for individuality and autonomy their mothers had failed to fight.

On a very personal level, the tumult of the 1960s allowed these women to accomplish what many psychologists believed normal women in the past had not: it allowed them to break away from their families, away from the docile, dependent mode expected of them. It allowed them to challenge old gender roles, to put off marriage and childbearing in order to become independent human beings. It also allowed young women to challenge their mothers, to break away from them, yet at the same time to try to right the wrongs done them—often in solidarity with other women.

Experts at the time assured worried parents, educators, and anyone else who would listen that after a period of experimentation in the world outside the home, our generation would soon marry, have children, and

110

maybe, eventually, find "suitable" jobs.[25] But the women I interviewed did not turn back: they kept right on going. Most put off marriage and children for an extended period to enter professions that in the past had been reserved for men, to embark on what promised to be a revolution of major proportions.

7

Success and Struggle: The 1970s

The 1970s were heady years for women. In 1972, the U.S. Senate passed an Equal Rights Amendment to the Constitution and a majority of Americans thought the states should ratify it. The percentage of women entering architecture, business, engineering, law, and medical schools increased fivefold or more; by the end of the decade, women made up some 12 percent of the doctors, lawyers, and judges in the country, and nearly a third of the managers and college professors. Backed by a strong feminist movement, professional women felt a sense of solidarity; what we were doing seemed important.[1]

For women to congregate at all could even be seen as a political act. When a group of women writers at the newspaper where I worked went to lunch after a 1974 editorial meeting, the editors (all male) asked if we were "organizing." Magazines wrote about us; we were the first women pilots, surgeons, stock traders. Women I've met since still speak of their accomplishments then with pride. "I never accepted any job that another woman did before me," said a pioneer in the electronics industry. An investment banker told me, "I got off on being the only woman in the boardroom." It was exciting, special, to be a professional woman.

More than that, for many women, the idea was to catalyze social change.

Janet Peters, now an architect, wanted "to do things for the cities."

Clara Zolen, now a consulting-company executive, started out as a community organizer.

Nancy Kelly, today a corporate lawyer, hoped to bring class action lawsuits to help the poor.

Abby Nathan, a doctor, first became an abortion counselor because she wanted to help women.

Women wanted equality—for minorities, for the poor, for other women, and for themselves. The best way to gain equality, it seemed, was through the economic system. Progress could be measured in terms of salaries and promotions, and if women did not depend on husbands for financial support, they would no longer be at men's beck and call. If both parents worked, their children would grow up androgynous—able to make comfortable use of traits once considered either male or female—and men and women alike would be able to achieve and to nurture.

This, theoretically, would not only create more egalitarian marriages and healthier families; it would also, on a broad, societal scale, open opportunities for women still further. Women in positions of power might then change the ways in which companies, institutions, even nations, did business and thus liberate women and men alike from the constraints of work in a competitive, industrial marketplace.[2] The key to it all was to overcome the barriers that held back working women.

What were those barriers? When economist Eli Ginsberg interviewed well-educated women in the early 1960s, nearly half of them said they had faced discrimination, but the biggest factor in their failure to advance was children: the more children she had, the less likely a professionally trained woman was to work outside the home.[3]

Sociologist Alice Rossi believed many women with children dropped out in large part because they were afraid society and their families would disapprove if they did not. Once they dropped out, even if only for a few years, they could never catch up with men because they had been at home with children during their peak creative years.[4]

According to Cynthia Fuchs Epstein, women who chose traditionally feminine careers like social work or nursing—or even psychiatry, matrimonial law, or government work—exhibited "a sort of minority group self-hatred" and perpetuated such fields as female ghettos. Women in predominantly male professions were, then, considered masculine or aberrational and were rarely promoted; consequently, men easily dominated the most highly paid and prestigious fields.[5]

In Rosabeth Kanter's analysis, career women's greatest problems stemmed from the lack of power all minorities hold in groups that perceive of them as different. "Token" women tended to overcompensate by overachieving, by hiding their successes, or by turning against other women; they faced special pressures because they were seen as representing all women, or they were forced to fit into stereotypes that did not suit them. Socialized differently from men, women were often not prepared for the aggressive worlds of professions and business.[6]

113

The solution, Kanter wrote, as part of a chorus that included Rossi and Epstein, among others, was to encourage more women to enter predominantly male fields, in order to change the structure of organizations to make the workplace, and, in turn, the society, more humane.

◆　◇　◆

Enter: a generation ripe for change. By the time they started their careers, the women I interviewed had the benefit of much of this analysis. Many had trained early and put off marriage and children, resolved to establish themselves, first, in their fields. Backing them were new civil rights legislation, the women's movement, and an ever-increasing number of female colleagues.

Sandy Smith was the first woman in her medical school to enter surgical residency. She sailed through with flying colors, pleased, for the first few years, with her choice.

> If you came in with belly pain, I examined you, I decided probably you had appendicitis and I got to open you up and find out and get immediate satisfaction. And if I took your appendix out you were never going to have appendicitis again and you were cured. And I cured you. It was very immediate in terms of both blame and success. I liked that.

Robyn Sparks, active in student politics, convinced a state senator to run for Congress. He ran and won; after graduation she moved out west to work in his campaign, then, when he won again, she moved to Washington, where she continued to work for him. "It was great," she says. "We got the [Vietnam] War to end."

With each of Eleanor Valera's promotions came "a rush, creative fulfillment." At her newspaper,

> There was only one woman senior to me. I was always trying something new; there was no one to follow. My successes were applauded. There was an esprit de corps, reinforcement from everyone, that you wouldn't believe. The confidence that I developed in myself gave me the confidence to lead people.

Like most women I spoke with, Sandy, Robyn, and Eleanor moved up steadily in their careers. Some married men who supported their ambitions and even shared household responsibilities; others refused to get involved with or divorced men who did not. To all appearances, women were succeeding well, even brilliantly, in their careers and marriages. In interviews, however, as each woman described the experiences of her twenties, she revealed that beneath the surface of all this success, she had felt serious doubts—about herself, her capabilities, her identity.

For Patricia Alcorn, the most anxious time was when she was deciding whether or not to go to medical school. Even though she had wanted to be a doctor since she was five years old, she said, "I felt like I was going crazy." She had "nightmare dreams about the awful instruments" and, for some reason she could not explain, about not knowing how to treat men injured in farm accidents.

Clara Zolen had problems starting her job in a consulting company. "I had to learn to work in a corporate culture, with all these macho men," she said.

Marjorie Babson, a social scientist, described a period in which she felt absolutely driven to achieve. "I was having trouble remembering the things that were important to me, my faith, my husband, children."

When Sandy Smith finished her surgical residency, she became profoundly depressed. "I'd passed the boards, I had a paper in a prestigious journal," she said. "I knew I'd always eat. I said to myself, 'That's all? This is it?'" That is when she began to consider suicide.

All of these women had questions about who they were as women and as professionals—and all had difficulties reconciling these two apparently irreconcilable roles. Why, despite all of the advantages these women had enjoyed, should the role of women and the role of professional still seem miles apart?

Part of the problem was that they had moved farther, faster, than they—and society—had ever imagined they would. The world of work had been designed for men with wives to care for them; work schedules and the demands of their careers left little time or energy for personal lives; women with children felt guilty because they had too little time to spend with them.

There was also discrimination to reckon with: rather than lessen as women proved their competence, resistance often seemed to deepen. One study showed that when the proportion of women in management reached about 33 percent, advancement for all women seemed to cease. In another study, only three of seventy-six high-level women managers believed they could become presidents of their companies. In 1976, a group of minority women scientists reported that while in college and professional school, racism and ethnic discrimination had presented the greatest obstacles, as they advanced in the world of work, sexism increasingly reared its head. At this time, white men earned "far more" than minority men, who earned "somewhat more" than white women, who made "slightly more" than minority women.[7]

For minority professional women in predominantly white settings, the situation was particularly complex. Although some researchers in the 1970s believed that black professional women were taken more seriously than white women by their white male colleagues, others found that black professional women experienced a "double jeopardy," in being judged against both black men and white women. According to Aida Hurtado, Asian-Americans, blacks, and Chicanas have long been especially subject to sexual objectification as a result of stereotyping that still persists.[8]

In the 1970s, as today, Asian-American women faced the myth of the "erotic oriental." Black women encountered "rude caricatures" of themselves, and in leadership positions "were expected" to comfort the weary and oppressed as well as champion equality and justice. They were often viewed as black first, women second, and professionals third. One Choctaw Cherokee physician who later went to law school was told by her anatomy teacher that she was not worth teaching; along with another woman, two blacks, and two Jews she was segregated at one end of the laboratory to work on cadavers—and taught by a research assistant.[9]

Among my interviewees, Dana Clavier, a labor negotiator, grimaced when she described the time a rather meaty opponent blew cigar smoke in her face. Several women said they were completely ignored when they presented their views at meetings, and a senior partner in Becky Wilson's law firm had advised her to "be more ladylike." Molly Walden noticed she was not asked to sit in on negotiating sessions; she suspected it was because the partners in her law firm could not take her seriously once she became pregnant.

In another study, a woman who was the only black and the only female lawyer in a large multi-national corporation reported that she had been intentionally misdirected into the clerk's office when she was looking for the president's. At a conference, a black scientist was brought in for questioning by a hotel security representative who thought she must be a prostitute, and in hospitals, female doctors of all races were commonly taken for secretaries or cleaning staff.[10]

Many women faced opposition from their families as well. Leila Davis, a business executive, said her lawyer father had actively discouraged her from becoming a lawyer; he thought she should study home economics. Marie Harrison, a television journalist, had been told by her father, a doctor, that she was "too emotional" for medical school. Banker Cynthia Jones's father had not spoken to her in the eight years since she had graduated from college and moved to New York City rather than return to live at home.

Patricia Alcorn's mother told her that if she went to medical school, she would never find a husband. Marie Harrison's mother seemed to boast about her daughter's accomplishments. "She's going to be just like Barbara Walters," her mother once told a friend, then added, in a nasty tone of voice, "She's so aggressive." When Peggy Talbot got into a top law school, her mother asked, "Why do you have to go there? Why don't you go to a school that is less competitive?"[11] Becky Wilson's husband, a professor, tried to steer her away from high-paying litigation work, and a lawyer interviewed in a study of black women professionals said she had to be "schizophrenic" and consciously switch off her professional role when she got home in order to keep her husband.[12]

Most women took all of this in stride. They had been warned there would be obstacles and most of these they overcame, often with flying colors. Many viewed the opposition they encountered from colleagues, parents, or mates as problems of misguided individuals who needed be set straight, rather than as monolithic, systemic problems. For many of the women I interviewed, despite the difficulties of challenging the stereotypes imposed on them by others, the most difficult dilemmas were inside themselves. A central question was how they could be different from their mothers and equal with men.

Take Clara Zolen. When she graduated from Harvard Business School and started working at a consulting firm, she "had a hard time going in."

> I had never worked in a large organization before; I had always been with people who had the same values as I did. I didn't know how to work in a small group, and I didn't realize the volume of work they expected from me. I didn't know what to do, how to communicate, how to ask for help. I had never seen a culture like this one.

The scene was "very intense, and you had to be able to respond to all different kinds of people." In her group, there was a man who liked to overpower others. "Even today, I expect he could still make me cry," she said.

The problem was not just that she'd had no corporate experience. In order to gain the respect of her male colleagues, she found she had to emulate them. To her, that meant she had to seem quite different from her mother; to express herself in a new way. "My mother kind of babbles," she explained. "That's different from what's valued in my work. In speaking, I have to say, 'one, two, three.' I have to make points. It's more male than female. I had to learn how to do that."

Sandy Smith chose surgery because "it was easy. I liked working with my hands, and I liked the way surgeons approached problems. There

was much more black and white and less ambiguity than in other specialties." But a few months into her training, surgical residency began to feel

> like being in the army, or in any very regimented, very male-
> dominated thing. The work in the hospital is supposed to be the first
> priority at all times. There's an old saying that the only trouble with
> being on call every other night is that you lose half the problems.
> You should be on call every night, and you shouldn't consider them
> problems. You want to get in there, do more, bigger, better opera-
> tions. The masculine image is the one that's held up as good, and
> the feminine is bad, so that being more macho and detached and
> aggressive and a little bit unfeeling is positive, and caring about the
> patients and being more involved with them and more conservative
> about operating is bad.

Sandy was well aware that by becoming a surgeon she was "going
completely counter to what (her) mother would have wanted," but even
so, her own "mothering impulses bubbled up." She responded by trying
to damp them down. One way she did this was by competing with the
men she worked with—to prove she was just as good as they were.

> It exended to all kinds of things. For example, I never called in sick.
> I worked many nights with temperatures of 103 when I was sicker
> than any patient I was taking care of. But God forbid you should
> ever stay home when you were sick or ever admit you were tired
> after being on call three nights in a row. You had to be tougher than
> anybody else, and you had to love it. And when you go down to the
> emergency room and there's a big operation, you can't say, "Oh, shit,
> I don't like to do big operations." You have to say, "Oh, wow! Boy,
> can we take this guy in!" That's what a surgeon is supposed to be.

Most women surgeons Sandy knew didn't "fit the mold." Most men, she
said, did not either.

> But they would never admit it. That's the ideal you're supposed to
> love, and your family and your life and everything else is secondary
> to the hospital and the patients. And how can any woman or man
> that you're involved with complain if you're going out to save lives?
> If you admit you don't like to do the macho operations, it means
> you're not a real surgeon.

Marjorie Babson, a social researcher who chose a career much like
her mother's, protested, "Everyone thinks that because my mother
worked, this has been easy for me. But it hasn't." As we sat in her office—

she at a hardwood desk on which the only objects were a single red maple leaf in a dark blue glass—Marjorie told me that like her mother, she had chosen to work as a social scientist. Like her mother, who earned more money than her husband, a minister, Marjorie also earned more than her husband, an artist. Unlike her mother, who failed to advance at work because she did not have a doctorate, Marjorie made sure to get a Ph.D. She chose a dissertation topic, however, that required her to work with a group of high-powered male professionals in an academic medical center—and, just as her mother had, she soon found herself in a "one-down" position at work.

> I worked with a psychologist and psychiatrist; we had the same job but I was called research assistant and they were called research associate directors. They got $40,000 a year; I got $5 an hour.

Her work was good, and within a year, Marjorie was promoted to associate director.

> I think it was because the director wanted to split the power three ways, to make the two other men less powerful. I think it must have been awful to the psychiatrist; I was a young girl. But it made me mad, because I had the title but not the authority.

At work, Marjorie had to learn to play a different game—one whose rules were set by men.

> In meetings, I couldn't get a word in. I had to learn to keep my voice going when I was interrupted. Their style at meetings was symbolic of a whole different way of operating, a style that was not assertive but aggressive. Before I'd had a quiet style. I was learning new skills I didn't have any respect for.

> Although Marjorie was proud of her title, she began to hate her job, in part because her coworkers were unwilling to do anything unless they got something in return.

> We were a steering committee, working together; theoretically whatever advanced one of us advanced us all. Instead, we were always battling over who owned what, who wrote what, who got credit for which study. You couldn't say, "this is what's good for me, now let's see what's good for you." It was more, "If you'll help me with this, I'll help you with the director for that."

They wouldn't acknowledge what was going on. To Marjorie, "Nothing seemed honest."

In entering these male-dominated professions, women had a lot to deal with. They were not unlike female corporate executives who, as described in one study, were subjected to contradictory expectations: they had "to show their toughness and independence and at the same time count on others. It was essential that they contradict the stereotypes that male executives and coworkers had about women." They had to be seen as different,

> better than women as a group. But they couldn't go too far, to forfeit all traces of femininity, because that would make them too alien to their superiors and colleagues. In essence, their mission was to do what wasn't expected of them, while doing enough of what was expected of them as women to gain acceptance.[13]

Making matters even more complicated were the conflictual images of masculinity and femininity these women held within themselves.

The women I interviewed grew up in the 1950s, usually with mothers who were homemakers. When opportunities for women broadened in the 1970s, many of these women felt that they held within them the potential to follow two very different life paths—one like their mothers', which in some ways seemed safe, secure, and suffocating, and a second, like their fathers', which offered freedom and power, but seemed unknown, foreign, even dangerous. That second path was a challenge to the roles their mothers had played, but at a far deeper level, it was also a challenge to each woman's inner self, a challenge to old images of femininity each woman carried within her, images by which she still defined herself yet from which she wanted desperately to escape.

The result, when these women entered male-dominated organizations, was a deep and complex set of reactions—all related to the same push-pull struggle for connection and separation from their mothers that had gotten them where they were in the first place.

Most of the analysis that follows is based on studies done primarily on white women because psychological research on women of differing race, nationality, and ethnicity is still in its fledgling stages. However, I would hypothesize that the push-pull pattern described below exists, but is expressed in different ways, depending on the expectations for men and women brought up in differing familial and cultural constellations.

Many psychologists describe women's development as a mirroring process starting in infancy, in which a female infant internalizes the image of herself in the way it is reflected in her mother's face and in the way her mother treats her. This is not to dismiss the importance of fathers and other aspects of women's upbringing, but for most women, the struggle for connection with and separation from a maternal figure is primary and intense.

Mothers tend to see themselves in their infant daughters and to feel a strong emotional connection to them. If a mother likes and respects herself, so much the better: she will reflect a positive image back to her infant daughter—which is likely to give her daughter the confidence she needs to stand strong in making her way in the world, even in a workplace that feels foreign. But if a mother feels put down or denigrated as a female, she will reflect that, also, back to the female child, who will incorporate those negative feelings into her own self-image.[14]

Some of the women I interviewed had mothers with more self-respect than others—and these women were most easily able to simply see the ways in which they were "different" from the men around them, perceive of these differences as strengths, and use them to their advantage. Other women, especially those women whose mothers had particularly low self-esteem, found it more difficult to stand strong.

Take Janet Peters, who graduated from night architecture school with honors and landed a job in the same architecture firm in which she had once worked as a secretary. Her mother had divorced, and had remarried a man who beat her. Janet was also divorced—largely, she believed, because her husband could not deal with her career success. But Janet did not feel all that successful. As an architect, she felt that she was too often relegated to "programming," or assessing the needs of clients, a skill at which she happened to excel.

"Most of the women I know are better at pulling that information out of clients than any of the men I've worked with," Janet said. Although she was convinced it was important to be a good programmer, her special talent was not valued by the men who made the decisions in her company. How could she tell? "The only way to the top as an architect is to be on a design team," she said.

> But in order to get assigned to a project that I want to work on, I have to ask constantly. I have to keep on putting in plugs for myself. Whereas the men don't ask. They are selected, sought after. I do a good job but each time I get on a team I feel I haven't proven anything because the next time they need a design team member, I have to ask again.

Sometimes, she wondered if sexism were to blame. "Maybe the men on the projects aren't comfortable working with women, or they want me to be on their project but they want me to do something that they think a woman could handle," she said. Then again, it was partly her own

121

fault, she said, because she rarely placed her work where others could see it easily.

> The young men who come in are very careful to display their work on their board because that's their hallmark, the reference board, the tack surface that's in front of your desk. It speaks for you. You pin your work up so everybody who walks by can see it. It says, "That guy can draw." But I don't see that on women's desks. Seldom if ever.

The reason she hid her own work is that it appeared different from the work the men did, and she questioned her ability and compared herself—negatively—with her male colleagues.

> The men I really admire are the ones who draw fantastically well. And they draw with gusto. The pencil in their hand is really an extension of their brain. They just draw and think at the same time. As for me, drawing is my weakness and I am very timid at it. But even if a man's sketch is ugly, even if what he's done is rough, somehow . . . it's really respected. And I do these very timid little drawings and hide them in the corner because they're not beautiful. Sometimes I look at myself and say, well, Janet, you just haven't practiced enough but you'll be able to do it. Then I think, on the other hand, I think my way of doing things is just as valid as men's so why should I change?

As hard as she tried to overcome the negative self-image she had inherited from her mother, Janet still saw herself as she saw her mother, a secretary who did her boss's work but did not get credit for it. In describing herself, she used exactly the same words she had used to describe her mother. She was "constantly struggling," she said.

Psychoanalyst Doris Bernstein explains that because the bond between mothers and daughters is so intense, for both, at each new stage of development, old anxieties come to the fore—and grip all the harder. Adding to the difficulty if a mother feels devalued, as her daughter grows up and tries to establish her own life, the daughter may seem to be rejecting her mother's values, which can make her mother feel even more devalued. While a mother may feel proud or gratified when her daughter tries to achieve independence, she may simultaneously feel competitive, afraid of losing her daughter, and fear for her daughter's safety and try to hold her back.

Hence, as daughters reach adulthood, the push-pulls between them and their mothers may become even more intense and conflictual. The harder a daughter asserts herself to be unlike her mother, the more she may feel that she is betraying her mother—or the images of her mother she has internalized.[15] So that as a daughter tries to differentiate herself from her mother, she may also cling to those old images of her mother—which are also a part of herself.

In order to minimize the conflict she feels about surpassing her mother, a woman may negate her intellectual worth or her sexuality. If she is successful, she may attribute her success to chance, or, like Janet, she may resist changing the idea that she is inadequate and inferior. By overvaluing men and undervaluing women, she may be holding on to a fantasy that a man will come along to help.[16]

For many of the women I interviewed, a big part of the problem was that the male-dominated environments in which they wished to prove their worth felt much like the male-dominated families in which they had grown up—and they wanted approval from the very same men whose attitudes toward women they were trying to change. Often, women found themselves being treated as their mothers had been treated. And, often, in spite of themselves, they found themselves fighting much the same battles their mothers had refused to fight.

As we sat in Peggy Talbot's office—what I remember most are gray metal filing cabinets, gray metal shelves, a gray desk, and a lamp with a frilly white shade on which were perched two small cloth parakeets—Peggy told me she had, with her parents' encouragement, trained through high school as a professional musician. In college she'd switched to economics and law, which she described as "rational, logical and cognitive states" poles apart from her mother's spiritualism and far away from her working class parents' values, which she dismissed as "nouveau bourgeois." Graduating with degrees in economics and law made her part of an intellectual community, and when she married a professor and joined a law firm, she knew she'd "made it." But within a few years, the law firm began to seem very hierarchical and competitive. "I'm not really that competitive. I couldn't relate to the work at all," said Peggy. "I couldn't see why it was important that I make somebody a little extra money by filing something a day earlier or a day later. I felt no identity of interests."

Then there was the sexism like that which her mother, intelligent but uneducated, had failed to confront when her husband, a factory worker-turned-corporate manager, pushed her around. As it had angered her mother, Peggy said, "It angers me when I see men who are successful, when I know I'm smarter than they are." As a result, Peggy had two major run-ins with men because they would not to listen to her.

I refused to deal with those guys. I told them off; I wouldn't work with them. I see now I was projecting my father onto them; the tough guy, the bully. I always saw him as saying, "I'm a man and I don't have to do anything about it." That pushes my buttons when I come up against it but the degree to which it riles me up isn't good, especially when I have to go up against a sexist judge. But now I'm seeing it more clearly as my mother's resentment about my father's success when she thought she was better than he was.

Even Marjorie Babson, who had a working mother whose husband and family respected her, found herself fighting . . . yet repeating . . . her mother's pattern. Like her mother in her office, "I was so angry at the way things were done, about the duplicity. I was furious all the time. But I didn't know how to let people know I was furious; I was passively aggressive," Marjorie said. At home, like her mother, she became "a screaming meanie," constantly complaining about her work.

I was lucky that I had a husband to tell everything to. It was hard on him to hear about it all the time, and it was hard for me to have only that to talk about. But being able to talk about it with him helped me survive and get through, to keep working. I was sure I would make it somehow. I was there four years. It was awful.

At this time, Marjorie said, "the achievement goals had me in their grip. I felt like I had to keep chasing them. It was never enough. I couldn't claim my achievement. It was a wild horse dragging me." Yet she thought constantly about quitting: "I kept saying to myself, 'don't forget you have a choice.'" Why didn't she leave?

Carrying on my mother's battles was part of it. Having seen my Mom do the same thing, it didn't feel unnatural to be in those kinds of situations. My mother couldn't distance herself, either. I told myself, "you have to fight these battles. Wherever you go, it's going to be like this."

♦   ◇   ♦

For some women, having children mitigates the inner push-pull struggle by reaffirming a maternal quality central to their self-definitions. But for other women, having children can lead to anxiety above and beyond that created by the demand on their time and energy. Eleanor Valera, for example, admired her mother in many ways, and attributed much of her own success as a manager to her ability to avoid conflict—just as her mother had. But after three years as section editor on a newspaper, she started to feel stale. "Here I was, doing exactly what I would have told you in college was my ultimate goal, to be an editor at a good newspaper, and I was doing it and getting tired of it and couldn't figure out what else to do," said Eleanor. She felt as if she wasn't running her own life, that she was climbing a ladder, by rote, to please others.

It was as if there was always somebody outside me directing me. I would sit there and stew and I would just keep working but feel depressed . . . but I didn't get off my ass and do anything about it. I didn't make changes happen. I went through the year thinking, "what do I want to do with my life?" I found myself overanalyzing situations. I thought to myself, "I ought to start doing some things, damn it."

Her doctor, "who was very conservative," had said she should have children before she was thirty, and her husband "really wanted to have children." So she decided to get pregnant. She also got yet another promotion. But once her son was born, instead of feeling more fulfilled, Eleanor soon felt stretched to the limit; she went back to work after two months' leave. Her husband, a self-employed computer consultant, took over most of the child care and household responsibilities, and Eleanor drove herself harder than ever at work.

I worked seven to seven and ate at my desk. I went to two movies in two years. My idea of sheer heaven would have been to go home to a quiet, empty house. I didn't want to cook, I didn't want to talk, I just wanted peace and quiet. When I would go home a little part of me would respond to my husband and son, but I was so ragged out that I had nothing to give. I was just into work. I wanted peace. I didn't want anyone around me. I was burned out.

One reason for her exhaustion was that the very same traits she believes accounted for her success in the first place began to work against her. On the one hand, Eleanor said, "the emotional side is a help to you in reporting in a way that it may not be in other professions. It doesn't hinder you because it makes you sensitive to stories, to others, to what the management needs." On the other hand, the sensitivity that helped her as a reporter began to hurt her as a manager because "every nuance of facial expression would register" and she "internalized everything." Besides, she did not like to exert power. "I wanted to achieve consensus to influence people rather than tell them what to do. I wasn't comfortable saying, 'I know you don't agree with this but we're going to do it,'" she said.

Much as Eleanor had tried to break her mother's pattern by achieving professionally, she had been successful precisely because she used her mother's techniques. At home, her mother had absorbed the conflict when her father got angry unjustly; when Eleanor protested, her mother had told her not to make waves. "She did everything a mother was supposed to do—but there was never any feeling of joy, any feeling that she or my father was happy," Eleanor said. Despite Eleanor's attempts through work to avoid a marital situation like her mother's, she fell into a situation much like it, only in a different setting. At work, Eleanor was as much at the beck and call of her male superiors as her mother had been at her father's. Like her mother, she said, she felt desperate for approval, for reassurance—and for love.

> I'm always thinking I should do more. I have a terrific need to achieve but I am terribly afraid of failing. I'm so afraid of failing that I don't take all the risks one must take in order to achieve. I need to achieve on a day-to-day basis so badly, to be reassured for success so constantly that I can't achieve anything great. I have an insatiable need to achieve, and part of that insatiable need to achieve is that I also want everyone to love me.

Eleanor punctuated these comments with sheepish laughter. Though she was laughing at herself, the situation was not all that funny. In her thirties, as hard as Eleanor tried to break her mother's pattern, she was repeating it—by absorbing or avoiding conflict, in order to be loved. She resented her situation—just as her mother had.

> I was put as mother hen of interns, this year. I would say, I'm no more mother than John Smith, over there, is a mother hen. But the damn fact was, I was thirty-two, my second in command was thirty-nine, and we *did* feel like parents. I *did* feel like their mother. They were younger. They were immature. I didn't want to mother, to teach. I wanted someone to teach *me*.

As she told her story, Eleanor sounded much like the "superwomen" various psychiatrists and psychologists have described treating in therapy.

Esther Menaker, M.D., explains that women whose mothers are denigrated or who play inferior roles in their families may work all the harder at their careers to offset the inner images of inferiority they carry within them. Often, they feel compelled to achieve and to please male bosses not because they feel a positive sense of self-worth but because they desire desperately to be thought well of, as their mothers were not. According to psychiatrist Alexandra Symonds, when they marry, such women may feel reaffirmed as women. But as time goes on they may get less and less nurturance. At the slightest conflict they automatically repress their own needs and extend themselves to support their husbands or children, without even being aware of it.[17]

That is in part because when they become mothers themselves their unconscious identifications with their own mothers may surface; they feel guilt and anxiety over having careers and not spending all of their time with their children. In many such women, psychiatrist Doris Bernstein explains, the mother of early childhood is idealized as totally nurturing, at the beck and call of the infant's needs. In each new stage of a woman's development, the fantasy of the all-giving mother is reawakened, and puts totally unrealistic pressures on women both from outside and inside. This creates guilt in working women when they are not catering to their families' needs. At the same time, Symonds explains, the more a woman feels she is like her mother, the harder she feels she must strive at work. As a result, many professional women refuse to give up any part of either the housework or their careers. In fact, one national study of executive women reported the astonishing news that married women with children spend more hours at work than single women.[18]

Such "super-wives" and "super-moms" thus become even more alienated from their own needs. While they may not be aware of this process, they are aware of an undercurrent of dissatisfaction. They work extremely hard but never seem to feel satisfied or fulfilled. Often such women attract husbands who are excessively dependent, which adds to their burdens. Most such patients, Symonds writes, come to see her complaining of depression or psychosomatic symptoms. They do well in therapy, she finds, when what emerges is a tremendous repressed anger and competitiveness toward their husbands, as well as a long-standing despair and hopelessness—dating back to childhood—of ever having their own "child needs" for nurturance recognized and fulfilled.[19]

◆   ◇   ◆

Another way in which professional women may try resolve the inner push-pull struggle (to be unlike their mothers yet retain connection with them) is by becoming romantically involved with powerful men. Robyn Sparks is an attorney who dated her boss. "It was hard because we were intimate outside of work and then at work, he'd be telling me what to do. The relationship ended because he was in charge at work," she said. "We didn't talk about it at the time; we didn't want to see it as a problem."

As Robyn described the relationship, it sounded much like the relationship between Robyn's parents. Robyn's father had made all of the decisions in the family. "You could disagree with my mother," Robyn said, "but you didn't disagree with him." Likewise, her boss always "decided what we did." Robyn resented that just as she had resented her father's attitude toward her mother. Even worse, she found it hard to act professionally at work. Like her mother, she had trouble remaining autonomous and independent; she found herself catering to her boss's whims as her mother had to her father's. "I found it difficult to be serious, to make a strong case for my side in an argument," she said. And, of course, there was sex. "We were new lovers; you could tell from my smile. I felt everyone could see," she said. The relationship lasted for several months; then, through mutual agreement, they called it off.

After that relationship broke up, Robyn, naturally enough, needed to feel nurtured, feminine, and attractive. "I got to know someone else intimately at work," she said. But that relationship soured, too. "I wore my private life on my sleeve. We had discussions; sharp words were said. I couldn't keep at a distance. Other people knew; it was hard to juggle," she said. Eventually, Robyn ended the relationship, and for the last few years had not been involved with anyone at all.

Yet another "solution" for a daughter who sees that her father does not respect her mother is to try to be like her father in order to please him, in the belief, perhaps unconscious, that she will win his love by proving that she is unlike her mother and other women. Some such women seem to emulate men in their quests for career success, but this can lead to problems because as such women enter adulthood, both their fathers and coworkers may find them competitive, threatening, or confusing. For the women themselves, it means that they hold particularly negative attitudes about themselves as women—which makes them especially vulnerable as women in male-dominated situations. It may also make them extremely driven to success in the world of work—often at the expense of their personal lives.[20]

Patricia Alcorn, a pediatrician, seemed such a woman. She sat on a well-worn couch, a brown springer spaniel asleep at her feet. To her right stood a music stand holding a Bach piece; behind it, on a bookshelf, lay a violin. "I knew when I was five years old that I wanted to be a doctor," she said. "It wasn't that I particularly wanted to take care of patients; it was that it was a man's field, and I believed that men were more special than women." Patricia had always admired her father much more than she had her mother, "who spent fifteen years keeping house." The smartest among five siblings, she worked hard in school because she "knew it pleased him."

When Patricia started medical school, however, she hated it. Even though she was one of just ten women in her medical school class, when

128

I pressed her, she denied that any of her negative feelings had to do with being female in a world of men. The problem, she said, was that

> I hated medical school and internal medicine. I found it degrading, a grind that squeezes humanity and life out of you. I came close to quitting. I was scared of entrapment in work. I didn't like the people who were teaching. I was depressed throughout medical school. I went from being a superstar in college to being an average medical student. I never felt smart.

She did not like the attitude with which "they just pulled a body out of a bag and you were supposed to dissect it." She didn't like internists—and she didn't like the "big smelly bodies" of adult patients. So when she finished her internship, instead of continuing as an internist, Patricia decided to work with children. "I was interested in psychology, developmental issues," she explained. At age thirty, she found a male mentor and what she thought would be her career. "I felt successful in my career, with my mentor. I loved pediatrics," she said.

Though she had a few close friends, she worked all the time, including weekends and evenings. But after six years, her career came to a standstill. She could no longer rely on her relationship with her mentor to move it forward.

> The years with my mentor were great, but I couldn't do it on my own. I was never able to carry out research on my own; I felt a lot of insecurity and instability at having to support myself by writing grants. I wasn't good at climbing the academic and political ladder. I wanted my own family life, to build a social network. I decided, painfully, to take a break from my career.

Patricia then turned down several prestigious offers in academic medicine in favor of a staff job in a health maintenance organization to assure herself regular hours and time to concentrate on her social life.

Patricia had not wanted to be like her mother, "a non-entity" compared to whom, growing up, she had felt like a superstar in her father's eyes. In her career, however, Patricia acted much as her mother had in her marriage: dependent on a man. Although Patricia did end up working with children, when it came time for her to establish herself on her own, despite her intelligence and talent, she found she could not function without a male mentor.

Finally, recognizing that she did in fact want a life more like her mother's than she had once imagined she would, Patricia left her high-powered career in hopes of establishing an intimate relationship. In the four years since, she said, she had dated a number of men but had yet to meet one with whom she cared to spend the rest of her life.

◆   ◇   ◆

Yet another way in which some women play out the struggle for connection with and separation from their mothers is in the arena of physical appearance. One successful journalist, forty pounds overweight, told me she chose to work in radio because she could not imagine being both sexy and smart; in radio, because no one could see her, she felt free to "seduce people" with her voice. Suzanne Lewis, also a journalist, said she "hides behind" her weight.

> In some way I think it changes how men might think of me. If I'm overweight, I'm less threatening, so somehow I think I can get away with doing everything else I want. But my weight has varied by as much as fifty pounds. And I've lost that huge amount of weight five different times. Usually I lose it after I've been somewhere for awhile and have gotten everybody to like me. Then usually I move on and gain it all back.

As Suzanne explained the syndrome, "My mother is very tiny and cute and always takes meticulous care of herself." While Suzanne's mother encouraged her daughter to have a career, she also "drummed into me her preoccupation with fitness." At this point, Suzanne apologized for "exploding," then raised her voice to emphasize her points. "There's some rebellion in me," she said. "I don't *want* to be a doll mannequin figure! I don't *want* to be that neat and that popular." But very much caught in her mother's conception of femininity, she added, "But I *do*. I *do* want to be neat and popular. Part of me wants nothing more than that."[21]

When she was growing up, Suzanne said, her mother expected her to have a career, but reserved the job of being popular for Suzanne's younger sister.

> She was cute as a button and very sociable and everybody liked her. All the way through school I saw her as the pretty one, the feminine one, the one that everybody liked. I was left with the role of the bookish one who wore glasses. It was very destructive to both of us. My sister came out lacking confidence in her intellectual ability and I came out lacking confidence in my appearance.

Suzanne's mother, who had once wanted a career herself but instead settled down to raise her family, evidently had trouble reconciling her own competence with a feminine image that revolved around her physi-

130

cal qualities. As a result, she projected different aspects of her own personality onto each daughter and made it difficult for either daughter to feel whole. This may be why Suzanne did not feel that she could be both attractive and successful in her career, and why, just as her mother had, she pitted these aspects of herself one against the other.

Not surprisingly, Suzanne had also found it difficult to establish an intimate relationship with a man. As she explained it, she was "badly shocked" when an intimate relationship with one of her professors ended after college.

> I think I had a great fear about men and relationships and part of me was more than willing to shut that part out. I was not going to put myself in that vulnerable position again where my whole world would fall away and I would be standing in air. So I haven't had any great sense of loss. I've set it up that way; I've chosen.

This created a third piece of the dilemma. Perhaps because she could not get wholehearted approval from her mother (or from herself, because her image of what it meant to be successful and female was as mixed up as her mother's), Suzanne looked to her job for nurturing, connection, and approval. This, in turn, complicated her life, she said, because needing emotional fulfillment from colleagues held her back.

> On the newspaper, I was getting, "We like you, we're rooting for you, you're one of us." I always get it, and I think I must have given up other things to get that. Work is the nurturer. If I get a good story, there is no question that I get great sustenance from my work, from my peers.
>
> There are times when I don't think it would have taken me quite this long, had I been a man, to get where I am now. I had a talk recently with my publisher about whether I should move to a bigger newspaper and he told me, "We had no right to expect to keep you this long. A person of your talent should have flown the coop long ago." This has been an exciting paper to work for but it has been a paper in great turmoil, so good people tend to come for a few years and then fly off to something better. I stayed and I've been rewarded. Nobody else has worked for them this long.

While Suzanne's parents had once encouraged her to have a career, now, when her mother saw her on national television, she would criticize her clothing; Suzanne's father would tell her she ought to have a child. In their eyes, nothing she did seemed right. Because she was successful in her career, they seemed to be saying, she was unsuccessful as a woman.

Not surprisingly, she expressed serious doubts about continuing to progress at work.

Suzanne's "greatest fear" was that by becoming a great reporter she would also become "a laughingstock," she said. "The real cost to a woman in journalism is the same as the cost to a man. And that is to make you a harder, more brutal, more cynical, person." For women, that is less acceptable than it is for men. Naming a well-known female reporter, Suzanne said,

> I want to get out before I turn into a woman like that. Because she is everything you want a reporter to be. She's tough, she doesn't care what people think about her, and when she asks questions at press conferences, she doesn't care if the whole press corps is laughing at her. Sometimes she asks really good questions amid the laughter. To me, it would be tragic to end up like that.

At the time of our interview, there were plenty of well-respected women journalists serving in the White House Press Corps or as anchorwomen on television. Although all was not smooth sailing for them, Suzanne's fears no doubt had more to do with her parents' mixed up definitions of feminine identity than with the attitudes of others. Unable to integrate those definitions for herself, Suzanne projected the negative attitudes she absorbed from her parents onto others, possibly in order to avoid recognizing or furthering her own potentially destructive inner turmoil.

◆ ◇ ◆

Although most of the women I interviewed were white, and most psychological research has been done on white women, this does not mean that minority professional women do not experience inner conflict in relation to their mothers. I would suggest that this inner conflict varies by degree and kind, and is particularly complicated when the gender and cultural expectations with which a woman is raised differ from those of the dominant society. The ease or difficulty with which a woman develops a strong positive sense of herself may be affected by her mother's place within the family constellation, the attitudes toward women in a given culture, as well as by the attitudes held by American society toward a particular cultural group.

Some researchers suggest that because most black women in this country have had working mothers, black professional women experience less guilt or role conflict than do white professional women who did not have working mothers.[22] Even if this is true, it does not mean the going for black female professionals has been easy. One black female executive described her experience as "an uncharted journey through rough psychological waters"; several black attorneys told a researcher that they were in counseling due to crises over gender-role conflict.[23]

Certainly, black professional women, whose families may have come from many different nations, classes, and cultures, have had to fight racism as well as sexism. Like many white women, some may also have grown up in households with mixed-up attitudes about the roles of men and women.

Although throughout American history most black women have worked to help support their families, studies show that some black husbands, like some white husbands, want their wives to fit what one researcher calls the "dainty, pedestal-sitting, subordinate" image of the white woman as idealized by white society. According to Roberta Morse, some black men—their own possibilities limited by discrimination—have wanted working but submissive wives; others may have resented their working wives or felt threatened by stereotypes of black women as of super-strength or overly-domineering. One black journalist I spoke with told me that her father, a professional man, would not allow her mother to have a job.[24]

Such attitudes, passed along generationally, would explain why in one study, several black attorneys spoke of the difficulty of having to buck "the feminine ideal" of white society in the workplace, but of trying to match it in their personal lives. One lawyer told researcher Gwyned Simpson that it was difficult to maintain personal relationships. "You learn professionally to take people apart and it's difficult to turn that off," she said.

> There was a time when if a man made a statement that I felt needed to be challenged, I would deal with him no differently than if he were a woman. But I also found that if you continue to deal like that you may wind up very lonely and without a relationship. . . . Although I hate to admit it, I'm seriously considering trying to change.

In the same study, a married woman described her husband, also an attorney, as "very traditional." Although they earned equal salaries and he wanted her to excel, he also thought that it was fine for him to stay late to work on briefs on the library but that she should be at home in the evenings.[25]

Asian-American women, who, after black women, make up the second largest group of minority professionals, may exhibit a high level of

133

success on the surface, according to researcher Farah Ibrahim, but it "may be at the expense of their personhood." In certain Asian cultures, female children are believed less valuable than males; daughters are encouraged to have no personal goals.

A college administrator who grew up in a Chinese family in Hong Kong told me her ancestors deemed it "noble" for women to remain uneducated. In many Asian-American families, however, education is encouraged but free thinking is not; Asian-American daughters may experience considerable conflict between Asian familial values and American ones. According to Ibrahim, as Asian-Americans, daughters are "forced to preserve their ethnic identity in a racist and hostile environment." Yet, the same values they defend may become a source of oppression and discrimination against them as women.[26]

Not surprisingly, their relationships with their mothers can be problematic. For example, Kesaya E. Noda, a Japanese-American sociologist, found it easier to "know herself" in Japan and to see her place in America than it was to accept her "line of connection" with her own mother. "She was my dark self, a figure in whom I thought I saw all that I feared most in myself," Noda writes. "Growing into womanhood and looking for some model of strength, I turned away from her."[27]

In many Mexican-American families, another study shows, several generations may live together, so that a Chicana may experience herself as closely connected not only with her mother but also with her grandmother, godmothers, or aunts. Rather than a "triangular object relational constellation," of mother/daughter, a Chicana may develop in a more complex "relational configuration" of daughter/mother/aunt/grandmother/godmother/father. As a result of the complicated process of identity development that would ensue "to recreate this internal psychic world," one researcher suggests, having children may be even more important to Chicanas than to European-American women, as might be maintaining relationships with other women in the family system. This theory could explain in part why a group of Mexican-American women scientists in a 1976 study said that their self-concepts and behavior had been strongly influenced by their internalizations of cultural gender role expectations. They had been brought up to assume responsibility for the home and to respect man's authority as the head of the household and spokesperson to the "outside" world.[28]

There is no doubt that daughters from cultures or families that devalue women struggle in retaining connections with both their mothers and with their cultures. To develop a strong sense of her own identity,

Ibrahim writes, a woman must understand her own family and cultural histories without denying the difficulties they represent.[29]

♦　◇　♦

In this chapter, I have described the experiences of the women I interviewed and others who entered professional careers in the 1970s, when most of them were in their twenties. In the early twenties, according to psychiatrist Roger Gould, people often define success in their parents' terms, but in the late twenties begin to come into their own and realize that they have incorporated images of their parents as a part of their own identities. In their thirties, they begin to accept that and to define the ways in which they are different from their parents as well.

Gould finds that the women he treats in his practice find it particularly difficult to redefine their goals as separate from their mothers' because they so crave connection with their mothers. Rather than understand the negative attitudes about succeeding in careers as originating within themselves, he writes, his clients tend to project those negative attitudes onto husbands or colleagues and to blame others for holding them back. More often than not, Gould writes, it is women's attempts to fit their mothers' definitions of feminine success that get in their way.[30]

The women I spoke with did in reality encounter negative attitudes at work and from their families. They fought hard to avoid falling into traps like those that had virtually crippled their mothers—and they went through complicated processes of sorting out which definitions of success were their parents', which were their professions', and which were their own. When they reached their thirties, most reached what seemed to be a point of impasse.

8

IMPASSE: THE 1980s

By the mid-1980s, the Equal Rights Amendment had failed, abortion rights were at risk, a conservative government touting "family values" had come into power, and affirmative action programs had weakened.[1] A quarter of the American public believed the women's movement had improved their lives, but two-thirds thought it had not, and 29 percent were actively hostile to it.[2] Women now occupied a third of executive and managerial positions, compared with a fifth just ten years earlier. But in top companies, the proportion of women in upper management appeared to be shrinking. *Fortune* magazine declared that in corporate America, no woman was on the fast track to the top, and a greater proportion of working women held secretarial and support positions than in 1950.[3]

With two-thirds of working women clustered in just ten occupations—most of them low paying—most married women were still economically dependent on their husbands. Overall, women earned just 64 percent of what men did—the same ratio as in 1955.[4]

In law, in 1987, women held fewer than 8 percent of the partnerships at the top 250 firms, and in medicine, in 1989, although women made up 37 percent of the first-year students, women doctors still earned 30 percent less than men. In medicine, law, and engineering, women were resegregating themselves into the lower paid, less entrepreneurial, and more bureaucratic areas of their professions. Nearly 60 percent of black women lawyers worked in government jobs rather than in law firms.[5] Women students were still being discouraged from entering careers in science; many who received M.D.s and Ph.D.s were stuck in non-tenure track positions in which they could not compete for research funds.

136

Women in industry had to contend with sexism, low pay, and paternalistic attitudes that questioned their talents.[6]

In journalism, women made up 66 percent of the graduates but less than 5 percent of upper management; and while women could now get jobs in engineering as easily as men and many felt fairly treated, sooner or later most reached barriers to advancement. Executive women were paying for what success they did have through a tremendous rise in cocaine abuse, cigarette smoking, and eating disorders—results of feeling powerless and "overly harried."[7]

Single women in their thirties and forties wished for families and were afraid of growing old alone. Black professional women found it particularly difficult to meet appropriate men, and many minority women found themselves professionally and socially isolated. Single women no longer organized their lives around the search for Prince Charming, but "in some inchoate way," they assumed he was "around the corner." He was not; the "new men," who were supposed to be open to sharing rights and responsibilities, had been "feminized" without becoming feminists; they liked cooking and decorating, but cared more about status and career success than about equality, and they were terrified of commitment.[8]

Married women were not faring much better. They had health and stress problems and if you counted the hours put into housework and child care, married women worked roughly fifteen hours longer each week than men. The higher the level of a woman's job, the less likely her husband was to help out at home. Married women tended to devote proportionately more of their time to housework and less to child care than did their husbands; men took the kids on "fun outings" to the park, but women washed the toilets and scrubbed the bathrooms—and continually apologized to interviewers for the amount of sleep they needed. Black women lawyers complained about "traditional" husbands who didn't help out, and spoke of "soft-pedalling" their assertiveness and catering to husbands' "delicate" temperaments.[9]

Divorce did not help. "Enlightened" laws passed in the 1970s to divide property equally between men and women ended up depriving divorced women (especially older homemakers and mothers of young children) of the legal and financial protections that the old laws had provided. Instead of recognizing contributions of homemakers and mothers and compensating them for years of lost opportunities and impaired earning capacities, judges now expected women to be as capable of supporting themselves after divorce as men. But they were not.

A year after divorce, the average woman had experienced a 73 percent loss in her standard of living, and the average man a 42 percent gain in his. In California, where property was divided fifty-fifty, one lawyer explained, "the wife gets the kids and half the money from the house, which is not enough to buy a new place. He walks off with the cash and she's left with the problem."[10] The result was a new group of poor single housewives with children to raise on their own.[11]

Then there were the children. Some researchers found long hours spent in day care were good for children, but others decried the lack of parental nurturing. Sylvia Ann Hewlett pointed out that hundreds of thousands of preschool children were spending most of their days in poor-quality, often unlicensed day care facilities, and between two and five million schoolchildren aged six through thirteen were without adult supervision for several hours a day because both parents were working. Many of these latchkey children expressed feelings of fear, loneliness, depression, bitterness, anger, and rejection.[12]

Young women—who, incidentally, were now graduating from college in smaller proportions than their male peers—said they were sick and tired of hearing about how hard it all was. A graduate physics student at Stanford said she would rather switch than fight. "If I'm going to be a mother, I'm not going to work 60 or 80 hours per week," she said. "I would sacrifice my career. It's a shame. But you can't do both as well as you would like."[13]

Women at a group of elite Eastern women's colleges said they expected to interrupt their careers in order to stay home with children for a few years. Other college women felt considerable anxiety over achievement and, far more than their male peers, underestimated their abilities and set inappropriately low goals for themselves. A study of eighty-one high school valedictorians showed that women's estimations of their own intelligence declined as they went through college; young women were more vague than their male peers about their career plans.[14]

A Harvard law school graduate in her late twenties told me she felt no need to fight, to struggle for equality. "I feel obligated to work at least part time," she reported, "but nothing beyond that." Having graduated from a class which was 30 percent women, she added, "I don't feel I have to prove anything." Susan Jacoby's students expected to take five to ten years off from rewarding, well-paid jobs to raise children. They described feminists as "bitter, angry" women who were "unattractive to men" and emphasized careers at the expense of romance and family life. Meanwhile—with so many mothers working—teenage daughters were taking on family responsibilities at younger and younger ages.[15]

As if that were not enough, the media once again began to play up the ways in which men and women differ. A front page *New York Times* story highlighted a study purporting to show that women's decision-making abilities are impaired at certain times of the month. *Newsweek* magazine reported that men and women experience the world differently—not merely because of the ways they were brought up in it, but because they feel it "with a different sensitivity of touch," hear it "with different aural responses," and "puzzle out" its problems "with different cells in their brains."[16]

The new vogue in psychology was to suggest that women, unlike men, operate best within the context of human relationships and should be encouraged to do so. In business, women managers who appeared to conform to sex-role stereotypes were perceived as better leaders than those who did not; employees preferred women bosses who were "considerate" but male bosses who were more "structured" and "dominant." Not a few authors suggested that in business, women's unique abilities would complement those of men.[17]

In contrast to the seeming solidarity of women a decade earlier, rifts among women appeared to widen. In a debate that echoed—or continued—debates of the nineteenth and early twentieth centuries, feminists divided among themselves. Some believed that differences between men and women should be minimized whenever possible, and that women ought to have the same rights and responsibilities as men. Other feminists touted "caring" and "maternal" values as women's special strengths, and questioned whether women were well-served in attempting to prove themselves in fields once reserved for men.[18] In the confusion, the women I spoke with and others expressed discouragement and despair.

Becky Wilson, a corporate lawyer, liked earning a lot of money, enjoyed arguing cases before the Securities and Exchange Commission, and was proud when a major client who left her firm retained her to do his securities work. She was soon to be considered for partnership. One partner, however, had already told her she should be more feminine—and she was not even sure she wanted to be a partner, partly because her husband seemed envious of her work. Asked where she saw herself in five years, Becky outlined three possible life scenarios. In the first, she was a successful corporate lawyer but felt bored. In the second, she quit work to become a faculty wife, run a junior year abroad program with her husband, and have three children. In the third, she left her husband, who didn't want children, continued working as a lawyer, and tried to meet a man who wanted children. It was already too late for this last scenerio, she feared.

Molly Walden, a corporate lawyer pregnant with her first child, questioned "mainstream" values.

I am successful in terms of society at large, held out as a standard. I make a lot of money, my job is prestigious and if I play my cards right I can really participate in corporate America. But in terms of achieving something of real worth or value, I think success involves making a mark, doing something good, producing something beautiful—not just helping somebody making money. I am always considering quitting. I don't plan to stay in the law firm; I am trying to figure out what to do; I can't quite see the way.

At thirty-two, Clara Zolen had her first child and as we spoke two years later, she was pregnant with a second. "Sometimes I feel like packing it all in and staying home," she said. She was also weighing a job offer that would involve a more prestigious title, more responsibility, and a huge pay increase. It would also mean a long commute. She wondered aloud: "Should I tell the new company I am pregnant and will need a maternity leave? But then they might take back their offer. Maybe I should just turn it down. Or maybe I'll just accept it and see what happens." She looked at me, sighed, and said, "I feel anxious all the time."

Andrea Schwartz, a specialist in ear, nose, and throat surgery, was also thinking of quitting work; the overhead in her private practice was so high that it made more financial sense for her to quit working entirely than to cut back her work week from seventy hours to forty so she could spend more time with her two children.

Anna Bart, a gastroenterologist in private practice, had married her high school sweetheart, who became a lawyer for a large corporation. They had a six-month-old daughter. Anna earned a sizable income after just a year in practice but at the price of working twelve to fourteen hours a day. When she got home, she said, she woke up the baby, who spent most of her time with a housekeeper, in order to play with her for two hours. "I am constantly exhausted," Anna said. "When Gloria Steinem stood up there and told us we could do it, she obviously hadn't looked to see how many hours there are in the day." When I pointed out that Anna could have chosen a less demanding medical specialty she said, "If I'd wanted to have a woman's job I'd have been a nurse." Still later, she said, "I've proved I can do it. Now I want to stop."

Peggy Talbot, a lawyer, wrote in the margin of a questionnaire, "The women's movement provided the external impetus for me to break out of traditional female career choices and put pressure on me to be untraditional. I am not sure these pressures were in my best interest."

Another lawyer told a researcher studying black women, "I expected to combine career and homemaker roles. I was not prepared for nor did

I expect to have to sacrifice one for the other. I was not prepared to live my life as a single woman and I'm having a great deal of trouble coping with the situation. I wonder if the career was worth it."[19]

Other minority professional women, caught in a clash of career, family, and community, found themselves isolated from all three. Leanita McClain, a thirty-two-year-old journalist who committed suicide, was the first black person to become a member of the *Chicago Tribune*'s editorial board, and in 1984 was selected as one of the ten most outstanding working women in America. She had written, "I have fulfilled the entry requirements of the American middle-class, yet I am left, at times, feeling unwelcomed and stereotyped."[20]

These women had travelled long, rocky transition paths. Most women—those I spoke with and others—went through an initial period of turmoil on making their career decisions. Many described difficulties in starting their jobs because they felt different from and perhaps not as competent as men. For a time, each bought into "masculine values," at the expense of what she considered the more "feminine" ones she had inherited from her mother. For a time, each felt torn in two. In her early-to mid-thirties, each woman seemed to hit what surgeon Sandy Smith described as "a wall": a period of anxiety, turmoil, or depression in which many wondered, in spite of their successes, whether they could or even wanted to continue at work.

"In terms of transition," Clara Zolen told me quite formally, "there are three stages. First you wonder if you can be successful. Then you prove you can be successful. Then you wonder if you even want to be successful."

These conflicts were not restricted to white women; many black women lawyers interviewed by another researcher experienced sex-role conflicts brought on by cultural and occupational inconsistencies, and a study in progress suggested that many were facing life crises resulting from the unpredicted state of their personal relationships.[21]

Some of the difficulty came from the strain of breaking new ground in the workplace, from the exhaustion that came from trying to prove themselves again and again in terms that felt alien. Some of it stemmed from the lack of institutional and familial support they needed to both work and raise families. On a very personal level, the central issue for each woman I interviewed was her relationship with her mother.

◆　◇　◆

Sandy Smith may have felt her inner conflicts more deeply than some women—perhaps because the definitions of feminine and masculine she had internalized as a child were particularly rigid and stereotypical—

but I have chosen to tell her story because it so clearly highlights the developmental processes of most of the women I interviewed.

After working almost nonstop for five years, Sandy finished her surgical residency. Then she got very depressed. She worked most of the time and spent the rest of the time sleeping or not doing much, in her apartment, making plans and not doing them. "The whole rest of my life stopped and the only thing I could just about manage was work," she said. At this point, Sandy spoke almost offhandedly, with a slight turn of the head, a shrug of the shoulders, as if to minimize the impact, the importance, of what she must have been feeling at the time, of what she was saying.

> I could only deal with people as a surgeon. I could only meet people and say, "I'm Doctor Smith." I had to have my beeper on as sort of a badge. I couldn't go out and wear playclothes. I couldn't go out in my jeans and my dirty tee-shirt. I might meet people, and if they didn't know me, if they didn't know I was a surgeon, I wasn't worth anything. I had nothing as a person.

Then, she had a complication while doing an operation. "That can happen in surgery, and in fact, now I'm getting sued for it," Sandy said. "But that was like . . . gee, if even work doesn't hold together, then it's all over." That is when she started ordering knives through the mail. "I had decided that was how I would kill myself," she explained. What had gone wrong?

As Sandy talked, I began to see her depression as a product of her struggle to earn her father's admiration by proving, again and again, that she was not like her mother. Sandy got along better with her father, growing up. Wanting to please him, she had always thought of herself as the oldest son, taking charge of her siblings—two younger sisters and a brother.

> My father was always the one who ran the show and took care of everything. Even though we never really had a lot of money growing up, if people really needed something he always found it. When I was in medical school he said he envied me because he would have loved to have been a doctor.

Sandy acknowledged that by going into surgery, she was disregarding her mother's wishes.

> My mother had five kids and she was into running the family and she was very into appearance. We always had a lot of conflicts over it. I'd buy books when she thought I should buy clothes. So in one

way I was rebelling by doing surgery. I was really going completely counter to what my mother wanted.

The result was a constant struggle with her mother's values.

The impression I always had—my mother died about two years ago—was that it was all right for me to be a surgeon because it was a good excuse as to why I wasn't married. The one memory that drives me crazy is of the first week I was an intern, which was just disastrous. You're sure that you're supposed to know everything and that all of these patients are going to live or die on the basis of what you do. Which is all baloney but you're sure it's true. Anyway, after the first ten days it was July Fourth and I was going to be able to sleep for a few hours and I called home and the first thing my mother asked me was how many single men there were in my group. That was typical. That was her perspective of what was important.

Perhaps in response, Sandy gave up all social life and devoted herself to proving she could be as "macho" as the male surgeons she worked with. She progressed, but as she did, she began to have problems with her father, a man who "comes from a generation where making money and having money define your masculinity." As a medical resident, she earned more money than he did, which, she said, "must have threatened him." Then, in hopes of doing something "nice," she made matters worse.

I paid for my parents' vacation in England toward the end of a year's rotation and took them around. My father and I at that point and for about a year or two years after that had a lot of problems. It was basically that I was surpassing him financially, that I could do things for him because I was really making more money.

Then Sandy's mother developed cancer.

When my mother was sick, I was the one who had the power. I knew people in medicine and I knew how to pull strings and get her taken care of and I had the authority in a medical situation that my father didn't have. We had a power struggle for a couple of years that neither of us was comfortable with. Because I really didn't want to have the power. In one way, I'd just as soon have been the little girl and have him take care of me and make it all better.

That was several years ago, and since then, Sandy and her father have worked out their relationship, she said, although she makes considerably more money than he does now. When people in her family need money, they go to her, not to him. "It was a big shift of power that took a while to even out. Now he's proud of me and we get along very well," she said. "We're both living our lives as two adults and we've sort of reconciled some of that stuff."

Not as well reconciled, however, was Sandy's relationship with her mother—and with her own sense of self as a woman—which led to an inner struggle and to the lowest point in her life so far. As Sandy explained it, she worried that by not having children, she had disappointed her mother.

> I'm the one who did the things that my father would respect the most. But it's not what my mother respected most. My mother got along best with the sister who got married and had two kids and lived down the street. She had the traditional standard relationship with my mother and would come and leave the kids off. As I envisioned it, that was my mother's ideal. I've never wanted to do that but I always feel guilty that I didn't. Some part of me feels that I'm not totally a success because if I were really a success I wouldn't be a rich and famous surgeon. I'd be married with 12 kids.

Growing up, Sandy was often expected to care for her siblings. Having been asked to take on too much responsibility as a child, she didn't particularly want to have children now. "I wouldn't mind if I were involved with somebody who really wanted to have kids. I'd put in the nine months for that reason. But the man would have to be the primary caretaker," she explained. Besides, she said, she *does* a lot of mothering in caring for patients "and maybe that fulfills enough of those needs that I don't feel an obligation to do it on somebody else."

So, for Sandy, life was still to be primarily career. She hoped that within five years she would become a nationally recognized surgeon. She had a good shot at it. "I'm certainly recognized in this city now, and I have patients coming from all over," she said. But the part she was "a little more up in the air about" was what she would be doing in her private life. "Ideally I would like to be involved in some type of long-term relationship. Not necessarily married with five kids living in the suburbs, but something . . . warmer and committed," she said.

Whereas once Sandy had been "all career," with the help of some therapy, in her thirties she was beginning to feel more comfortable with the aspects of herself she considered feminine. That brought up new issues for her. Since she did not enjoy doing "big macho" operations, she was thinking of subspecializing in a field of surgery she considered "female." But among general surgeons, who tended to be sexist, the subspecialty was not considered prestigious and Sandy still wanted very much to prove that she could compete in "men's" terms. To her, subspecializing meant "giving up the macho stuff for the female stuff." And, she asked, "should you really do that?" On the other hand,

> already my practice is changed and it's worked out well. It's half women, and the thing that I'm making my reputation for is *not* doing big gory operations. That's what's much more comfortable to me. But I feel a little bit guilty that I'm a women's surgeon and not a macho trauma save-the-world surgeon. Am I lowering my standards to do what's all right for a woman to do? To do less surgery? There's still that conflict, because still the ideal is to be the big macho surgeon, and do the big macho operations.

Sandy explained her concern as political: she believed she ought to serve as a role model, to prove to her colleagues and to other women that women could compete successfully in men's terms. It may also be that she had internalized the beliefs that women and women's fields were second class. But as we spoke, I realized that Sandy had come nearly full circle in her struggle—from wanting desperately to prove she was nothing like her mother to developing a new respect for herself and for other women.

In her mid-thirties, Sandy said, she was developing relationships with women friends for the first time.

> When you're buying it and trying to be one of the boys and all that stuff, you don't have a lot of women friends. Now I'm developing a fairly large support group of women friends, and becoming reacquainted suddenly with being a woman. The woman's side of things isn't bad anymore. But it's something to be able to associate with other women whereas God forbid you would never do that before. Mostly it's other women physicians, and it supports that whole side of the conflict, which is really quite interesting: that it's not so bad after all.

What was not so bad after all?

> Being a woman, or having women friends, or the female aspect of being a doctor. That there are other people who have had the same conflicts and complaints. That you're not as bizarre as you thought you were.

Like Sandy, for a time, most of the women I spoke with tried to be assertive, objective, unemotional, and oriented toward tasks rather than toward people. Most also, for a time, tried to damp down what they considered their feminine attributes—defined, by each woman, as the more predominant aspects of her own mother's personality. Failing to express the aspects of themselves that they shared with their mothers further jeopardized their feelings of worth as females—all the more so in workplaces that did not seem to value those traits. The harder they worked to prove their competence, the worse they felt—because they were breaking the societal and familial rules for successful females that they had internalized. They also felt more distanced from their mothers.

Eventually, most women began to feel competent as professionals— and dared to begin expressing aspects of themselves they considered feminine. At this point, several decided to have children. While having children made some women more secure in their feminine identity,[22] for Abby Nathan and others, it led to heightened inner conflict.

◆   ◇   ◆

In her third year of residency, Abby Nathan began to feel competent as a doctor; she decided to marry the man she lived with and to have a child. Knowing that women in their thirties often had trouble conceiving, she went off birth control thinking that if all went well, the soonest she would have a child was when she finished her training. Instead, she got pregnant right away. She resolved that being pregnant would make no difference in her work.

> During my first trimester I was tired. I felt I was getting no support. I couldn't let anyone know that being physically different made a difference. I had to act as though pregnancy had no effect. Inside, I felt like I was going to die. My back hurt, I'd had no sleep. People would ask me how I felt and I'd say, "Great."

Her residency program made no special provisions for pregnant residents. "The administration is anti—they think it's a bad precedent, that I shouldn't have gotten pregnant," she said. Her coworkers agreed. Eight months pregnant at the time of our interview, she said,

> Two women residents are mad at me. One woman is gay, the other has a kid; I would have expected support from them. People say I'm irresponsible, unfair to other people; I partly agree. But then, one of the men has a child and another is trying to; no one is mad at them. The woman who is mad at me did a half-time residency; she may be afraid that if I can't work as hard, she will have to do even more work. But I planned carefully so that having the baby doesn't affect anyone else in any way. I'm taking all my night call now and will be working on elective time and clinic, just daytime, after the baby comes. I'll have the kid, then come back for three months. Then I'll

look for a job in primary internal medicine in a community health center.

Abby now planned to work just nine to five, and felt disappointed. "In medical school I had higher hopes for myself. I wanted to be in public health, to make a difference. Now, I am settling to do just practice, when the men around me are going on to big jobs, writing grant proposals," she said.

Other women might have described a choice of this sort as between career and family. In addition, Abby was struggling with the self-image she had inherited from her mother, whom she had seen as incompetent. "The question is, do I feel I am not capable or is it just that I want to have a family? Sometimes I ask myself if I'm going to practice in the health center because that's all I think I *can* do," she said.

Still, Abby was not willing to make the sacrifices necessary to be a success, a state of grace which meant to her that "you have a brilliant career, a mentor, that you are at the top of the field, judged the most competent by your peers; that you're publishing, being a leader." She did not want to put in the time it would take to do that.

I feel guilty, but now even men are saying that living is important. Or maybe it's being pregnant and not knowing what will happen once the child is born. Preparing for the child is diminishing my goals and aspirations. It's hard, finishing residency at thirty-two, with only a few more years for child raising.

Many of the difficulties Abby ran into had to do with the fact that she was one of the first women in her training program to become pregnant during residency—the least flexible period in any doctor's training. Medicine is a field known for requiring tremendous commitment and long hours.

On an emotional level, pregnancy can complicate matters still further—not just because it takes extra energy and can raise the ire of colleagues, but also, according to psychiatrist Carol Nadelson, because it often brings up a woman's guilt, anger, ambivalence, or remorse about her early relationship with her own mother—as she takes on her mother's role. In addition, a pregnant woman's own mother may begin to see her as an equal and no longer a child; she may compete to prove she is a better mother than her daughter, or she may have trouble with the idea that she is old enough to be a grandmother and become angry and jealous.[23]

Some of this may have been at play for Eleanor Valera, who at the time of our interview, felt caught in a bind. She had been offered

147

a promotion which would have made her the highest-ranking woman at her newspaper—but she also wanted another child. She could turn down the promotion to work part time and have the child, she said, but she also felt it was important to be a role model to prove that women do not have to compromise their careers to raise children. She also wanted more time for herself. "I need to be more selfish and less self-sacrificing," she said, but what she meant was unclear. Would it be more or less self-sacrificing to continue striving for the sort of career success her mother had given up or to tone down the career and spend more time at home, given her mother's unhappy experience?

◆   ◇   ◆

Robyn Sparks was not yet ready to consider children; the central issue for her at this point was marriage itself. Without fully understanding why, she started to feel bored and burned out in the public defenders office. She quit her job not knowing what she would do next, then she opened her own private practice. At the time of our interview, Robyn felt "transitional."

> I don't have a rhythm, yet, I don't have a sense of the new territory. I make less money now than I did in my old job because I have a lot more expenses; now I have to make $50,000 or $60,000 to take home $37,000 because of the overhead, paying for my office. I won't be bringing in any settlements for a couple of years.

Still, she said, workwise, "I am where I should be," but "work has an end every day."

Knowing of a study showing that while in their twenties many women define success in terms of their careers but in their thirties begin to define success as balancing career and family,[24] I asked Robyn how successful she felt. "I'm doing O.K.," she said. How did she define success? "It's when you're satisfied with yourself, and other people perceive you as positive, competent, a good person in your field," she answered. I noted that Robyn seemed to be defining success only in terms of work. Where did she see herself in five years?

> I see myself doing an interesting job that I enjoy but I wonder if I won't want to have a family. I don't know how to resolve it. I see that the biological clock is running out but it may be that my life is to be all career and no family. Have I *chosen* that or did it just happen? I think if I were to say I want to be married, I could do it. I have had goals and have reached them. If I wanted to save $3,000 for a vaca-

148

tion, or to lose weight, I could do it. If I were to commit myself to getting married, I could probably do it.

Then she added with a twinkle in her eye, "Of course, I don't know what kind of man I would come up with." Twinkle or not, she was not entirely joking. Clearly ambivalent about marriage, she did not want to end up trapped with a man who did not respect her as an equal.

> I keep looking at my parents' marriage. I see that they have grown to like each other. But their marriage was no model; my mother was stuck with kids, she felt she had to be there. I ask myself, "Would I feel the same way?" I wouldn't want it to be like it was for my mother.

Even though Robyn was successful at work, she doubted that she could do any better than her mother at choosing a man to live with. "You do see people work it out," she said, but she knew that marriage was no panacea. Although at work she felt able to relate to men, she believed intimate relationships were a different story. "You learn a lot about the men you work with when you meet their wives," she said. "When they're with their wives, they're bastards. I ask myself, 'How do you really know?'"

Robyn, here, could almost have been talking about her father, whom she still admired, even though he apparently walked all over her mother. "I would want to project myself publicly like my father," she said. But, she added, "his only interests are law and politics. I want more than that." However, even though Robyn had, through her work, established an independent role in the world, she now sometimes worried that she was beginning to "get like" her mother, who was "bright," but "dominated" by her father.

Sadly, Robyn remained as dominated by work as her mother had been by her father, afraid even to try to relate on an intimate basis with a man lest she be trapped in as unhappy a situation as her mother had been. Or perhaps Robyn feared that succeeding in both a career and marriage would make her very different from her mother, hence less emotionally connected with her and with the images of femininity she had internalized, based on her mother's model, in childhood.

However, generally, the women I interviewed did not believe that having careers had prevented them from marrying. "Heck, my career is the best part of my life," said Cynthia Jefferson, a lawyer. "The fact that I'm not married has nothing to do with that." She explained her single state in terms of her childhood. Her mother, once a journalist, had breakdown after breakdown when her four children were small, and as the oldest, Cynthia had taken much responsibility for the family. As a result, at thirty-four, Cynthia was just beginning to learn how to develop her own relationships with men.

Jennifer Howe, a scientist who had been divorced, said she had no interest in remarrying because she wanted to spend most of her time in the lab. She considered herself nurturant, but she saw her students as the children she would never have. "That's enough for me," she said.

♦　◇　♦

While these women described their conflicts—and what they considered feminine attributes—along the traditional lines of nurturing, marriage, and children, not all women did. Janet Peters considered the artistic vision she brought to architecture as feminine. Unlike architects who concentrate on the forms and shapes of buildings, she said,

> I see rooms filled with things that give me pleasure, like the way the light hits the room, the color of natural daylight, how it will fall on the desktop. I don't see a sterile box; I would let you arrange it the way you want to arrange it. There wouldn't be mammoth spaces; there would be more intimate spaces, not monumental halls and lobbies.

Marjorie Babson felt that she had "a gift, a spark," in doing research.

> But I felt I had a gift, a spark, from being raised, too. I had other values, and I had better not let them get lost. I felt, as a woman, different: like I was a person that could make some sense out of life. I realized I had to keep a balance. I had to keep work in a different context. It had to come from me.

Peggy Talbot knew she had "spiritual, creative, celestial parts" which she had a hard time expressing through law; she missed her music, which she had dropped as a career because it seemed too feminine.

Defining "feminine" and "femininity" is tricky. Webster's dictionary gives the rather solipsistic definition of feminine as "having the qualities regarded as characteristic of women and girls, as gentleness, weakness, delicacy, modesty." Susan Brownmiller describes femininity as societally defined, "a romantic sentiment, a nostalgic tradition of imposed limitations" which goes beyond the biological to become "a set of compromises"—in dress and behavior—designed to make men feel superior. "Masculinity," she writes, "is known to please by displays of mastery and competence while femininity pleases by suggesting that these concerns are beyond its intent." Feminist writers Suzanne Gordon and Sarah Ruddick define femininity or feminine nature, if there is such a thing, in terms of caring and nurturing.[25]

150

Throughout *Broken Patterns,* I have described the societal ideology of femininity as confused, as simultaneously portraying women as powerful, nurturing, and spiritual, yet also as weak, dependent, and overly emotional. That ideology, those idealizations, I believe, are based on projections and internalizations through which both males and females deal with feelings of helplessness and desire in relation to the all-powerful caregivers we need or experience in our infancy.

Given the differences in mothering styles, and the positions women hold in families of differing religions, races, and ethnic backgrounds, those idealizations clearly do not do justice to the complexity of female experiences and capabilities. Based on my interviews, I would describe feminine *identity*—as opposed to femininity or the *ideology* of femininity—as a central if intangible set of qualities defined by each woman for herself in relation to her own biological, familial, and spiritual heritage and molded by her own experiences and the societal influences of her time. Especially important are the characteristics a woman shares with her own mother and grandmothers.

When I started *Broken Patterns* I had hoped to chart a transition path along which women worked their way through to an adult feminine identity. Some psychologists, who had studied mainly men, believed that the normal human being developed in a linear way—that is, through a series of steps or stages—starting out connected with the mother, and eventually reaching a point of autonomy. Some psychologists described women as never becoming fully adult, getting stuck in relationships, unable to compete or excel on their own. Others believed both men and women grew more independent and autonomous through experience; still others thought that personality was pretty much set in childhood, a result of genetics and family dynamics.

What I found was that women's development seemed to combine all of the above. The women I interviewed did seem to go through steps or stages, and at each step women seemed to be dealing with the same central issue—how to be independent of her mother yet not lose touch with her. At each step, as different life questions emerged, the dilemma was posed in a slightly different way. Psychologist Irene Stiver suggests the difficulty with which a woman resolves the issue and moves beyond it may be more or less severe—depending on the degree of subjugation a woman's mother appeared to experience. (As described in the previous chapter, differing family structures and ethnic and cultural backgrounds might tend to complicate the process.)[26]

The women I interviewed appeared to be at different stages of resolution.

Janet Peters, for example, had long hoped to design public housing because she wanted "to contribute something to society." But in the prestigious architectural firm in which she worked, she was continually asked to design shopping centers and parking lots, work which, she said, "does nothing for [her] soul."

Despite her certainty about what she wanted to do, when I asked Janet how she could gain the influence to reach her goal, her answer showed that she still measured herself according to "masculine" values, that she believed that as a woman, like her mother, she was not good enough. "First I have to erase everything that they once thought about me to show that I do everything they can do. You have to play it as a man," she said. Paradoxically, Janet felt that in order to succeed she had to negate the very attributes that were crucial to her own self-expression, to her own definition of herself as a full person in the world.

Peggy Talbot, who described her mother as powerful but angry, may have started out with a more positive self-image than Janet, whose mother had been beaten by Janet's stepfather. Peggy had married another lawyer just after graduating from law school and the marriage remained strong, she said. But after eight years in a corporate law firm, she had begun to feel that law and economics did not reward the artistic and spiritual aspects of her being. So, just a few weeks before our interview, she had left the corporate firm to take a lower-paying job in government.

> In this context, I can be a good writer as well as an analytic person, an advocate; I can treat that fellow I talked to on the phone as a human being, giving him advice; I can step beyond my role, connect to people outside my role. Government and public policy issues affect the caring part of me; I can feel good about that; it's not just straight power.

Still, Peggy said she missed her music and wondered if she had made the right decision. "There still isn't a way to integrate the spiritual side here in the way music can take you above reality," she said. But maybe there was no way to do that through her work, she suggested. "That I'll have to do on my own."

Marjorie Babson, who followed her mother into a career in social science research, had perhaps come the closest to finding a personal and professional balance. Over the four years she held her job in a medical center, Marjorie got better at standing up for herself.

> Eventually my fury was channelled at work into appropriate places but I was still worried and anxious and angry all the time. I had the skills to manage myself so I did not get put down: I knew how to

watch out for myself and there were rewards to the job. But finally, I asked myself, "Is this what I want?"

Feeling that her real self was not being expressed in her career, Marjorie cut her work schedule to part-time in the medical center—and took a second part-time job directing her own research project at a women's college.

Although that compromise allowed her to do the sort of work she wanted in an environment in which she felt comfortable, she worried that she might be falling into the trap of part-time work that had kept women in the past from reaching influential positions. And, though she was happily married to an artist, she wondered what would happen to her career when she decided to have children.

◆　◇　◆

The women I interviewed had all started out wanting to be quite different from their mothers. In many ways they had succeeded. By the 1980s, few felt trapped in marriage as their mothers had been; regardless of their marital status, they took full responsibility for the decisions they had made—blaming neither society nor men for their situations. In their early to mid-thirties, when they "hit the wall," though many women were undecided about what to do and in turmoil, unlike their mothers, most eventually took action. Several women changed jobs or moved into part-time work; others decided to have children.

For all of them, somewhere along the way, the central question changed. Once, they had asked how they could be different from their mothers and equal with men. Now, they were wondering how they could be more *like* their mothers, how they could retrieve and express the traits that made them as women special, "feminine"—yet still be equal with men.

This same question—which divided women earlier in this century and in the last one—reemerged, in the 1980s, in the form of fierce debate in the courts, among policymakers, and among feminists themselves.

In a sex discrimination case against the Sears Roebuck Company, the Equal Employment Opportunity Commission argued that the fact that far more men than women held lucrative sales jobs showed that the company discriminated against women. Sears took the position that women rarely applied for such jobs, so, evidently, they did not want them.

Feminists divided among themselves. Some testified that women might want and excel at sales jobs but did not apply because they knew Sears preferred to hire men and would not accommodate the family pressures women disproportionately faced. Other feminists argued that there are real, possibly innate differences in the desires and capabilities of men and women and that companies should not be held responsible for the different career choices of men and women. In the view of this faction, to say that discrimination alone kept women in low-paid, "traditionally female" jobs denigrated what might have been the genuine—and equally worthy—job preferences of many women workers.[27]

A related issue, heated in the 1980s and still smoldering today, is "comparable worth." Should women be encouraged to do the same jobs as men, so that they can earn as much money as men do? Or should the pay scales for "traditionally female" jobs be raised, even if that might mean more women than men would be attracted to such jobs? If the pay scales for "women's" jobs are to be elevated, how can the intrinsic values of the jobs be compared—except by what the market will bear? Should a secretary be paid the same as a truck driver?[28]

Then there is pregnancy leave. A 1978 California law required that companies with fifteen or more employees treat pregnancy like any disability. A group of California employees challenged the law on the grounds that it discriminated against men and non-pregnant women, and was destructive to women because it was based on the stereotype that women needed special protection to be brought up to the level of men. The law's supporters held that it simply corrected for a biological burden that only women and not men in the workplace face. "Men can father children without risking their jobs," one lawyer pointed out.[29]

Rather than single women out for special treatment, many feminists instead favored federal legislation—which has since passed—mandating family or parental leave to allow both men and women to take time off to care for family members.[30]

There are also questions about the impact of day care on both parents and future generations. If corporations provide it, will women hesitate to leave their companies for better jobs to avoid uprooting their children? Should the government fund day care to allow—force?—poor women to work in order to leave the welfare roles? What is the impact of day care on child development? If women continue to hold most child care jobs, what happens to the egalitarian ideal of raising children with both male and female role models?

And how about insurance? Since women generally live longer than men, should women pay more for health and disability benefits and annuities that will be likely to pay out more to them over the years? If women have fewer automobile accidents than men, should they be charged lower rates than men—even if that would reinforce cultural and economic distinctions between men and women?[31]

Finally, consider "post-feminism." Does the fact that women quit their jobs or go half-time mean, simply, that they are doing what fulfills them? Or are they leaving work because husbands, employers, or society have failed to make it feasible for them to do otherwise?[32]

By the end of the 1980s, in part because of dissension and debate among women themselves, the media had declared feminism dead. American society was, in regard to questions of "difference" and "equality," at an impasse. With feminists divided among themselves, the struggle that had once felt like a great common effort had become for many women a solitary one. Psychologist Irene Stiver described the professional women she treated as lacking connection either to their mothers or to a feminist movement. "They feel so lonely," she said.[33]

Still, Sandy managed to be hopeful. "This is really a transitional age, where we were raised unliberated, and we got liberated. I think with our relationships and with everything else there's a whole lot of conflict," she said. Perhaps future generations "who are not raised with quite so much garbage will be able to deal with it better," she suggested. Despite the difficulties, "I think it'll work out in the end," she said.

But how? How will the women I interviewed resolve their dilemmas? And how will society?

9

Spirals: Present, Past, and Future

By now, most of the women I spoke with have moved on in their lives, and American society has begun to ask new questions about the meaning of equality. Increasingly, Americans are recognizing that the polarization of men and women and rigid definitions of race and class do not serve the common good; new models, new ways of defining and achieving equality are being sought through a developing diversity movement.

At the same time, the end of the cold war has brought major disruptions in the world order. Americans, facing increasing economic uncertainty and demographic changes, are redefining themselves in their own homes and workplaces and as a nation. A major question is, can we avoid, in what seems likely to be a continuing period of turmoil on many levels, a resurgence of old beliefs, oversimplifications, and repolarization as has occurred again and again in the past?[1]

In *Broken Patterns,* I have shown a historical and generational process in which women leave the home for paying work, lose momentum, divide among themselves, and although they may continue to work, face a deepening societal belief that they should not. One generation makes tremendous strides, only to see its accomplishments resented, diminished, or forgotten by the next. Subsequent generations of women find ways to synthesize the gains of their predecessors, to move forward once again.

It is possible to view this history as a relatively straight line leading to autonomy and freedom for women. Demographer Charles Westoff, for instance, writes that since the colonial era, women have been increasingly freed from domestic duties. A steady decline in the infant mortality rate has meant that women have needed fewer and fewer children to ensure that at least some would survive; as the economy shifted from farm to factory, families no longer needed large numbers of children to work the land.[2]

Historian Carl Degler points out that smaller families and longer life spans have allowed women to spend fewer years caring for young children and more time pursuing their own interests, and that within the family women have gained strength—both through the development of legal rights and through greater control over their own destinies. Degler even interprets the sexual repression of the late nineteenth century as an expression of women's increasing control—unconscious though it may have been—over their own bodies and the number of children they would bear. Historian Sarah Evans and others describe steady progress for women in the world of work from 1900 on and predict the same for the future.[3]

Others look at the very same history as cyclic. Social psychologist Marcia Guttentag suggests that in times when there are more marriageable women than men, women tend to be free to (or are forced to) work outside the home; in periods when there are too few women to go around, men, who compete for mates, tend to marry younger, view wives as possessions, and try to keep them at home.[4]

According to demographer Richard Easterlin, generations that are relatively small in population believe they will have an easier time earning livings than their parents, so they marry younger and have larger families than their parents, which allows women less time before marriage to pursue careers. The next generation, relatively large in contrast, faces greater competition for education and jobs so it puts off having children. In large generations, Easterlin says, women can—or must—seriously pursue careers, and in turn, they and their husbands put off having children and produce relatively small generations.[5]

Also in keeping with a cyclic theory, some social scientists suggest that in times of war, plague, or famine, women are blamed for misfortunes and made to play subservient roles. Susan Faludi argues that feminism is blamed when the economy gets rough and men fear they are losing jobs to women. Others believe that during societal crises, women are called upon to use all of their skills and talents, but when crises abate, women's roles are curtailed as the society pulls back to a deeper conservatism than before.[6] What *Broken Patterns* shows is a progression for women—on a historical and personal level—that is neither linear nor cyclic but spiral.

◆   ◇   ◆

During the colonial era, women worked alongside men in farms and families, and later, as the nation industrialized, were the first to work in factories. As a middle class developed, so did an ideology proclaiming that men and women were meant to play very separate roles. Although some women continued to work outside the home (mainly those who had no other choices) the ideology of domesticity deepened. As it did, a small number of privileged women saw their mothers' lives of domesticity as too constrained. From the Civil War on, these daughters entered colleges and professions. Some became active in a movement for women's rights and suffrage.

Women's gains in politics and professions continued into the 1920s, after women had won the vote and were entering colleges and some careers at nearly the same rate as men. During the Great Depression and after World War II, hostility to working women deepened; by the 1950s, their gains seemed largely forgotten and the next generation of women was encouraged to return to the home. In the 1960s and 1970s, *their* daughters, many of them granddaughters of career women of the 1920s, began in unprecedented numbers to seek equality by entering professions once reserved for men.

In this spiral pattern, women in each generation have, in some way, surpassed their mothers—with some generations viewing it as a luxury to be able to remain at home with children, and others seeing careers as freeing them from the drudgery of housework and child care. Certainly each generation at home has benefited from technological progress, and each generation of professional women has been larger and has had more rights, responsibilities, and possibilities than those that came before.

On a grand social scale, the spiral is driven by economics, politics, demographics, the opening of possibility, and the closing of it. Just as important, the spiral affects and reflects a natural human need for connection and separation, for nurturing and achieving, for independence and autonomy. The spiral is an historical expression of the developmental path of the young child, who moves away from the mother to explore the world in ever-widening circles—but always checks back to be sure her mother is still there. It is the push-pull between generations that seek to break the patterns of their parents, yet remain connected with them. It is the societal manifestation of a psychodynamic process in which, especially during times of crisis, confusion, or chaos, we wish for the idealized all-powerful mother of our infancy, the mother who was our whole world, and who, we hoped, could make all well—yet from whom we ran in fear.

In itself, the spiral is not terrible: it can be a creative process in which we move forward and make our own way, then return to reintegrate the people, images, and values of the past we care about. In every generation, individual women have done so. For example, women of the early nineteenth century moved into the world outside the home through religious activities deemed in keeping with women's special, spiritual character; later, settlement house workers referred to women's "maternal" nature to justify their work on behalf of the poor.

Likewise, most of the women I interviewed found ways, by the time they reached their forties, to retrieve what they considered the feminine aspects of themselves, defined largely as aspects of their mothers that, for a time, they seemed to have left behind.

One of those women was Molly Walden, the student radical-turned-corporate lawyer, who now has three daughters. After her second daughter was born, she switched to part-time legal work, then moved full-time to a government environmental agency where she can fulfill her early social action goals and keep a relatively flexible schedule. Molly's husband, also a lawyer, works from their home; an au pair helps with housework and child care.

Sandy Smith is now a renowned surgeon who operates almost entirely on women; she lives with another woman and, though she said in our interview that she did not expect to have children, she now has a child of her own. Suzanne Lewis, now a New York reporter, is happily married to a business executive with grown children from a previous marriage.

Eleanor Valera, an editor, has two children in grade school and some health problems; she has turned down several promotions in order to maintain a work schedule that allows her to spend time with her sons and to garden.

Although these syntheses work for the women who chose them, too often, solutions like these are ignored or considered insignificant. "These women are not successful," one editor wrote, in response to a draft of this book. What she meant was that none of them has both reached the pinnacle in her field of work and become a perfect wife and/or mother, as defined by the mythic stereotypes many of us carry within ourselves.

It is these stereotypes, of the super-achieving, all-providing father, and the always-available, all-nurturing mother, that turn what could be a positive spiral into a negative one. These stereotypes are conjured up by generation after generation, especially in times of crisis. At these times, individuals who are traumatized or feeling out of control may wish for protection and order. Feeling disempowered and disconnected, they tend to fall back, psychologically, to a time in their lives when their world seemed safer and simpler, and to view the world through child-like eyes.

At such times, both personally and politically, people seem to expect of themselves and project onto one another impossible, simplistic, and rigid images of weakness and strength, sometimes incorporating them into law and social policy. Women who do not fit the crippling stereotypes ascribed to them are demeaned as unfeminine, and men, as unmasculine; those who struggle to match the stereotypes limit themselves.

When parents try to conform to images that do not fit, or when there is a power imbalance between them, sons and daughters may perceive either parent as all-weak or all-powerful; mothers may be experienced as inferior to men or to some feminine ideal. Children of both genders grow up wanting to be unlike their mothers—to denigrate women, to reject aspects of themselves they consider feminine, and to exaggerate the power of the masculine. They perpetuate in their own families and workplaces and society what has become a vicious generational and social spiral in which, no matter what women do, they are considered not good enough.

Alison Hartley, for example, was one of several women I spoke with who could trace their family histories back four generations. Her great-grandmother came from a wealthy family but evidently fell on hard times and had to work as a milliner in the 1890s. She also had an abortion, which to this day the family still considers scandalous.

As described in an earlier chapter, her daughter, Alison's grandmother, worked as a legal secretary even after she was married because, Alison explained, her husband "couldn't afford to buy the furniture." Because Alison's grandmother wished to live out the image of the ideal Victorian lady of leisure as her mother, the milliner, had not, Alison's grandmother was "furious" that she had to work, even in an era when many women wished to do so. Alison considered her grandmother "shallow," especially in contrast with her daughter, Alison's mother, whom Alison described as "sweet" and "artistic." Alison's mother, however, ended her own life before she turned thirty, soon after her fifth child was born.

Each of Alison's forebears aimed to be different from her own mother, but never seemed to match up to the feminine societal ideal of her time, and none was considered successful, no matter what she did. While Alison herself admired many of her mother's qualities, she saw her mother as weak. Not surprisingly, like other women I interviewed, Alison grew up divided within herself—uncertain, in her mid-thirties, of what it meant to be a successful woman. She did look to her paternal grandmother, who had had just one child, as a role model for her career as a writer, but at the time of our interview, Alison was unmarried and felt unclear about her life goals.

Not all of the women I interviewed managed to navigate even as successfully as Alison, and virtually all described periods of anxiety and despair. While such emotions are not exclusive to women, the point is that for the women described in *Broken Patterns,* inner conflict was heightened because of the way they developed in relation to their mothers. The women I interviewed identified with their mothers as oppressed and wished to remain connected with them and to help them, but at the same time, they also wanted desperately to escape the "feminine" role and the conflicting images of femininity they had internalized from early childhood on.

In a previous chapter, I described how the difficulty of resolving such conflicts led Sandy to consider suicide; one journalist I spoke with actually did take her own life—possibly as a result of the combination of her own chemistry and the impossibility of integrating the horrors of her mother's experience as a Jew in Germany during the Holocaust in the 1930s and 1940s. (Of all the women I interviewed, this journalist was the only one who claimed not to feel any conflict with her mother's values. She was also the only woman to say that she did not feel conflict between success in a male-dominated field and success as a woman; rather she felt that her success brought her love. Her suicide came soon after her love affair with a married coworker ended; she became so upset that her journalistic judgment appeared questionable, and she was demoted.)

◆   ◇   ◆

Today, given the personal and professional difficulties so many working women are experiencing, combined with a rapidly changing world order, economic uncertainty, and continued questions about gender roles, we are in danger of perpetuating the negative spiral. Women are entering politics and careers in ever greater numbers and are approaching pay equity with men, but progress is slow and we are experiencing a resurgence of concern for the "traditional" family. There is denial of—yet, at the same time, resistance to—women's progress in the workplace, and sexual harassment is widespread.[7]

As in the 1920s, women are divided among themselves. Sixty-three percent of American women do not consider themselves feminists, 54 percent say the women's movement had no effect on their lives, and 50 percent say it does not reflect the views of most women. Former supporters of the National Organization for Women question whether the organization can be effective if its leader is an acknowledged bisexual, and a "new breed" of feminists attack "radical" feminists for being anti-male and for portraying women as victims, rather than as victors in the struggle for equality.[8]

Some films and television programs portray career women as vicious, deserving of "nannies from hell." In Texas, it was male legislators, not female ones, who allied with a female state senator to pass laws requiring insurance companies to pay for mammography as well as chest x-rays. It was a woman who led the National Federation of Independent Businesses' opposition to the unpaid Family and Medical Leave Act. Even success is problematic: in two states, qualified women running against one another for the U.S. Senate split feminists and the vote. Despite the fact that women increasingly own companies, their companies are not always supportive of women; the *Wall Street Journal* reports that women-owned companies can be "positively antidiluvian when it comes to hiring or promoting women into management."[9]

In pockets of the middle-class and upper-middle-class "the stay-at-home mom is fast becoming the newest status symbol" partly because it is a luxury that few families can afford.[10] Working-class women charge that professional women fail to respect them, and women of color, ethnic minorities, and foreigners find their talents and achievements ignored. The antipathy expressed by blacks, Hispanics, and Asian-Americans toward one another nearly equals the resentment they collectively feel toward whites.[11]

Meanwhile, the proportion of mothers who are poor and single continues to rise, as do reports of physical and mental violence against women in all income groups. Although the Family Leave Act granting twelve weeks of unpaid leave for family medical emergencies was enacted in 1993, its benefits are not available to many workers in small companies. With an increasing need to supplement family incomes and a lack of adequate child care, a greater proportion of women today work in low-paid, part-time secretarial and support positions than twenty years ago. Women still earn only 75 percent of what men do. Two-thirds of all part-timers and nearly 60 percent of all temporary workers are women.[12]

Despite hopes that working women would provide positive role models for their sons and daughters, because working women (and men) have so little time away from work, the condition of children since 1979 has worsened in what one analyst called "a pattern of national child and family neglect." Many families are without access to health care, adequate education, or housing; millions of infants and toddlers are so deprived of medical care, loving supervision, and intellectual stimulation that their growth into healthy and responsible adults is threatened.

The number of children entering foster care jumped by more than 50 percent from 1987 to 1991, and reports of child abuse are rising. One of every three abused children is a baby less than one year old. American children are among the least likely in the world to be immunized, and an increasing number of very young children grow up witnessing stabbings, shootings, and beatings.[13] Once they get to school, they find that gender bias is still rife, and the majority of girls who drop out of high school

162

give as reasons sexual harassment from their male classmates or family responsibilities at home.[14]

One reason girls have those family responsibilities is that even though more than half of women with children work outside the home, only 2 percent of corporations provide full day care for employees' children. While large employers are beginning to offer at least unpaid leaves for family matters, many workers do not use them for fear of jeopardizing their performance evaluations or of becoming targets for layoffs if companies downsize. Such fears are not unfounded; in recessionary times, minorities and women, the last hired, are usually the first let go.[15] What is more, although in coming decades most women will have to work to support themselves and their families, if past experience holds true, we can expect that working women will be blamed for the demise of the "traditional family" and the ills of society that ensue.

All in all, despite our generation's efforts to break the patterns of our parents, our society is paving the way for yet another generation of children to grow up in dire need of the safety of home, who become adults with impossible, idealized images of absent parents, and who are angry at those who do not or cannot meet their needs. We are perpetuating a pattern in which working women are blamed for deserting the family, for neglecting what are continually categorized as women's—and only women's—nurturing responsibilities.

Professional women, now approaching their prime within their fields and an increasingly powerful force in the society at large, must take the lead. We must gather our strength as individuals and join with others to turn a potentially destructive spiral into a creative one. On many different levels, we must use our understanding of the needs for connection and separation to rethink not only the nature of feminine identity, but also the nature and measurement of equality itself.

As individuals, professional women must give themselves credit for how far they have come. It is a mistake to listen when people say professional women have gotten nowhere, that all they have done is for naught—just as it is a mistake to assume that women have reached all of their goals. Professional women have come far, but there is a long way to go. We must recognize that each of us is a participant in an ongoing struggle, both individually and historically. It is a struggle in which there are losses and gains, but which will ultimately lead to progress.

Rather than measure this progress in terms defined by and for mythic men or women of the past, or resort to simplistic definitions of male and female, each woman must measure her success and value in her own context. We must acknowledge that men and women alike grow and change along the life cycle, and see both setbacks and successes as

163

steps in a process of discovery in which we seek individuality yet connection with others. It is this quest that moves us forward in our own lives and as a group.

Women must accept that gains and growth—that equality itself—need not always be measured in terms of money, power, or position. New research in psychology and psychiatry, for example, is leading to better understanding of the relationship between women's life cycles and the stages of family and career development. It also suggests ways in which education can best bring out the talent in both boys and girls. In medicine, increased attention to the health and disease processes of women could lead to greater longevity and quality of life. In Boston, three female hospital administrators are encouraging their hospitals to address breast cancer, obstetrics, and gynecology in new ways. This new knowledge, these new methods, mean gains for us all.[16]

We can all also take pride in the development, in academe, of women's and gender studies and of feminist criticism; classroom discussions and reading about women's contributions in all fields are already providing added insight on bias, and are imbuing young women with a solid sense of their own places in history. Young women are beginning to apply these new perspectives in their chosen careers—international relations, management, law, and the arts.[17] All of these advances will lead, one day, to new values, to new organizational forms, to new definitions of equality we are only beginning to imagine. But there is a long road ahead.

◆   ◇   ◆

Throughout *Broken Patterns,* I have shown that generations of American women have wrestled with the questions of how different women are from men, of what causes those differences, and of what those differences mean in regard to equality. In the early nineteenth century, Margaret Fuller argued that women deserved the same rights and responsibilities as men, while Catharine Beecher wrote that women wielded tremendous power through their family roles. Later in the century, female lawyers debated the more-than-symbolic question of whether they ought to wear hats in court or remove them, as men did. In the 1920s and again in the 1980s, the women's movement developed serious, nearly fatal divisions over the question of whether women would be strengthened or weakened by special legal protections or an Equal Rights Amendment, which would require—and guarantee—that women receive the same treatment as men.

Today, in the 1990s, we are still struggling to answer these age-old questions concerning "difference" and "equality." Clearly, there are biological differences between men and women, but we do not yet know the extent to which these are influenced by environment, by hormones, by the interaction of the two. We are ever-more cognizant of the vast differences—biological and cultural—that exist among women, and among men, and it is as difficult as ever to define equality when individuals have different origins, talents, and goals. Our challenge is to find new, complex approaches to the relationships of men, women, and society, and a new definition of equality that will take into account the differences and similarities not just between men and women, but among us all.

After long impasse, we are beginning to make inroads.

In terms of social policy, for example, the courts are beginning to assess when differences between men and women matter and when they do not, and rather than assume that there is just one approach to equality, to develop strategies to fit different circumstances. As political scientist Nancy Gilson explains, equality does sometimes mean treating women and men exactly the same—as in assuring the same pay for the same work or the same rights to educational funding and opportunity.[18] This might mean, as economist Barbara Bergmann advocates, ending sex segregation in engineering and vocational education and requiring that all high school students learn construction skills, cooking, and parenting skills. Bergmann also advocates ending discrimination against part-time workers—the vast majority of whom are women who have no pensions and who earn proportionately less than full-time employees.[19]

In other cases, we should acknowledge that our society is still in a state of transition and, rather than use the exact same treatment for people who may come from differing backgrounds, develop treatment that will lead to equivalent outcomes. Legal scholar Martha Minow suggests that because women still earn far less on average than men, in calculating social security benefits, it is appropriate for women to exclude more low-earning years than men. In some cases, it may be fair to promote women ahead of men in jobs from which women have traditionally been excluded. In divorce, rather than assume that all men and all women are equally capable of supporting themselves and impose a 50-50 property split, judges might proceed on a case-by-case basis.[20]

Under other circumstances, we might look to women's experience as the norm. For instance, health payment policies based on the situation of the "average" elderly person fall far short of meeting the financial and health care needs of elderly women. This is because women tend to outlive men, are less likely than men to remarry when they lose their spouses, are less likely to be cared for by their families, and are more likely than men to be poor because they lose income from private pensions when their husbands die. Women are also less likely than men to die suddenly of heart attacks or accidents and are more likely to live on, chronically ill, in nursing homes. Providing benefits that meet the needs of such women would also help men in comparable straits.[21]

In still other situations, gender should not be taken into account at all. Consider a case in which a woman five feet tall shoots a much larger and inebriated man who advances on her in a threatening way. Law professor Kathleen Sullivan explains that rather than ask whether a man or woman could reasonably believe the man would kill her, the court might throw out both "masculine" and "feminine" tests of reasonability entirely and come up with a "reasonable person" standard based, perhaps, on a new category—such as "height"—to determine, in this case, what is fair on the basis of the perceptions of a short person.[22]

A second strategy in dealing with the differences between men and women is to better understand how institutional frameworks contribute to gender inequality. Sociologist Rosabeth Moss Kanter explains that men (and women) at the bottom of a hierarchy, who have little power, often exhibit stereotypical characteristics most commonly attributed to women, such as passivity and lack of commitment to their jobs. In contrast, women who lead organizations more closely resemble male executives in their levels of ambition, competitiveness, and methods of attacking problems. Kanter proposes equalizing opportunity by restructuring work organizations to increase mobility for people at the bottom, and substituting rewards and values other than upward mobility at the top.[23]

A third strategy is to recognize that men and women alike need to both nurture and achieve, and to make it easier for all parents to spend more time with their children. This might mean expanding the Family Leave Act to include more workers; building residential communities easily accessible to work, shopping, child care, cleaners, restaurants, and pediatric facilities; or lowering the average number of hours people work, which is now the same as it was in the 1930s.[24]

Perhaps family considerations should structure the workplace. Some companies already hold peer discussion groups for people at different stages along the life cycle and allow a range of support strategies such as in-house child care, after school programs, care for sick children or the elderly, or voucher systems so that employees can choose the support most appropriate to their needs. While only a few companies provide full-time day care for their employees' children, of 1,006 major employers, some 66 percent offer some type of child care assistance, 36 percent give elder-care assistance, and 53 percent allow flexible schedules. Approximately ninety large corporations employ "work-family coordinators" to serve as liaisons between employees and high-level executives,

166

designing and managing policies and programs to help employees balance home and work.[25]

On an expanded scale, allowing such choices could, ultimately, empower women (and men) both in the workplace and in the family by legitimizing the many different family forms that have always existed.[26] This would, in turn, strengthen the identities of boys and girls alike by allowing them all the best material and emotional chances for survival.

While addressing the question of male-female difference is important, it is just as crucial that we recognize and address the differences that exist among women. So far, in *Broken Patterns,* much of the discussion about women's advancement has assumed white middle-class values—in large part because professions have always been predominantly white and middle-class, and because those values have been the societal norm.

The more we advance as women and as a society and the more we learn about ourselves and about women as a group, the more we understand that women themselves have different histories, different interests, and different hopes. Asian-Americans, African-Americans, Hispanics, and Native Americans, as do white Americans, come from a wide range of nations, social classes, cultures, and religions. Most of us are descended from a mix of people from different backgrounds. Certain class, family background, and educational levels make it easier for some than for others to advance, and these categories change historically. At some times, concerning some issues, women may have more in common with men in a particular group or class than with other women.[27] Since all women grow and change along the life cycle, young, middle-aged, and elderly women have very different needs.

In the past, assuming that all women were alike and had similar values divided women again and again and weakened their common progress. Our new challenge—and the challenge of the next generation—is to find ways to target individual needs yet also promote women as a group, to live out our individual destinies, yet strive for the common good. We must recognize that, paradoxically, as individuals we are all members of intersecting yet competing groups. Yet, also paradoxically, despite the differences among us, all women are in this together, potentially subjected to the same stereotypes, put-downs, and primal reactions, regardless of class, race, religion, political belief, income, or occupation. We must tease out the ways in which women are similar and the ways in which they differ, and we must establish that it is respecting and enhancing not just the similarities but also the differences among us that will strengthen women as a group.

This, too, is starting to happen. In science, psychology, and medicine, studies strictly of women are beginning to enable researchers to determine the impact and interplay of various environmental and genetic factors on biological and psychological development as well as on disease. Educators and counselors are developing models of multiracial identity development, and in the management area, researchers are beginning to assess the impact of culture, class, and educational background within different racial and ethnic groups. While it is still unclear which differences are definitive and which are not and what they ultimately might mean, by focusing on every person as a person of difference we will find ways to make creative use of each person's unique talents, skills, and understanding.

Some corporations are conducting workshops in attempts to build trust that all differences will be heard and respected. Through storytelling and other exercises, team members may articulate a variety of approaches toward common goals, and members of all groups may be encouraged to see the ways in which they are privileged.[28] Ideally, these sorts of interactions ensure that different voices are heard, but also require that each person take responsibility for being heard and for listening—first steps in breaking down stereotypes and making settings safe for creative approaches to problem solving.

Such workshops and training are already leading to new organizational forms. In one large company, individuals volunteer to participate in "core groups" based on their own particular interests—race, sexual orientation, or expertise. These groups cut across function lines and are company-wide; they provide for creative interchange, strengthen individuals, and make top management aware of employees' needs. Such "cross-structures" also help to break down traditional gender-based hierarchies, and can make corporations more responsive to "the real world." In addition, some companies are beginning to judge managers on how well minorities and women—as well as white males—are taught, perform, and move up in the ranks.[29]

These programs are crucial because by the year 2000, minorities and women will be the majority of new hires in the workplace; new, more culturally sensitive management structures must evolve not just to make work environments pleasant but to ensure that companies remain competitive.[30] Training in negotiating based on respect for differences may also be useful beyond the workplace. Within the family, it could provide couples with skills to help work out equitable household and child care arrangements. On a larger scale, acknowledging the legitimacy of many voices could give more individuals the confidence to bring creative solutions through avenues of politics and civic life.

In times of economic downturn and national crisis, however, new initiatives are often lost. To prevent this from happening, professional women must form new alliances. Within the workplace, professional women must join with others to advocate diversity training, a multicultural workforce, and to make it possible for all employees to both achieve and nurture. Professional women must also maintain the alliances they already have with female coworkers and clients, advocating on their behalf with sensitivity to the special strengths and needs of individuals, women, and members of different groups.[31]

In the community, professional women must support grassroots organizations aimed at empowering the underserved either financially, or by volunteering skills and time. As feminists, we must recognize that while some women have made great strides, others have had fewer opportunities; while many have overcome obstacles, countless others remain victims. On a national level, professional women must join with others through the vote and social action to make priorities of health care, education, adequate subsistence, and job opportunities for all.

Ultimately, this nation must bring all Americans to a standard of living that provides children material security and allows each parent to stand strong, within the family, as well as in the workplace. It is only when sons and daughters do not experience fathers or mothers of any class, race, or religion as downtrodden—or conversely as all-powerful—that they will not have to adhere to, project, or fight off rigid, internalized stereotypes as they go to school, compete in the workplace, and raise families of their own.

It is in these ways, as individuals engaged in dialogue, interacting and wrestling with issues of connection and separation, similarity and difference, that we can transform relationships—within ourselves, within families, within the workplace and in the broader society. Seemingly small solutions will become larger ones in a synergistic process until one day, our society will be ready to consider gender, race, class, and generation as just several of a wide range of categories to be taken into account in policy formulation and in our lives. Success will come to be measured not just by money and power—but by quality of life, by self-respect, and by the existence of equal possibility for all to pursue life, liberty, and happiness.

There will always be historical, generational, and individual spirals and there should be—because it is through exploration and reconnection that we grow and change, building on the past but not bound to it. There will always be divisions among us and there should be—because it is our individual histories and genetics that make each of us unique and special. By joining together to explore our similarities and our differences, we will build new forms of relationships, of organizations, of community. These may come and go, but if we can interact out of mutual respect rather than fear or disdain, if our conflicts can become fuel for creative interaction, we will have joined together in a future in which everyone can flourish.

From us, I hope generations to come will learn that there is no one feminine identity—there never has been, there never will be—but that our individual choices, combined, determine the future for us all. It is not enough just to have freedom. It is *using* our freedom to embark on a quest for answers that has created for each of us—and will assure for each woman of the future the freedom to create—her own new feminine identity.

NOTES

Chapter 1

1. Carol Gilligan, interview with author, Bunting Institute, Radcliffe College, Cambridge, Mass., Nov. 4, 1982.
2. Steven D. McLaughlin, John O. Billy, Terry R. Johnson, Barbara D. Melber, Linda D. Winges, and Denise M. Zimmerle, *The Cosmopolitan Report on the Changing Life Course of American Women* (Seattle, Wash., Battelle Human Affairs Research Centers, 1985) p. vii points out the demographic similarities between women born between 1946 and 1964 and their grandmothers.

Chapter 2

1. I place the word "traditional" in quotation marks because, while many Americans believe women's historic role has been as homemakers, *Broken Patterns* shows that women have worked in a myriad of occupations for centuries. The term may also have different meanings within particular racial, ethnic, religious or cultural groups. Alice Rossi, "Barriers to the Career Choice of Engineering, Medicine, or Science Among American Women," in *Women in the Scientific Professions,* edited by Jacqueline A. Mattfeld and Carol G. Van Aken (Cambridge: M.I.T. Press, 1965) p. 57.
2. Richard Easterlin, *Birth and Fortune, The Impact on Personal Welfare* (New York: Basic Books, 1980); Helen Guttentag and Paul Secord, *Too Many Women: The Sex Ratio Question* (Beverly Hills: Sage Publications, 1983); David Herlihy, *Medieval Households* (Cambridge: Harvard University Press, 1985); Anita Harris and Shirley Wershba, "Will There Soon be Another Baby Boom?" *MacNeil-Lehrer Report,* Public Broadcasting System, May 9, 1977; Susan Faludi, *Backlash: The Undeclared War Against American Women* (New York: Crown Publishers Inc., 1991).
3. Elizabeth Douvan and Joseph Adelson, *The Adolescent Experience* (New York: John Wiley and Sons, 1966); James Davis, *Great Aspirations* (Chicago: Aldine Publishing Co., 1964); Charles Westoff and Raymond Potvin, *College Women and Fertility Values* (Princeton, N.J.: Princeton University Press, 1967); Sandra Tangri, "Role Innovation in

Occupational Choice Among College Women," Doc. diss., University of Michigan, 1969, Reprinted by University Microfilms Ltd., 1970, 1979) pp. 15, 16, 118.

4. Mirra Komarovsky, *Women in College: Shaping Feminine Identities* (New York: Basic Books, 1985) p. 196; Tangri, "Role Innovation," pp. 46, 103–105, 118.

5. E. H. Plank and R. Plank, "Emotional Components in Arithmetic Learning, As Seen Through Autobiographies," in *The Psychoanalytic Study of the Child,* Vol. 9 (New York: International Universities Press, 1954) pp. 9, 274–296, 954, described by Ravenna Helson, "Women Mathematicians and the Creative Personality," *Journal of Consulting and Clinical Society* 36:2, (1971) pp. 210–220, in *Readings on the Psychology of Women,* edited by Judith Bardwick (New York: Harper and Row, 1972) p. 93; Cynthia Fuchs Epstein, *Women in Law* (New York: Basic Books, Inc., 1981) pp. 25–26.

6. Shirley Mahaley Malcolm, Paula Quick Hall, and Janet Welsh Brown, eds., *The Double Bind: The Price of Being a Minority Woman in Science* (Washington, D.C.: American Association for the Advancement of Science Report No. 76-R-3, April 1976) pp. 31–40.

7. Tangri, "Role Innovation," pp. 39–46, citing Davis, *Great Aspirations,* and Alice L. Dement, "The College Woman as a Science Major," *The Journal of Higher Education* 33:9 (1962) pp. 487–490; Malcolm et al., *The Double Bind,* p. 8.

8. Cynthia Fuchs Epstein, *Woman's Place: Options and Limits in Professional Careers* (Berkeley: University of California Press, 1971) p. 29.

9. Helene Deutsch, *The Psychology of Women,* Vol 1. (New York: Bantam, 1973) pp. 286–333 (Originally published by Gune and Stratton, 1944). Ferdinand Lundberg and Marynia Farnham, *Modern Woman: The Lost Sex* (New York: Harper & Brothers, 1947), pp. 143, 235, quoted in William Chafe, *The American Woman* (New York: Oxford University Press, 1974) pp. 204–205.

10. Plank and Plank, "Emotional Components in Arithmetic Learning as Seen Through Autobiographies," in *Psychoanalytic Study of the Child,* Vol. 9, cited in Tangri, "Role Innovation," p. 18; Helson, "Women Mathematicians," in Bardwick, ed., *Readings,* pp. 93–99 (Helson found mathematical creativity to be associated with an "androgenous" mental temperament in which both men and women exhibited "cross-sex parent ties," and felt free to use the "cognitive resources generally attributed to the opposite sex." They had "considerable flexibility of mind" and were able to maintain and coordinate what for many people were "antithetical cognitive processes." This did not make either the men or women "sexless." But it did make the creative women seem less sociable, more eccentric, and less interested in social rewards than the less creative women. The creative women, unfortunately, also showed more early psychopathology and felt more conflict about their sex roles than other women, though they were not actually more masculine than other women.) Donald Brown, "Some Educational Patterns," *Journal of Social Issues,* vol. 12, 1956, p. 54, cited in Tangri, "Role Innovation," p. 18.

11. Epstein, *Women in Law,* pp. 96, 30–31, also citing Rita Lynn Stafford, "An Analysis of Consciously Recalled Professional Involvement for American Women in New York State," Ph.D. Diss. School of Education, New York University, 1966; M. V. Lozoff, "Father and Autonomy in Women," *Annals of the New York Academy of Sciences* 208 (March 15, 1973) cited in Nora Reiner Gluck, Elaine Dannefer and Kathryn Miles, "Women in Families," in *The Family Life Cycle,* edited by Betty Carter and Monica McGoldrick (New York, Gardner Press, Inc., 1980) pp. 299–300; Margaret Hennig and Anne Jardim, *The Managerial Woman* (New York: Doubleday, 1976; Pocket Books, 1977) pp. 99–108.

12. Elizabeth Douvan, "Employment and the Adolescent," in *The Employed Mother in America,* edited by F. I. Nye and L. W. Hoffman (Chicago: Rand McNally, 1963) pp. 142–143; Douvan and Adelson, *The Adolescent Experience,* cited in Tangri, "Role Innova-

tion," p. 17; Grace Baruch, "Maternal Influences upon Women's Attitudes toward Career Achievement," Doc. diss., University of Michigan, 1969, in archives of Henry A. Murray Research Center, Radcliffe College; Malkah Notman, M.D., and Carol Nadelson, M.D., personal interviews, April 13, 1983, Dec. 10, 1983; Robert Stevens, "Law Schools and Law Students," *Virginia Law Review* 59, no. 4 (April 1973) pp. 551–707 cited in Epstein, *Women in Law*, pp. 60–62.

13. Eleanor Maccoby, "Sex Differences in Intellectual Functioning," in *Readings on the Psychology of Women*, edited by Judith M. Bardwick (New York: Harper and Row, 1972) p. 43; reprinted from Eleanor Maccoby, Ed., *The Development of Sex Differences* (Stanford, California: Stanford University Press, 1966) pp. 25–36, 38–44, 46–66.

14. Tangri, "Role Innovation," 1969, pp. 112–118, 196–200.

15. Gwyned Simpson, "The Daughters of Charlotte Ray: The Career Development Process During the Exploratory and Establishment Stages of Black Women Attorneys," in *Sex Roles: A Journal of Research* (New York: Plenum, July 1984) Vol. 11, Nos. 1/2, pp. 125–127.

16. For a discussion of changing questions and studies, see Diane Tickton Schuster, "Studying Women's Lives Through Time," in *Women's Lives Through Time: Educated American Women of the Twentieth Century*, edited by Kathleen Day Hulbert and Diane Tickton Schuster (San Francisco: Jossey-Bass Inc. Publishers, 1993) pp. 3–31 and 417–443. On expectations of researchers: Alice Rossi, "Equality Between the Sexes," in *The Woman in America*, edited by Robert J. Lifton (Boston: Beacon Paperback, 1967) p. 116 (first published in *Daedalus*, Spring 1964).

Chapter 3

1. Erik Erikson suggests that "socioeconomic and cultural panics" which involve the family can cause "individual regressions to infantile atonements and a reactionary return to more primitive moral codes"; societally, such panics can lead to "reactionary returns to the content and form of historically earlier and stricter principles of behavior." Erik Erikson, *Identity, Youth and Crisis* (New York: W. W. Norton and Co. Inc., 1968) pp. 54–56; also see pp. 257, 260.

2. Gretchen M. Bataille, ed. *Native American Women* (New York: Garland Publishing Company, 1993) p. xiii; also see Sara M. Evans, *Born for Liberty: A History of Women in America* (New York: Free Press, 1989; London: Collier MacMillan, 1989) pp. 1–11, citing Carolyn Niethammer, *Daughters of the Earth, The Lives and Legends of American Indian Women* (New York: Collier Books, 1977).

3. Gerda Lerner, "The Lady and the Mill Girl, Changes in the Status of Women in the Age of Jackson, 1800–1840," in *A Heritage of Her Own: Families, Work and Feminism in America*, edited by Nancy Cott and Elizabeth Pleck (New York: Touchstone Books, 1980) pp. 183–184.

4. Laurel Thatcher Ulrich, *Good Wives: Image and Reality in the Lives of Women in Northern New England 1650–1750* (New York: Vintage Books [first published 1980], 1991) p. 38.

5. Steven Mintz and Susan Kellogg, *Domestic Revolutions: A Social History of American Family Life* (New York: The Free Press, 1988) p. 40 citing Carr and Walsh, "The Planter's Wife: The Experience of White Women in Seventeenth Century Maryland" in Cott and Pleck, *A Heritage of Her Own*, pp. 42–43; Ulrich, *Good Wives*, pp. 9, 36–50, 238, citing Daniel Blake Smith, "The Study of The Family in Early Colonial America: Trends, Problems and Prospects," *William and Mary Quarterly*, 39:9 (1982) pp. 9–10.

6. Mintz and Kellogg, *Domestic Revolutions*, p. 37, citing Edmund Sears Morgan,

American Slavery, American Freedom, The Ordeal of Colonial Virginia (New York: Norton, 1975) 158–162.

7. Carol Hymowitz and Michaele Weissman, *A History of Women in America* (New York: Bantam Books, 1978) p. 3, citing Daniel Boorstin, *The Americans: The Colonial Experience* (New York: Random House, 1958) p. 350.

8. Jeanne Boydston, *Home and Work: Housework, Wages and the Ideology of Labor in the Early Republic* (New York: Oxford University Press, 1990) p. 7, citing Nathaniel B. Shurtleff, ed., *Records of the Governor and Company of the Massachusetts Bay in New England* (Boston: Press of William White, 1853), *Massachusetts Records,* May 14, 1645, 2:116–117.

9. Nancy Cott, *The Bonds of Womanhood: "Women's Sphere" in New England, 1780–1835* (New Haven, Yale University Press, 1977) p. 27, citing the *Oxford English Dictionary;* Alice Kessler-Harris, *Out to Work: A History of Wage-Earning Women in the United States* (New York: Oxford University Press, 1982) p. 18, quoting Edith Abbott, "A Study of the History of Child Labor in America," *American Journal of Sociology* 14:21, 23 (July 1908); Evans, *Born for Liberty,* p. 35.

10. William Chafe, *Women and Equality, Changing Patterns in American Culture* (New York: Oxford University Press, 1979 ed.) p. 19, citing Julia Cherry Spruill, *Women's Life and Work in the Southern Colonies* (New York: Norton, 1972), Chapters 11–14, esp. pages 240–245; Mary Ryan, *Womanhood in America: From Colonial Times to the Present* (New York: New Viewpoints, 1975) p. 34.

11. Kessler-Harris, *Out to Work,* pp. 14–15, citing Spruill, *Women's Life and Work in the Southern Colonies,* p. 290.

12. Kessler-Harris, *Out to Work,* pp. 14–15, citing Linda Grant DePauw, *Four Traditions, Women of New York During the Revolution* (Albany, New York: New York State Bicentennial Commission, 1976) p. 13.

13. Hymowitz and Weissman, *A History of Women in America,* p. 7, citing Daniel Boorstin, *The Americans: The Colonial Experience* (New York: Random House, 1958) p. 217; Regina Markell Morantz-Sanchez, *Sympathy and Science* (New York: Oxford University Press, 1985) p. 12, citing Mary Putnam Jacobi, "Women in Medicine," in *Women's Work in America,* edited by Annie Nathan Meyer (New York: Henry Holt, 1891) p. 141.

14. Hymowitz and Weissman, *A History of Women,* p. 6.

15. William Chafe, *Women and Equality,* p. 20.

16. Mary Beth Norton, *Liberty's Daughters: The Revolutionary Experience of American Women, 1750–1800* (Boston: Little Brown, 1980) p. 38; Evans, *Born for Liberty,* pp. 26–29, based on Russell Menard, "Immigrants and their Increase: The Process of Population Growth in Early Colonial Maryland" in *Law, Society and Politics in Early Maryland,* edited by Aubrey C. Land, Lois Green Carr and Edward C. Papenfuse (Baltimore: Johns Hopkins University Press, 1977) pp. 88–110; Lois Green Carr and Lorena S. Walsh, "The Planter's Wife: The Experience of White Women in Seventeenth Century Maryland," *William and Mary Quarterly,* 3d series, 34 (1977) p. 552.

17. Evans, *Born for Liberty,* pp. 26, 29, citing Carr and Walsh, "The Planter's Wife," pp. 524–571, Allan Kulikoff, "The Origins of Afro-American Society in Tidewater Maryland and Virginia, 1700 to 1790," *William and Mary Quarterly,* 3d series, 35 (1978) pp. 22–26, and Peter Wood, *Black Majority* (New York: W. W. Norton, 1974) pp. 599–662; Bell Hooks, *Ain't I a Woman: Black Women and Feminism* (Boston: South End Press, 1981) pp. 23–25.

18. Boydston, *Home and Work,* pp. xix, 35.

19. Norton, *Liberty's Daughters,* pp. 215, 63–64, 117.

20. Mintz and Kellogg, *Domestic Revolutions,* p. 11, citing Lyle Koehler, *A Search for Power, The Weaker Sex in Seventeenth Century New England* (Urbana: University of Illinois Press, 1980), pp. 137–142.

21. Cott, *Bonds of Womanhood,* p. 6; Mary Beth Norton, *Liberty's Daughters,* pp. 228–242.

22. Evans, *Born for Liberty,* p. 50, citing Linda K. Kerber, *Women of the Republic: Intellectual Ideology in Revolutionary America* (Chapel Hill: University of North Carolina Press, 1980) p. 46.

23. Hymowitz and Weissman, *A History of Women,* pp. 30–31; Darlene Clark Hine, *Black Women in America* (Brooklyn, New York: Carlson Publishing Company, 1993) pp. 447–448.

24. Evans, *Born for Liberty,* p. 53, citing Gary Nash, "The Forgotten Experience, Indians, Blacks and the American Revolution," in *The American Revolution: Changing Perspectives,* edited by William M. Fowler, Jr., and Wallace Coyle (Boston: Northeastern University Press, 1979) pp. 27–46; also citing Francis Jennings, "The Indians' Revolution," in Alfred F. Young, *The American Revolution: Explorations in the History of American Radicalism* (DeKalb: Northern Illinois University Press, 1976) pp. 319–348.

25. Hymowitz and Weissman, *A History of Women,* pp. 30–41, citing Sally Smith Booth, *The Women of '76* (New York: Hastings House, 1973) pp. 264–265, and Alice Brown, *The Women of Colonial Times* (New York: Scribner's, 1869) p. 88.

26. In New Jersey, women over 21 who had at least 50 pounds worth of property and who were one-year residents could vote in state elections. Mary Frances Berry, *Why ERA Failed: Politics, Women's Rights and the Amending Process of the Constitution* (Bloomington: Indiana University Press, 1986) p. 30.

27. Norton, *Liberty's Daughters,* pp. 228–250.

28. Kessler-Harris, *Out to Work,* pp. 23–24.

29. Cott, *Bonds of Womanhood,* p. 35, citing Maris Vinovskis and Richard M. Bernard, "Women in Education in Ante-Bellum America," Unpublished Working Paper 73-7, June 1973, Center for Demography and Ecology, University of Wisconsin, Madison, pp. 13–14 and graph 6.

30. Judith Sargent Murray, "On the Equality of the Sexes," *The Massachusetts Magazine* (March 1790) pp. 132–135, in Alice Rossi, ed., *The Feminist Papers from Adams to Beauvoir* (New York: Bantam Books, 1973) pp. 17–22.

31. Alexis de Tocqueville, *Democracy in America,* edited by Richard D. Hefner (New York: New American Library, 1956) bk. 3, chapter 41, p. 244.

32. Kessler-Harris, *Out to Work,* p. 57, citing *New York Daily Tribune* Sept. 30, 1845, p. 1.

33. Kessler-Harris, *Out to Work,* p. 57; Mary Roth Walsh, *Doctors Wanted: No Women Need Apply. Sexual Barriers in the Medical Profession, 1835–1975* (New Haven: Yale University Press, 1977) pp. 5–9.

34. Carl Degler, *At Odds: Women and the Family in America from the Revolution to the Present* (New York: Oxford University Press, 1981) p. 368, citing Helen L. Sumner, *History of Women in Industry in the United States,* Vol. 9 of 19 in "Report on Condition of Woman and Child Wage-Earners in the United States" (Washington, D.C., 1910) p. 37.

35. Evans, *Born for Liberty,* p. 40; Boydston, *Home and Work,* p. 42.

36. Harris, *Beyond Her Sphere,* p. 33.

37. John Ruskin, "Of Queens Gardens," in his *Sesame and Lillies* (New York: Thomas Y. Crowell and Co., N.D.) pp. 115–117, quoted in B. Harris, *Beyond her Sphere,* p. 34.

38. Bernard Wishy, *The Child and the Republic* (Philadelphia: University of Pennsylvania Press, 1972) p. 28, quoted in Kessler-Harris, *Out to Work*, p. 50. See also Carroll Smith-Rosenberg, *Disorderly Conduct: Visions of Gender in Victorian America* (New York: Alfred A Knopf, 1985) pp. 85–86.

39. Carl Degler, *At Odds*, pp. 249–278.

40. Mintz and Kellogg, p. 50, citing Tocqueville, *Democracy in America*, Vols. 1, 3, and 5; Vol. 2, pp. 209–214, 222–225.

41. Cott, *The Bonds of Womanhood*, p. 61; Lerner, "The Lady and the Mill Girl, Changes in the Status of Women in the Age of Jackson, 1800–1840," in Cott and Pleck, *A Heritage of her Own*, p. 191.

42. Kessler-Harris, *Out to Work*, pp. 38–39, 50–56, 64.

43. Smith-Rosenberg, *Disorderly Conduct*, p. 89.

44. Steven Mintz, *A Prison of Expectations, The Family in Victorian Culture* (New York and London: New York University Press, 1983) p. 67, drawing on Walter Houghton, *The Victorian Frame of Mind* (New Haven: Published for Wellesley College by Yale University Press, 1957, 1985) p. 343.

45. Sarah Stage, *Female Complaints: Lydia Pinkham and the Business of Women's Medicine* (New York: W. W. Norton, 1979) p. 75.

46. B. Harris, *Beyond Her Sphere*, pp. 1–22.

47. Carroll Smith-Rosenberg and Charles E. Rosenberg, "Introduction," "Science, Society and Social Thought," and "The Bitter Fruit: Heredity, Disease and Social Thought," in Charles Rosenberg, *No Other Gods: On Science and American Thought* (Baltimore: Johns Hopkins University Press, 1976) p. 39; Stage, *Female Complaints*, p. 72, based on Augustus K. Gardener, M.D., *Conjugal Sins Against the Laws of Life and Health and Their Effects Upon the Father, Mother and Child* (New York: J. S. Redfield, Publisher, 1870) p. 82; George L. Austin, *Perils of American Women or a Doctor's Talk with Maiden, Wife and Mother* (Boston: Lee and Shepard Publishers, 1883) pp. 5, 105, 88; and Henry Maudsley, M.D., *Body and Mind* (London: MacMillan, 1870) p. 32.

48. Stage, *Female Complaints*, p. 85, quoting Frederick Hollick, *The Origin of Life and the Process of Reproduction* (New York: The American News Company, 1878) p. 677.

49. Nathaniel Hawthorne, *The Complete Novels and Selected Tales of Nathaniel Hawthorne* (New York: Random House, 1937) pp. 114, 499, cited in Stage, *Female Complaints*, pp. 74–75.

50. Stage, *Female Complaints*, pp. 68–69, quoting Maudsley, *Body and Mind*, p. 32.

51. Stage, *Female Complaints*, pp. 68–69 and 73, citing Hollick, *The Origin of Life and the Process of Reproduction*, p. 683, and M. L. Holbrook, *Parturition Without Pain* (1882); also cited in Carroll Smith-Rosenberg and Charles Rosenberg, "The Female Animal: Medical and Biological Views of Women and Her Role in the Nineteenth Century America," *Journal of American History*, LX (September 1973) p. 335.

52. Kessler-Harris, *Out to Work*, p. 106, citing Azel Ames, *Sex in Industry: A Plea for the Working Girl* (Boston: James R. Osgood, 1875) pp. 26–27.

53. Kessler-Harris, *Out to Work*, p. 98, citing *New York Times*, Feb. 14, 1869, p. 7, and Lillie Devereux Blake, testimony of September 18, 1883, in U.S. Education and Labor Committee, *Report Upon the Relations Between Capital and Labor*, 2:597.

54. Kessler-Harris, *Out to Work*, pp. 58, 98–105.

55. Kessler-Harris, *Out to Work*, pp. 98–99, citing *Daily Evening Voice*, Jan 7, 1865, p. 2, *Daily Evening Voice*, Dec. 17, 1864, p. 4; and "Marry the Women," *Birmingham Labor Advocate*, May 25, 1901, p. 1.

56. Kessler-Harris, *Out to Work*, p. 47.

57. Rosalind Rosenberg, *Beyond Separate Spheres: Intellectual Roots of Modern Femi-*

nism (New Haven: Yale University Press, 1982) p. 7, citing Edward Clarke, *The Building of a Brain* (Boston: Osgood & Co., 1874) p. 20; George Beard, *Eating and Drinking, A Popular Manual of Food and Diet in Health and Disease* (New York: G. P. Putnam & Sons, 1871) p. 103; T. S. Clouston, "Woman from a Medical Point of View," *Popular Science Monthly* 24 (Dec. 1883) p. 224.

58. Smith-Rosenberg, "Bourgeois Discourse and the Age of Jackson," in *Disorderly Conduct,* p. 88.

59. William Chafe, *The American Woman, Her Changing Social, Economic and Political Roles, 1920–1970* (New York: Oxford University Press, 1974) p. 11. Also in Eleanor Flexner, *A Century of Struggle* (New York: Atheneum, 1970) pp. 148–149; and Aileen Kraditor, *Up From the Pedestal* (Chicago: Quadrangle Press, 1968) p. 25ff.

60. Kessler-Harris, *Out to Work,* p. 59; Cott, *The Bonds of Womanhood,* pp. 5–6.

61. Evans, *Born for Liberty,* p. 90, citing Herbert Gutman, *The Black Family in Slavery and Freedom* (New York: Pantheon Books, 1976) ch. 5; Hooks, *Ain't I A Woman?,* pp. 48–49.

62. Evans, *Born for Liberty,* p. 91, citing Theda Purdue, "Southern Indians and the Cult of True Womanhood," in *The Web of Southern Social Relations: Women, Family and Education,* edited by Walter Fraser, Jr., R. Frank Saunders, Jr., and Jon L. Wakeley (Athens: University of Georgia Press, 1985) pp. 35–51, 41.

63. Nancy Theriot, *The Biosocial Construction of Femininity: Mothers and Daughters in Nineteenth Century America* (Westport, Conn.: Greenwood Press, 1988) p. 33.

64. Cott, *Bonds of Womanhood,* pp. 7–8.

65. Nancy Cott, *The Grounding of Modern Feminism* (New Haven: Yale University Press, 1987) pp. 16–20.

66. Alice Rossi, *Feminist Papers,* pp. 246; Cott, *Bonds,* p. 140; Carroll Smith-Rosenberg, "Beauty, the Beast and The Militant Woman: A Case Study in Sex Roles and Social Stress in Jacksonian America," in Carroll Smith-Rosenberg, *Disorderly Conduct,* pp. 109, 110.

67. Rossi, *The Feminist Papers,* pp. 246–248.

68. Cott, *The Grounding of Modern Feminism,* p. 16.

69. Catherine Beecher, *Treatise on Domestic Economy: For the Use of Young Ladies at Home* (Boston: T. H. Webb & Co., 1842) Chapter 1, cited in Kraditor, *Up From the Pedestal,* p. 130.

70. Margaret Fuller, *Woman in the Nineteenth Century,* quoted in Kraditor, *Up from the Pedestal,* pp. 131–134.

71. Harriot Hunt's remarks in "Proceedings of the Women's Rights Convention," October, 1851 (Boston: 1852) in *In Her Own Words: Oral Histories of Women Physicians,* edited by Regina Markell Morantz, Cynthia Stodola Pomerleau, and Carol Hansen Fenichel (Westport, Conn.: Greenwood Press, 1982) p. 17.

72. Kraditor, *Up From the Pedestal,* pp. 140–141; Kessler-Harris, *Out to Work,* p. 58; Patricia Hummer, *The Decade of Elusive Promise, 1920–1930* (Ann Arbor: U.M.I. Research Press, 1979) pp. 36–38.

73. Kessler-Harris, *Out to Work,* p. 143, citing Lucille Foster McMillan, *Women in the Federal Service* (Washington, D.C.: U.S. Civil Service Commission, 1941) pp. 5–9.

74. Evans, *Born for Liberty,* p. 114; B. Harris, *Beyond Her Sphere,* p. 98, citing Mary Elizabeth Massey, *Bonnet Brigades* (New York: Alfred A. Knopf, 1966) pp. 9, 52.

75. B. Harris, *Beyond her Sphere,* p. 98, citing Massey, *Bonnet Brigades,* p. 52.

76. Evans, *Born for Liberty,* p. 177, citing Lawrence W. Levine, *Black Culture and Black Consciousness: Afro-American Folk Thought from Slavery to Freedom* (New York: Oxford University Press, 1977) pp. 138–158.

77. Patricia Graham, "Women in Academe," in *The Professional Woman,* edited by Athena Theodore (Cambridge, Mass.: Schenkman Publishing Co., 1977) pp. 720–721.

78. Peter G. Filene, *Him/Her/Self: Sex Roles in Modern America,* 2nd ed. (Baltimore: Johns Hopkins Press, 1986), statistical table: Higher Education, 1870–1980, p. 238.

79. Morantz-Sanchez, p. 69, citing *Water-Cure Journal* 26(1858) pp. 26, 27, 28 and (1859) p. 10 and letter dated August 1869 to *The Revolution,* 1 August 1869, 98; and Ronald Numbers, "Health Reform on the Delaware," *New Jersey History* 42 (September 1974) pp. 5–12.

80. Hine, *Black Women in America,* p. 923.

81. Morantz-Sanchez, *Sympathy and Science,* p. 72.

82. Morantz-Sanchez, *Sympathy and Science,* p. 72, citing "The Admission of Women to Harvard University," *Boston Medical and Surgical Journal* 23 (5 June 1879) pp. 789–791; "Harvard Medical School and Women," *Boston Medical and Surgical Journal* 21 (22 May 1879) pp. 727–728; Degler, *At Odds,* pp. 371, 382.

83. Morantz, Pomerleau, and Fenichel, *In Her Own Words,* p. 17; Hine, *Black Women in America,* p. 923. In the 1880s, there were approximately 115 black women physicians.

84. Virginia Drachman, *Women Lawyers and the Origins of Professional Identity in America: The Letters of the Equity Club, 1887–1890* (Ann Arbor: University of Michigan Press, 1993) p. 4; information on Charlotte Ray is from Jessie Carney Smith, ed., *Notable Black American Women* (Detroit: Gale Research, Inc., 1992) pp. 922–923; also in Hine, *Black Women in America,* p. 965.

85. Degler, *At Odds,* pp. 371, 382; Drachman, p. 2, citing U.S. Bureau of the Census, The Tenth Census of the United States, 1880 (Washington, D. C., 1883) Vol. 1 at 788; and Eleventh Census of the United States, 1890 (Washington, D.C., 1897) Vol. 1 at 304; B. Harris, *Beyond Her Sphere,* p. 98; Morantz-Sanchez, *Sympathy and Science,* p. 17.

86. Evans, *Born for Liberty,* p. 147, citing Mary Church Terrell, *A Colored Woman in a White World* (New York: Arno Press, 1980); "The Oldest Woman Doctor Diagnoses Life," *New York Times,* 29 March 1925; Bertha Van Hoosen, *Petticoat Surgeon* (Chicago: Pellegrini and Cuday, 1947) p. 56, in Morantz-Sanchez, *Sympathy and Science,* p. 99.

87. Morantz-Sanchez, *Sympathy and Science,* p. 48.

88. Morantz-Sanchez, *Sympathy and Science,* p. 9, citing Dr. Elizabeth Keller, Woman's Medical College of Pennsylvania Alumnae *Transactions,* 1906, p. 36 and *Philadelphia Evening Bulletin,* 8 November 1869, clipping in Eliza Jane Wood Alumnae File, Medical College of Pennsylvania Archives; Drachman, *Women Lawyers,* p. 20, citing Dorothy Gies McGuigan, *A Dangerous Experiment: 100 Years of Women at the University of Michigan* (Ann Arbor: Center for Continuing Education of Women, 1970) pp. 32–33; Morantz-Sanchez, *Sympathy and Science,* p. 65.

89. Jane Friedman, *America's First Woman Lawyer, The Biography of Myra Bradwell* (Buffalo, N.Y.: Prometheus Books, 1993) p. 12, quoting Bradwell v. Illinois, 16 Wall 130 (1873); Jessie Carney Smith, ed., *Notable Black American Women* (Detroit: Gale Research Inc., 1992) pp. 922–923; Drachman, *Women Lawyers,* p. 20, citing Grace Hathaway, *Fate Rides a Tortoise: A Biography of Ellen Spencer Mussey* (New York: Putnam, 1937) no page number given.

90. Morantz-Sanchez, *Sympathy and Science,* pp. 101–113.

91. Morantz-Sanchez, *Sympathy and Science,* p. 93; Hine, *Black Women in America,* p. 924; Bataille, *Native American Women* p. 147.

92. Morantz-Sanchez, *Sympathy and Science,* pp. 93–110, quoting Bertha Van Hoosen, *Petticoat Surgeon* (Chicago: Pellegrini & Cudahy, 1947) pp. 54–55, and Belva Lockwood, "My Life as a Lawyer," in *Lippincott's* (June 1888) pp. 215–229.

93. Christopher Lasch, *The New Radicalism in America 1889–1963: The Intellectual as Social Type* (New York: Alfred A. Knopf, 1966) p. 36.

94. Filene, *Him/Her/Self: Sex Roles in Modern America* (New York: New American Library, 1976) p. 16.

95. Mintz and Kellogg, *Domestic Revolutions,* p. 57, citing Ann Douglas, "The Road to Marriage," *New Republic,* October 8, 1984, pp. 36–41; Cott, *Bonds of Womanhood,* pp. 80–83, citing Catherine Kish Sklar, *Catherine Beecher, A Study in American Domesticity* (New Haven: Yale University Press, 1973) pp. 28, 60, 193–195.

96. Theriot, *The Biosocial Construction of Femininity,* pp. 135–136; Lasch, *The New Radicalism in America,* pp. 54–68.

97. Filene, *Him/Her/Self,* p. 16, quoting Jane Addams, *Twenty Years at Hull House* (New York: Macmillan, 1910) pp. 72–73; Jane Addams to Ellen Gates Star, Feb. 7, 1886, in Lasch, *The New Radicalism in America,* p. 23.

98. Morantz-Sanchez, *Sympathy and Science,* p. 127, quoting Elizabeth Blackwell, "Pioneer Work," 28, Williams, Typescript Autobiography Chap. 2, p. 36.

99. Cott, *The Grounding of Modern Feminism,* pp. 18–19, citing Mary Austin, *Earth Horizon: Autobiography* (Boston: Houghton Mifflin, 1932) p. 128; Miriam Allen de Ford, "Feminism, Cause or Effect," box 573, de Ford papers, San Francisco Historical Society; Carrie Chapman Catt, "Why I Have Found Life Worth Living," *Christian Century,* March 29, 1928, Catt papers, LC reel 9; and Rheta Childe Dorr, *A Woman of Fifty* (New York: Funk and Wagnells, 1924) p. 13.

100. Lorine Pruette, "The Evolution of Disenchantment," *Nation,* 124 (February 2, 1927) pp. 113–115, in *These Modern Women,* edited by Elaine Showalter (Westbury, New York: Feminist Press, 1978) p. 70.

101. Showalter, *These Modern Women,* pp. 86–91, 74–77, 39.

102. Morantz-Sanchez, *Sympathy and Science,* pp. 5–7, 57–58, 60–63, citing Bertha Selmon, "Pioneer Women in Medicine," *Women's Medical Journal* 56 (January 1949) p. 48; and quoting Elizabeth Blackwell, "Criticism of Gronlund's Co-operative Commonwealth; Chapter X-Woman," given before the Fellowship of New Life, n.d., pp. 9–10; *The Influence of Women in the Profession of Medicine* (London, 1889), 11; "Anatomy," Lecture Notes, n.d., all in Blackwell MSS, Library of Congress.

103. Morantz-Sanchez, *Sympathy and Science,* pp. 119–120.

104. Morantz-Sanchez, *Sympathy and Science,* p. 121, citing Emily Dunning Barringer, *Bowery to Belleview* (New York: W. W. Norton, 1950) p. 99; Sara Josephine Baker, M.D., *Fighting for Life* (New York: MacMillan, 1939) p. 64; John B. Gabel, ed., "Medical Education in the 1890s: An Ohio Woman's Memories," *Ohio History* 87 (Winter 1978) pp. 59, 61.

105. Morantz-Sanchez, *Sympathy and Science,* pp. 135, 126, 127, 131, citing Rachel L. Bodley, "The College Story: Valedictory Address to the Twenty-Ninth Graduating Class of the Woman's Medical College of Pennsylvania," (Philadelphia: Grant, Faires & Rodgers, 1881); Emily F. and Augusta C. Pope and Emma L. Call, *The Practice of Medicine by Women in the United States,* (Boston: Wright & Potter, 1881); Anna Wessell Williams Typescript Autobiography, Anna Wessell Williams MSS, Schlesinger Library, Radcliffe College, Cambridge, Mass., Chapter 2, p. 36; also Williams notes, Williams MSS, Schlesinger Library, Folder 16, n.p.

106. Morantz-Sanchez, *Sympathy and Science,* pp. 135–137, 142. Morantz-Sanchez's own calculations show that approximately 337 out of 937 graduates of the Medical College of Pennsylvania in the years 1852–1900 married (about 35 percent). Material on black women physicians comes from Darlene Clark Hine, "Nineteenth Century Physicians," in Hine, *Notable Black American Women,* pp. 925–926.

107. Morantz-Sanchez, *Sympathy and Science,* p. 135, quoting Mary Putnam Jacobi, "Inaugural Address at the Opening of Woman's Medical College of the New York Infirmary," October 1880, reprinted in Women's Medical Association of New York City, *Mary Putnam Jacobi: Pathfinder in Medicine* (New York: G. P. Putnam, 1925) p. 390.

108. Cott, *The Grounding of Modern Feminism,* p. 232.

109. Drachman, *Women Lawyers,* p. 30, citing Catharine G. Waugh McCulloch to the Equity Club, May 2, 1988, Rockford Illinois, Equity Club Annal, at 51, Dillon Collection, Schlesinger Library.

110. Drachman, *Women Lawyers,* pp. 22, 23, 37, quoting Lelia J. Robinson to Equity Club, April, 1887, Calvert Texas, Equity Club Letters, Dillon Collection; and Ada M. Bittenbender to the Equity Club, May 1889, Washington, D. C., Equity Club letters, Dillon Collection.

111. Chafe, *The American Woman,* pp. 5–10; quoting on p. 9, Charlotte Perkins Gilman, *Women in Economics* (New York: Harper & Row, 1966 edition) p. 313.

112. Chafe, *The American Woman,* p. 96, citing "Ellen Key and Feminism," *Nation* CXXII (May 5, 1926) pp. 493–494.

113. Hooks, *Ain't I A Woman,* pp. 129, 169–170; Chafe, *The American Woman,* p. 15.

Chapter 4

1. Carol Hymowitz and Michaele Weissman, *A History of Women in America* (New York: Bantam, 1979) p. 221.

2. Patricia Hummer, *The Decade of Elusive Promise, 1920–1930* (Ann Arbor: U.M.I. Research Press, 1979) p. 12, citing Beatrice Doershuk, *Women in the Law: An Analysis of Training, Practice and Salaried Positions* (New York: Bureau of Vocational Information, 1920) pp. 36, 131–133; Peter Filene, *Him/Her/Self: Sex Roles in Modern America* (New York: New American Library, 1976) p. 27 citing Joseph Hill, *Women in Gainful Occupations, 1970–1920,* Census monographs IX (Washington D.C.: Government Printing Office, 1929) p. 42, table 32 and p. 83, table 57; William Chafe, *The American Woman: Her Changing Social, Economic and Political Roles, 1920–1970* (New York: Oxford University Press, 1972, pb. 1974) p. 49, citing Miriam Simons Leusch, "Women in Odd and Unusual Fields of Work," *Annals of the American Academy of Political and Social Science* CXLIII (May 1929) p. 166 and *New York Times,* Sept. 5, Dec. 26, July 20, 1920; March 3 and June 12, 1921.

3. Quoted in James Stanley Lemons, *The Woman Citizen: Social Feminism in the 1920s* (Urbana: University of Illinois Press, 1973) p. 20.

4. Darlene Clark Hine, *Black Women in America: An Historical Encyclopedia* (Brooklyn, N.Y.: Carlson Publishing Company, 1993) p. 1287.

5. Lemons, *The Woman Citizen,* p. 21.

6. Smith College Weekly 10 (Dec. 3, 1919), in Peter Filene, *Him/Her/Self,* p. 128; Chafe, *The American Woman,* pp. 56, 25, table titled "The Female Labor Force," based on U.S. Bureau of the Census Documents and others, p. 219.

7. Chafe, *The American Woman,* p. 22, from Mildred Adams, *The Right to be People,* (New York, W. W. Norton, 1967) p. 170.

8. Hummer, *The Decade of Elusive Promise,* p. 57, from "Medical Education in the United States," *Journal of the American Medical Association* (August 7, 1920) p. 391 and U.S. Department of the Interior, Bureau of Education, "Biennial Survey of Education: Statistics of Universities, Colleges, and Professional Schools, 1919–1920," *Bulletin No. 28* (1922) p. 5.

9. Hummer, *The Decade of Elusive Promise,* p. 10.

10. Vanessa Gamble, "Physicians, Twentieth Century," in Hine, *Black Women in*

America, A Historical Encyclopedia, p. 926; Jessie Carney Smith, ed., *Notable Black American Women* (Detroit: Gale Research, Inc., 1992) Table of Contents.

11. Lemons, *The Woman Citizen,* pp. 106, 108.

12. Rosalind Rosenberg, *Beyond Separate Spheres, Intellectual Roots of Modern Feminism* (New Haven: Yale University Press, 1982) p. 210, citing Ben Wattenberg, *Statistical History of the U.S.* (New York: Basic Books, 1970) p. 383.

13. Frederick Lewis Allen, *Only Yesterday, An Informal History of the Nineteen Twenties* (New York: Harper and Brothers, 1931) p. 97. Also published by Harper and Row, 1959.

14. Paula Fass, *The Damned and the Beautiful: American Youth in the 1920s* (New York: Oxford University Press, 1977, 1979) pp. 260–326, citing such college newspapers as the *Daily Illini,* the *UCLA Daily,* and the *Cornell Daily Sun,* 1920–1921, and 1926; quote on p. 307 from *Ohio State Lantern,* Jan. 9, 1922, p. 1.

15. Joanne J. Meyerowitz, *Women Adrift: Independent Wage Earners in Chicago, 1880–1930* (Chicago and London: University of Chicago Press, 1988) pp. xxi, xxiii, 124–146.

16. Allen, *Only Yesterday* (New York: Harper and Row, 1959), pp. 73–101.

17. Fass, *The Damned and the Beautiful,* pp. 19, 22.

18. Sara M. Evans, *Born for Liberty, A History of Women in America* (New York: Free Press, 1989) pp. 161–162.

19. Ben Lindsay and Wainwright Evans, *The Companionate Marriage* (New York: Boni and Liveright, 1927), pp. xiii, xviii, 156, in Nancy A. Costello, unpublished paper, "Moving from Homosocial to Heterosexual Relationships in the Early 1900s: Women's Gain or Loss?," Harvard University Extension School, 1984.

20. Nancy Cott, *The Grounding of Modern Feminism* (New Haven: Yale University Press, 1987) pp. 129–130; Alice Kessler-Harris, *Out to Work, A History of Wage-Earning Women in the United States* (New York: Oxford University Press, 1982) p. 122.

21. Allen, *Only Yesterday,* p. 347.

22. Crystal Eastman, "Mother-Worship," in *These Modern Women: Autobiographical Essays from the Twenties,* edited by Elaine Showalter (Westbury, New York: The Feminist Press, 1978) p. 5.

23. Fass, *The Damned and the Beautiful,* p. 3.

24. Fass, *The Damned and the Beautiful,* pp. 68–70, citing Irene B. Taeuber and Conrad Taeuber, *People in the United States in the 20th Century* (Washington, D.C.: U.S. Bureau of the Census, 1971) p. 284, ff. Proportionately more young urban men and women (aged 20–24) were married in 1920 than in 1890. Whereas for men in 1890, the median age at marriage was 26.1 years and for women 22 years, by 1920 the median age was 24.6 years for men and 21.3 years for women.

25. Chafe, *The American Woman,* pp. 104–106, citing: "Editorial" in *Ladies' Home Journal* XLVII (May 1930), p. 34; XLVI, (February 1929) p. 30, and "Editorial," *McCall's* LVI (April 1919) p. 2; Showalter, *These Modern Women,* p. 20.

26. Fass, *The Damned and the Beautiful,* p. 69; Allen, *Only Yesterday,* p. 347.

27. Marjorie Nicholson, "The Rights and Privileges Pertaining Thereto," *Journal of the American Association of University Women* 31, no. 3 (April 1938) p. 136, quoted in Patricia Graham, "Expansion and Exclusion: A History of Women in American Higher Education," *Signs* (Summer 1978) p. 765.

28. Cott, *Grounding,* pp. 145–147.

29. Of the men and women born in the twenty years after the Civil War, almost 10 percent never married; the median age at first marriage for the 90 percent who did marry was about 26 for men and near 24 for women. In the generation born thirty years later

(from 1895 to the outbreak of the Great War), who came of age from the late 1910s to through the Depression, the proportion who never married dropped to near 6 percent, and the median age at first marriage declined to about 25 for men and even further for women, to 22 and a half. Cott, *Grounding*, p. 147.

30. Cott, *Grounding*, p. 167.

31. Fass, *The Damned and the Beautiful*, p. 69.

32. Cott, *Grounding*, pp. 145–175, esp. pp. 171–175. Photo on page 145 from *American Magazine*, October 1932.

33. Ruth Schwartz Cowan, *More Work for Mother: The Ironies of Household Technology from the Open Hearth to the Microwave* (New York: Basic Books, 1983) pp. 151–191; Joan Wallach Scott, "The Mechanization of Women's Work," *Scientific American* (September 3, 1982) pp. 167–185; Betty Friedan, *The Feminine Mystique*, (New York: Dell Publishing Co., 1974) pp. 204–206 (first published by New York: W. W. Norton, 1963); Cott, *Grounding*, pp. 162–163.

34. Cott, *Grounding*, p. 164, citing Anna E. Richardson, "The Woman Administrator in the Modern Home," *Annals of the American Academy of Political and Social Science* 143 (May 1929) pp. 22, 28, 32.

35. Cott, *Grounding*, p. 223.

36. Penina Migdal Glazer and Miriam Slater, *Unequal Colleagues: The Entrance of Women into the Professions, 1890–1940* (New Brunswick, N.J.: Rutgers University Press, 1987) pp. 223–227, citing: Jerold S. Auerbach, *Unequal Justice* (New York: Oxford University Press, 1976) pp. 54, 75 and Chapter 3, and Rosemary Stevens, *Medicine and the Public Interest* (New Haven: Yale University Press, 1972), p. 72.

37. Hummer, *The Decade of Elusive Promise*, pp. 57–61.

38. Glazer and Slater, *Unequal Colleagues*, pp. 169, 225, citing Auerbach, *Unequal Justice*, p. 72.

39. Hummer, *The Decade of Elusive Promise*, pp. 37–87, 90, 105; Gamble, "Black Women Physicians," in Hine, *Black Women in America*, p. 926.

40. Glazer and Slater, *Unequal Colleagues*, pp. 225–226; Hummer, *The Decade of Elusive Promise*, pp. 57–61; Virginia Drachman, Brown Bag Lunch Talk delivered at Henry A. Murray Research Center, Cambridge, Mass., May 13, 1986.

Female enrollment in medical school increased to a high of 1030 in 1923, then fluctuated in the 900s until it hit 955 in 1930. The rate of growth for the female enrollment over the entire decade was only 16.7 percent, compared with a 59 percent increase for men. During the 1920s, both Columbia and Harvard Law Schools refused to consider women applicants; as late as 1937 the New York City Bar Association excluded women, as did most county law societies. Hummer, *The Decade of Elusive Promise*, pp. 61, 41.

41. Hummer, *The Decade of Elusive Promise*, pp. 41–70, 75.

42. Glazer and Slater, *Unequal Colleagues*, pp. 161–163, citing Jonathan Cole, *Fair Science, Women in the Scientific Community* (New York: Free Press, 1979) pp. 214, 219–220; Margaret Rossiter, *Women Scientists in America: Struggles and Strategies to 1940* (Baltimore: Johns Hopkins University Press, 1982), pp. 160–217.

43. Glazer and Slater, *Unequal Colleagues*, pp. 160–163 and 209–222, based on Alice Hamilton, Exploring Dangerous Trades (Boston: Little Brown, 1943) pp. 115–128; Cole, *Fair Science*, pp. 219–222; also see Rossiter, *Women Scientists*, pp. 160–217.

44. Rossiter, *Women Scientists*, pp. 160–217; Marian O. Hawthorne, "Women as College Teachers," *Annals of the American Academy of Political and Social Science* 143 (May 1929) in Cott, *Grounding*, p. 222.

45. Degler, *The American Woman*, p. 412, citing Alice Henry, *The Trade Union Woman* (New York: Burt Franklin, 1973; originally published in 1915) p. 225.

46. Hummer, *The Decade of Elusive Promise,* p. 88, citing Martha Tracy, "Women Graduates in Medicine," *AAMC Bulletin* 2 (January 1927) p. 23.

47. Virginia MacMakin Collier, *Marriage and Careers: A Study of One Hundred Women Who Are Wives, Mothers, Homemakers and Professional Workers* (New York: Bureau of Vocational Information, 1926) pp. 9–10, 17–19. Described in Degler, *At Odds,* p. 412, and in Cott, *Grounding,* pp. 196–197. Slightly over half of the women Collier studied said their husbands helped with home and children, though a number of women seemed dubious whether even a very willing husband could "take an even share of the responsibility." This group, however, was hardly representative; most professional women at the time were low-paid teachers who could not have afforded household help, which was a luxury of only about 5 percent of American families at the time.

48. Showalter, *These Modern Women,* pp. 7–10, 19–21 and essays, pp. 31–127; Rosenberg, *Beyond Separate Spheres,* pp. 203–207.

49. Hummer, *The Decade of Elusive Promise,* pp. 135–137; Glazer and Slater, *Unequal Colleagues,* pp. 145–162, quote on p. 157, citing Hamilton, *Exploring,* pp. 253, 268–269.

50. Hummer, *The Decade of Elusive Promise,* pp. 135–137; Lemons, *The Woman Citizen,* p. 41.

51. Chafe, *The American Woman,* p. 30, citing Emily Newell Blair, "Are Women a Failure in Politics?" *Harper's* CLI (October 1925) pp. 513–522.

52. Bell Hooks, *Ain't I A Woman: Black Women and Feminism* (Boston: South End Press, 1981), pp. 133–134.

53. Chafe, *The American Woman,* pp. 112–132, quote on p. 127.

54. Chafe, *The American Woman,* p. 119, based on Olive Colton to Mary Anderson, Feb. 23, 1926, *Anderson Papers,* Box 1; National Women's Party Press Release, Jan. 20, 1928, Smith Papers, Box 7. Alice Lee, "A Novice Visits Washington," League of Women Voters Papers, Box 31; Lemons, *The Woman Citizen,* pp. 184–191, 199–204.

55. Chafe, *The American Woman,* p. 131; Mary F. Berry, *Why the ERA Failed: Politics, Women's Rights and the Amending Process of the Constitution* (Bloomington: Indiana University Press, 1986) p. 60.

56. Sheila Rothman, *Women's Proper Place: A History of Changing Ideals and Practices 1870 to the Present* (New York: Basic Books, 1978) pp. 142–174.

57. Showalter, *These Modern Women,* p. 20.

58. William O'Neill, *Everyone Was Brave: The Rise and Fall of Feminism in America* (Chicago: Quadrangle Press, 1969) p. 313.

59. Ruth Milkman, "Women's Work and the Economic Crisis," in *A Heritage of Her Own: Families, Work and Feminism in America,* edited by Nancy Cott and Elizabeth Pleck (New York: Touchstone Press, 1980) p. 529.

60. Kessler-Harris, *Out to Work,* p. 256, citing Norman Cousins, "Will Women Lose Their Jobs?" *Current History and Forum* 41 (September 1939) p. 14.

61. Kessler-Harris, *Out to Work,* p. 257, drawing on Lois Scharf, *To Work and to Wed* (Westport, Conn.: Greenwood Press, 1980) Chapter 3.

62. Scharf, *To Work and to Wed,* Chapter 5, esp. pp. 90–93, in Cott, *Grounding,* p. 225; Elaine Tyler May, *Homeward Bound: American Families in the Cold War Era* (New York: Basic Books, 1988) p. 50.

63. Glen H. Elder, Jr., Geraldine Downey, and Catherine E. Cross, "Family Ties and Life Chances: Hard Times and Hard Choices in Women's Lives Since the 1930s," in *Life Span Development Psychology: Intergenerational Relations,* edited by Nancy Datan, Anita L. Greene, and Hayne W. Reese (Hillsdale, N.J.: Lawrence Erlbaum Associates, 1986) p. 155.

64. Kessler-Harris, *Out to Work,* pp. 250–253, 256, citing Dorothy Dunbar Bromley,

"Birth Control and The Depression," *Harper's* 69, (Oct. 1934) pp. 563, 564; William Haber, "The Effects of Insecurity on Family Life," *Annals of American Academy of Political and Social Science* 196 (March 1938) p. 25; and Edna McKnight, "Jobs—for Men Only?" *Outlook and Independent* 159 (Sept. 2, 1931) p. 18.

65. Kessler-Harris, *Out to Work*, p. 253, citing Claire Howe, "Return of the Lady," in *New Outlook* 164 (Oct. 1934) pp. 34–38; Jane Allen, "You May Have My Job: A Feminist Discovers Her Home," *Forum* 87 (April 1932) pp. 228–231.

66. Kessler-Harris, *Out to Work*, p. 255, citing Marion Elderton, "Unemployment Consequences on the Home," *Annals of the American Academy of Social and Political Science* 154 (March 1931) p. 62.

67. Kessler-Harris, *Out to Work*, p. 256, citing Cousins, "Will Women Lose Their Jobs?" p. 14; Hadley Cantrill, ed., *Public Opinion, 1935–46*, (Princeton: Princeton University Press, 1951) American Institute of Public Opinion Poll, p. 1044.

68. Milkman, "Women's Work," in Cott and Pleck, *A Heritage of Her Own*, p. 529.

69. In a longitudinal study of children who grew up in Oakland, California after the depression, Elder found while only 18 percent of the mothers of women he studied had gone to college, most of the mothers who attended college did graduate. While the women he studied were twice as likely as their mothers to start college, however, they were less likely than their mothers to graduate. Instead, many married younger than had their mothers and bore children at earlier ages. Their husbands were more likely to be better educated than they were, and were more likely to be professional or salaried workers than the fathers of these women had been. Elder et al., "Family Ties and Life Chances," p. 152; Glen H. Elder, Jr., *Children of the Great Depression: Social Change in Life Experience* (Chicago: University of Chicago Press, 1974) pp. 16–30, 93, 186, 236–240.

70. Milkman, "Women's Work," citing *U.S.D.L. Women's Bureau Special Bulletin Number 20*, "Changes in Women's Employment During the War" (1944) pp. 9, 15, in Cott and Pleck, *A Heritage of Her Own*, pp. 528–531.

71. Chafe, *The American Woman*, pp. 140–142.

72. Chafe, *The American Woman*, p. 148.

73. May, *Homeward Bound*, p. 59, citing Susan Hartmann, *The Homefront and Beyond: American Women in the 1940s* (Boston: Twayne Publishers, 1982) pp. 7, 194; Chafe, *The American Woman*, pp. 185–189.

74. Kessler-Harris, *Out to Work*, p. 295; Chafe, *The American Woman*, pp. 180–185; May, *Homeward Bound*, pp. 75–77, information on black women on p. 76.

75. May, *Homeward Bound*, pp. 79–80.

76. "Changes in Women's Occupations 1940–1950," *Women's Bureau Bulletin No. 253* (Washington, D.C., 1954) pp. 37, 41; Hadley Cantril, *Public Opinion 1935–1946* (Princeton, 1951) p. 1045, "The *Fortune* Survey: Women in America," Part I *Fortune* 34 (August 1946) p. 8; all cited in Chafe, *The American Woman*, pp. 182, 148, 189–190; also see May, *Homeward Bound*, p. 76.

77. Kessler-Harris, *Out to Work*, pp. 290, 295; Chafe, *The American Woman*, pp. 160–173; Milkman, "Women's Work," in Cott and Pleck, *A Heritage of Her Own*, p. 531, citing *Fortune* 27:2 (Feb. 1943) p. 37.

78. May, *Homeward Bound*, pp. 59, 102–103.

79. Joseph Adelson, "Is Women's Lib a Passing Fad?" *New York Times Magazine* CXXI: 41, 693, Section 6 (March 19, 1972) p. 94, cited in Elder, *Children of the Great Depression*, p. 216.

80. Friedan, *The Feminine Mystique*, p. 174.

81. Beatrice Whiting, Personal Interview, May, 1983; Judith Lewis Herman, M.D., and Helen Block Lewis, Ph.D., "Anger in the Mother-Daughter Relationship," in *The Psy-*

chology of Today's Woman: New Psychoanalytic Visions, edited by Toni Bernay and Dorothy Cantor (Hillsdale, N.J.: Analytic Press, 1986).

82. Norman Ryder, "The Cohort as a Concept in the Study of Social Change," *American Sociological Review* 30:6 (Dec. 1965) p. 851.

83. Elder et al., "Family Ties and Life Chances," p. 152; May, *Homeward Bound,* p. 88.

84. This idea is based on Kenneth Keniston's finding in a study of a group of Harvard men who turned out to be, quite often, sons of "new men" and "new women" of the 1920s. These "new men" and "new women," Keniston writes, had married one another to avoid becoming like their tradition-bound, Victorian parents. Deep down, Keniston suggests, the mothers of the men he interviewed were disappointed in their husbands for not being like the strong fathers they had once rebelled against. Their husbands, the fathers of Keniston's subjects, "secretly wondered" whether they were less "masculine" than their own fathers were. They may also have had mixed feelings about their wives, who were ambitious, talented, and energetic.

As a result, these fathers became distant and work-oriented, and these mothers tended to ask their sons to fill in for their absent fathers. Growing up, then, without strong father figures, these sons were encouraged by their mothers to look to idealized images of their Victorian grandparents for models of how the true men and true women should act. Kenneth Keniston, *The Uncommitted: Alienated Youth in American Society* (New York: Harcourt, Brace, Jovanovich, 1965) pp. 161–177.

Chapter 5

1. Betty Friedan, *The Feminine Mystique* (New York: W. W. Norton, 1973; Dell Paperback ed., 1983) p. 12.

2. Cynthia Fuchs Epstein, *Woman's Place: Options and Limits in Professional Careers* (Berkeley: University of California Press, 1970) p. 58; Table p. 58: College and University Degrees Earned by Women (U.S.) Source: 1968 *Handbook of Women Workers* (Washington, D.C.: United States Department of Labor Women's Bureau, Draft).

3. Alice Rossi, "Barriers to the Career Choice of Engineering, Medicine, or Science Among American Women," in *Women in the Scientific Professions,* edited by Jacqueline Mattfeld and Carol G. Van Aken (Cambridge: M.I.T. Press, 1965) p. 77, citing U.S. Bureau of the Census, *Census of the Population 1960,* Table 202, pp. 528–533.

4. Cynthia Fuchs Epstein, "Positive Effects of the Multiple Negative: Explaining the Success of Black Professional Women," *The American Journal of Sociology* 41:78 (January 1973) pp. 915–916; Natalie Sokoloff, *Black Women and White Women in the Professions: Occupational Segregation by Race and Gender, 1960–1980* (New York: Routledge Press, 1992) p. 6, citing USDC, Bureau of Census, 1963, Table 205; *1970 Census, "Occupational Characteristics,"* June 1973, Table G-WF-24B, and "Minority Women in the 1970 Labor Force, by Field," cited in *The Double Bind: The Price of Being a Minority Woman in Science,* Shirley Mahaley Malcolm, Paula Quick Hall, and Janet Welsh Brown, eds. (American Association for the Advancement of Science, Report No. 76-R-3, April 1976) p. 44.

5. Epstein, *Woman's Place,* pp. 10–11, quote on p. 2.

6. National Opinion Research Center, College Graduate Study (University of Chicago, 1961) cited in Rossi, "Barriers," in Mattfeld and Van Aken, *Women in the Scientific Professions,* p. 126.

7. I use the phrase "women of color" to describe women who may consider themselves black, African-American, Native American, Asian-American, Japanese-American, Chinese-American, Hispanic, Latina, Chicana, Puerto Rican, or members of other

nonwhite groups. Each group is culturally and ethnically diverse, and although women of color may not be the preferred term in some instances, the phrase does not suggest that there are not qualitative differences among and within different racial and ethnic categories. Epstein, "Positive Effects of the Double Negative," p. 915, citing Eli Ginzberg and Dale L. Hiestand, "Employment Patterns of Negro Men and Women," in *American Negro Reference Book,* edited by John P. Davis (Englewood Cliffs, N.J.: Prentice-Hall, 1966), pp. 210, 216; Malcolm et al., *The Double Bind,* p. 26.

8. As late as 1965, sociologist Alice Rossi, along with a number of other social scientists and economists, predicted that despite the relatively high numbers of women who had held jobs in the 1920s, 1930s, and 1940s, if the trends of the 1950s held, the proportion of professional women in relation to men would continue to decline. Rossi, "Barriers," in Mattfeld and Van Aken, *Women in the Scientific Professions,* p. 57.

9. In a 1962 Gallup Poll, which reported women's high satisfaction with marriage, only 10 percent of those sampled said they wanted their daughters to live the same sort of lives they had; most women said they wanted their daughters to get more education and to marry later than they did. George Gallup and Evan Hill, "The American Woman," *The Saturday Evening Post,* Dec. 22, 1962, cited by Rossi, "Equality Between the Sexes," in *The Woman in America,* edited by Robert J. Lifton (Boston: Beacon Paperback, 1967) p. 127. According to Epstein, whereas earlier women lawyers often had immigrant parents and working mothers who encouraged them to enter law, some of those who chose legal careers after 1970 appeared to have been influenced by their mothers as negative role models. Cynthia Fuchs Epstein, *Women in Law* (New York: Basic Books, Inc., 1981) p. 31.

10. Gwyned Simpson, "The Daughters of Charlotte Ray: The Career Development Process During the Exploratory and Establishment Stages of Black Women Attorneys," *Sex Roles* 11:1 and 2 (July 1984) p. 123.

11. Material on biological and hormonal differences between boys and girls is drawn from Anke A. Ehrhardt, "Psychobiology of Gender," in *Gender and the Life Course,* edited by Alice S. Rossi (New York: Aldine Publishing Company, 1985), pp. 82–86, 93; F. E. Purifoy and L. H. Koopmans, "Androstenedione, T and free T concentrations in women of various occupations," *Social Biology* 26 (1980) pp. 179–188, cited on p. 92. See also John Money and Anke Ehrhardt, *Man & Woman, Boy & Girl, The Differentiation and Dimorphism of Gender Identity from Conception to Maturity* (Baltimore: Johns Hopkins University Press, 1972; Signet, 1974).

12. Nancy Chodorow, *The Reproduction of Mothering, Psychoanalysis and the Sociology of Gender* (Berkeley: University of California Press, 1978), especially chapter 7; Carol Gilligan, *In a Different Voice* (Cambridge: Harvard University Press, 1982).

13. Denise A. Segura and Jennifer L. Pierce, "Chicana/o Family Structure and Gender Personality: Chodorow, Familism, and Psychoanalytic Sociology Revisited," *Signs; Journal of Women in Culture and Society* 19:11 (Chicago, University of Chicago, 1993) pp. 62–91, esp. p. 76; Farah A. Ibrahim, "A Course on Asian-American Women: Identity Development Issues," *Women's Studies Quarterly* 20: 1&2 (Spring and Summer 1992) pp. 41–58; Beverly Daniel Tatum, "Talking About Race," *Harvard Education Review* 62:1 (Spring 1992) p. 1; see also P. B. Pederson, *A Handbook for Developing Multi-cultural Awareness* (Alexandria Va.: AACD Press, 1988).

14. Sally Powers, interview with author, Henry A. Murray Research Center, A Center for the Study of Lives, Radcliffe College, Cambridge, Mass., November 14, 1985.

15. Irene Stiver, ongoing interviews and conversations with author, McLean Hospital, 1983–1994; Louise Kaplan, *Oneness and Separateness* (New York: Simon and Schuster, 1978); Janet Surrey, "The Relational Self in Women: Clinical Implications," in Judith Jordan, Jean Baker Miller, Irene Stiver, and Janet Surrey, *Women's Growth in Connection, Writ-*

ings from the Stone Center (New York: The Guilford Press, 1991) p. 38; Surrey, "The Self in Relation: A Theory of Women's Development," in *Women's Growth in Connection,* pp. 55, 57. Also see Margaret Mahler, Fred Pine and Anni Bergman, *The Psychological Birth of the Human Infant: Symbiosis and Individuation* (New York: Basic Books, Inc., 1975) pp. 6–7.

16. Simpson, "The Daughters of Charlotte Ray," pp. 126, 137.

Chapter 6

1. Ralph H. Turner, "Some Aspects of Women's Ambition," in *The Professional Woman,* edited by Athena Theodore (Cambridge: Schenkman Publishing Co, Inc., 1971) pp. 227–250.

2. Alice Rossi, "Equality between the Sexes: An Immodest Proposal" in *The Woman in America,* edited by Robert J. Lifton (Boston: Beacon Press, 1965) p. 99.

3. Cynthia Fuchs Epstein, *Women's Place: Options and Limits in Professional Careers* (Berkeley: University of California Press, 1971) p. 65; Epstein, "Positive Effects of the Double Negative: Explaining the Success of Black Professional Women, *The American Journal of Sociology* 78:41 (January 1973) pp. 915–916, citing Eli Ginzberg and Dale L. Hiestand, "Employment Patterns of Negro Men and Women," in *American Negro Reference Book,* edited by John P. Davis (Englewood Cliffs, N.J.: Prentice Hall, 1966) p. 210; Shirley Mahaley Malcolm, Paula Quick Hall, and Janet Welsh Brown, *The Double Bind: The Price of Being a Minority Woman in Science* (American Association for the Advancement of Science, Report No. 76-R-3, April 1976) p. 11.

4. Epstein, *Woman's Place,* p. 65.

5. Described in Jean Baker Miller, "The Development of Women's Sense of Self," in Judith V. Jordan, Alexandra G. Kaplan, Jean Baker Miller, Irene P. Stiver, Janet L. Surrey, *Women's Growth in Connection: Writings from the Stone Center* (New York: The Guilford Press, 1991) p. 9.

6. Erik Erikson, *Identity, Youth and Crisis* (New York: W. W. Norton Co., 1968) pp. 161–294, esp. pp. 282–283.

7. Epstein, *Woman's Place,* pp. 59–85; Matina Horner, "The Motive to Avoid Success and Changing Aspirations of College Women," in *Readings on the Psychology of Women,* edited by Judith M. Bardwick (New York: Harper and Row, 1972) pp. 62–67.

8. Various theories are described in Carol Gilligan, *In a Different Voice* (Cambridge: Harvard University Press, 1982) pp. 6–7, and in Nancy Chodorow, *The Reproduction of Mothering: Psychoanalysis and the Sociology of Gender* (Berkeley and Los Angeles: The University of California Press, 1978) esp. Chapter 4.

9. Horner wrote that women avoided achieving in non-traditional realms because they feared retribution and social ostracism; others later suggested that the stories Horner collected simply reflected reality of what happened to women who tried to achieve. Horner, "The Motive to Avoid Success," in Bardwick, *Readings,* pp. 62–67.

10. Gwyned Simpson, "The Daughters of Charlotte Ray: The Career Development Process During the Exploratory and Establishment Stages of Black Women Attorneys," *Sex Roles* 11:1&2: (July 1984) pp. 130–131.

11. Kenneth Keniston, "The Unholy Alliance," in his *Youth and Dissent: The Rise of a New Opposition* (New York: Harcourt Brace Jovanovich, 1971) pp. viii, 355.

12. Kenneth Keniston, *The Uncommitted: Alienated Youth in American Society* (New York: Harcourt Brace Jovanovich, 1965) pp. 426–427.

13. Sara Evans, *Personal Politics: The Roots of Women's Liberation in the Civil Rights Movement and The New Left* (New York: Random House, 1980; first published by Knopf, 1979) p. 14.

14. Doug McAdam, *Freedom Summer* (New York, Oxford University Press, 1988) pp. 18–20.

15. Todd Gitlin, *The Sixties: Years of Hope, Days of Rage* (New York: Bantam, 1987) pp. 21–26. In 1930 there were a million students and eighty thousand faculty; by 1970, there were seven million students, and half a million full-time faculty, which created a critical mass that could be readily reached and mobilized on campuses. Seymour Martin Lipset, *Rebellion in the University* (Boston: Little Brown, 1971) pp. xiv, xv.

16. Keniston, "You Have to Grow up in Scarsdale," *Youth and Dissent,* pp. 306–307.

17. Lewis Feuer, *The Conflict of Generations, The Character and Significance of Student Movements* (New York: Basic Books, Inc., 1969) pp. vii, ix.

18. Keniston, "Radicals Revisited, Some Second Thoughts," *Youth and Dissent,* pp. 274–275. Young men involved in radical politics often had parents who were permissive, liberal, or radical, and not formally religious. The activists, studies showed, tended to be intelligent, disproportionately concentrated in the social sciences and humanities, and underrepresented in pre-professional programs; they perceived of themselves as independent of authority, liked art, and saw themselves as altruistic, empathetic, open, and honest. In the North, activists tended to be sophisticated, well-educated, and sometimes doctrinaire; southern civil rights workers most often came from religious backgrounds, according to Richard E. Peterson, "The Student Left in American Higher Education," in *Students in Revolt,* edited by Seymour Martin Lipset and Philip G. Altbach (Boston: Houghton Mifflin Co., 1969) pp. 216–217.

19. Keniston, "Radicals: Renewal of the Tradition," pp. 218–219, and "Young Radicals," pp. 55–70, both in Keniston, *Youth and Dissent;* Gordon Allport, *Pattern and Growth in Personality* (New York: Holt, Rinehart and Winston, 1961) pp. 283–304; Lipset, *Rebellion in the University,* pp. 16–19; Christopher Lasch, *The New Radicalism in America 1889– 1963: The Intellectual as Social Type* (New York: Alfred A. Knopf, 1966); Erikson, *Identity, Youth and Crisis,* pp. 27–37, 54–56, 257.

Erikson, borrowing on a Freudian concept, describes youth rebellions as, in part, a generation's way of turning passive into active. Adolescents, in the process of changing their center of activity from their parents' homes to the wider world, he implies, may express outwardly their parents' dissatisfactions or abandoned ideals. In youth, Erikson writes, "life intersects with history; here individuals are confirmed in their identities and societies regenerated in their life style."

20. Evans, *Personal Politics,* pp. 35, 77–89, 111–125, 163; Gitlin, *The Sixties,* pp. 362–374. Also see Mary King, *Freedom Song: A Personal Story of the 1960s Civil Rights Movement* (New York: William Morrow, 1987) p. 445; McAdam, *Freedom Summer,* pp. 106–111.

21. Of the lawyers Simpson interviewed, 71 percent had gone to predominantly white public high schools and 38 percent had attended predominantly white Ivy League colleges. Simpson, "The Daughters of Charlotte Ray," pp. 130–131.

22. Ongoing conversations with Sally Powers, research psychologist at the Henry A. Murray Center, Radcliffe College, 1982–1986.

23. Carol Gilligan, "The Relational World of Adolescent Girls," talk delivered at the Bunting Institute, Jan. 14, 1991; Gilligan, Nona P. Lyons and Trudy J. Hammer, *Making Connections: The Relational Worlds of Adolescent Girls at Emma Willard School* (Troy, New York: Emma Willard School, 1989) pp. 9–19.

While early on it was believed that most women did not go through an adolescent crisis (and perhaps, given the times, they didn't), more recent studies, done on adolescents in the 1970s and 1980s, indicate that the entry into adolescence is indeed a crisis point for both sexes. Glen Elder, T. Nguyen, and A. Caspi, "Linking Family Hardship to Children's

Lives," *Child Development* 56 (1985) pp. 361–375; Gilligan, "Preface," *Making Connections,* p. 10.

Gilligan and others suggest that white middle-class girls from the ages of nine to twelve begin to "paper new selves over" their own responses to the world with "appropriate" feminine behavior encouraged by their mothers, and reinforced by schools, media, and other societal forces. By "disconnecting," in this way, they lose touch with their own senses of self, their bodies, and their own power. Gilligan, "Adolescent Development Reconsidered," in Gilligan, Janie Victoria Ward, Jill McLean Taylor, with Betty Bardige, eds., *Mapping the Moral Domain* (Cambridge: Harvard University Press, 1988) p. xi; Elizabeth Debold, Marie Wilson, and Idelisse Malave, *Mother Daughter Revolution: From Betrayal to Power* (Reading, Mass.: Addison Wesley Publishing Company, 1993) pp. 11–17; "papering new selves," p. 52.

Debold et al. suggest, based on current research, that adolescent African-American girls appear to hold onto their voices longer than white or Hispanic girls because they are better able to draw on family and community connections to retain their own identities. In a "protective but costly" maneuver, to do so they distance themselves from schools or other institutions that denigrate them—which is effective in the short run, but leaves them economically vulnerable for lack of career training in the long term.

Latina girls lose confidence in themselves later in adolescence, with 83 percent saying they would not like to be homemakers but a third expecting to become homemakers anyway. There is little research on Asian-American or Native American adolescents.

24. Ongoing conversations with Irene Stiver, chief of psychology, McLean Hospital, Belmont, Mass., 1983–1993.

25. Erikson, *Identity: Youth and Crisis,* p. 283.

Chapter 7

1. Jane J. Mansbridge, *Why We Lost the ERA* (Chicago: The University of Chicago Press, 1986) p. 1; Carol Boyd Leon, "Occupational winners and losers: who they were during 1972–80," *Monthly Labor Review* (June 1982) pp. 18–28; U.S. Department of Labor, Bureau of Labor Statistics Bulletin 2080, Table 11, "Employment of Women in Selected Occupations, 1950, 1960, 1970 and 1979," *Data book,* (1980) p. 10. The figure on college professors includes college presidents. Also, Daphne Spain, "Women's Demographic Past, Present, and Future," talk at Radcliffe Conferences, "Defining the Challenge: Emerging Needs and Constraints," Dec. 2, 1988.

2. Alice Rossi, "Equality Between the Sexes, An Immodest Proposal," *Daedalus, The Journal of the American Academy of Arts and Sciences* (Spring 1964), in *The Woman in America,* edited by Robert J. Lifton (Boston: Beacon Press, 1964) pp. 99–140. Suzanne Gordon, *Prisoners of Men's Dreams, Striking Out for a New Feminine Future* (Boston: Little Brown, 1991) p. 23.

3. This, Ginsberg suggested, was either because having children allowed women to drop out of the workforce if they wanted to—or because family demands forced them to. Eli Ginsberg, *Life Styles of Educated Women* (New York: Columbia University Press, 1966) pp. 83–94, 103–105.

4. Alice Rossi, "Barriers to the Career Choice of Engineering, Medicine, or Science Among American Women," in *Women in the Scientific Professions,* edited by Jacqueline A. Mattfeld and Carol G. Van Aken (Cambridge: M.I.T. Press, 1965) pp. 102–105, citing Harvey C. Lehman, *Age and Achievement* (Princeton, N.J.: Princeton University Press, 1953).

5. Cynthia Fuchs Epstein, *Woman's Place, Options and Limits in Professional Careers* (Berkeley: University of California Press, 1971) pp. 24–26.

6. Rosabeth Moss Kanter, *Men and Women of the Corporation* (New York: Basic Books, 1977) pp. 208, 234–239, 242.

7. Anne Harlan and Carol Weiss, "Moving Up: Women in Managerial Careers," *Working Paper #86* (Wellesley College Center for Research on Women, 1981); Ann M. Morrison, Randall P. White, Ellen Van Velsor, and The Center for Creative Leadership, *Breaking the Glass Ceiling: Can Women Reach the Top of America's Largest Corporations?* (Reading, Ma. Addison-Wesley Publishing Company, 1987) p. 140; Shirley Mahaley Malcolm, Paula Quick Hall, and Janet Welsh Brown, *The Double Bind: The Price of Being a Minority Woman in Science* (Washington, D.C.: American Association for the Advancement of Women Report No. 76-R-3, April, 1976) pp. 25–25; Paul Burstein, "Legislation and the Income of Women and Nonwhites," *American Sociological Review* 44 (June 1979) pp. 367–391, and Robert M. Jobu, "Earnings Differential of White and Ethnic Minorities: The Case of Asians, Americans, the Blacks and Chicanos," *Sociology and Social Research* 66:1 (Oct. 1976) pp. 24–38, cited in John P. Fernandez, *Racism and Sexism in Corporate Life: Changing Values in American Business* (Lexington, Ma.: Lexington Books 1981) p. 43.

8. Cynthia Fuchs Epstein, "Positive Effects of the Multiple Negative: Explaining the Success of Black Professional Women," *The American Journal of Sociology,* 78:4 (January 1973) p. 932; Natalie Sokoloff, *Black Women and White Women in the Professions: Occupational Segregation by Race and Gender, 1960–1980* (New York: Routledge Press, 1992) pp. 55, 94; Cheryl Bernadette Leggon, "Black Female Professionals: Dilemmas and Contradictions of Status," in *The Black Woman,* edited by La Frances Rodgers-Rose (Beverly Hills, California: Sage Publications, Inc., 1980) pp. 189–202; Aida Hurtado, "Relating to Privilege: Seduction and Rejection in the Subordination of White Women and Women of Color," *Signs: Journal of Culture and Society* 14:4 (University of Chicago, Summer 1989) p. 834.

9. Farah A. Ibrahim, "A Course on Asian-American Women: Identity Development Issues," *Women's Studies Quarterly* 1 & 2 (Spring and Summer 1992) p. 49; Roberta Morse, *The Black Female Professional* Occasional Paper No. 21, Mental Health Research and Development Center (Washington, D.C.: Institute for Urban Affairs and Research, 1983) p. 13; Stella M. Nkomo, "Race and Sex: The Forgotten Case of the Black Female Manager," in *Women's Careers: Pathways and Pitfalls,* edited by Suzanna Rose and Laurie Larwood (New York: Praeger, 1989) p. 140; Malcolm et al., *The Double Bind,* pp. 26–27; Dr. Shirley Hill Witt, "Native Women in the World of Work," speech delivered at the U.S. Department of Labor Conference on Native American Women and Equal Opportunity: A Federal Training Seminar, Nov. 13, 1978, in *Women of Color Forum, A Collection of Readings,* Wisconsin Department of Public Instruction, Nov. 1979, Bulletin #404.

10. Gwyned Simpson, "The Daughters of Charlotte Ray: The Career Development Process during the Exploratory and Establishment Stages of Black Women Attorneys," *Sex Roles: A Journal of Research* 11:1 and 2 (New York: Plenum, July 1984) p. 132; Malcolm et al., *The Double Bind,* p. 26; Malkah Notman, M.D., conversation with author, Henry A. Murray Center, A Center for the Study of Lives, Radcliffe College, Cambridge, Ma. April 5, 1994.

11. While many of the women I spoke with saw their mothers as overtly competitive with them, their mothers' attitudes, Irene Stiver explains, may also stem from the difficulties mothers tend to have in parting with their daughters, and with their reluctance to see them become individuals and adults. Dorothy Hilly, chair of the Department of Women's Studies at Hunter College, believes these mothers may have been trying to protect their daughters from what they had been brought up to believe happened to women who entered the real world of professional school and work. Stiver, ongoing conversations; Dorothy Hilly, conversation with author, New York, Dec. 31, 1986.

12. Simpson, "The Daughters of Charlotte Ray," p. 135.

13. Morrison et al., *Breaking the Glass Ceiling*, pp. 54–55.

14. Doris Bernstein, "Female Identity Synthesis," based on Annie Reich, "Early Identifications as Archaic Elements in the Superego," *Journal of the American Psychoanalytic Association,* 1954, in *Career and Motherhood, Struggles for a New Identity,* edited by Alan Roland and Barbara Harris (New York: Human Sciences Press, 1979) pp. 108, 115–116; Esther Menaker, "Some Inner Conflicts of Women in a Changing Society," in Roland and Harris, *Career and Motherhood,* pp. 89–90. Psychiatrist Alexandra Symonds describes mothers with low self-esteem, themselves the victims of cultural prejudice, who automatically project their own low self-esteem onto their daughters, treating them as second class citizens. A mother who feels she failed to please her husband by not having a son may reject her daughter, project onto her daughter her own self-hate, use her daughter as a surrogate mother to the younger siblings, or treat her daughter as a competitor for the father's love. The result is a daughter who fails to grow up with a healthy sense of security and confidence in her own identity. Alexandra Symonds, "The Wife as the Professional," *The American Journal of Psychoanalysis* (Association for the Advancement of Psychoanalysis) 39:1 (1979) pp. 59–60.

15. Bernstein, "Female Identity Synthesis," pp. 108–109; Menaker, "Some Inner Conflicts of Women in a Changing Society," pp. 92–93.

In a related theory, Luise Eichenbaum and Susie Orbach suggest that mothers, who may fear their own dependence or connection, require their daughters to be independent at early ages and train them to care for others too soon. As a result, their daughters remain needy, and when they become mothers themselves, in turn, perpetuate the same pattern of dependence and counter-dependence. Luise Eichenbaum and Susie Orbach, *Understanding Women, A Feminist Psychoanalytic Approach* (New York: Basic Books, 1983) pp. 42–50.

16. Irene Stiver, Brown Bag Talk, Henry A. Murray Center, Dec. 1983; also see Irene P. Stiver, "Work Inhibitions in Women," Stone Center for Developmental Services and Studies, Wellesley College, No. 82-03, 1983; also in Judith Jordan, Jean Baker Miller, Irene Stiver, and Jan Surrey, *Women's Growth in Connection, Writings from the Stone Center* (New York: The Guilford Press, 1991).

17. Menaker, "Some Inner Conflicts of Women in a Changing Society," p. 88; Symonds, "The Wife as the Professional," pp. 61–62.

18. Symonds, "The Wife as the Professional," p. 61; Bernstein, "Female Identity Synthesis," p. 92. Korn/Ferry International found that most of the women sampled tended to work fifty-three hours a week, the same as male executives. To the researchers' surprise, 47 percent of the married women executives indicated that they worked fifty-nine or more hours per week—even though they had additional time-consuming responsibilities at home, including the care of children. "Profile of Women Senior Executives" (New York: Korn/Ferry International, 1982).

19. Symonds, "The Wife as the Professional," p. 62.

20. Irene Stiver, director of psychology, McLean Hospital, Belmont, Mass., interviews with author, Nov. 3, 1983; April 20, 1983.

21. Kim Chernin, a writer and therapist, describes anorexia and bulimia as expressions of an internalized battle daughters have with their mothers: although they want to take advantage of opportunities their mothers never had, they feel guilty about doing so, because they feel they are in some way depriving their mothers of such opportunities. Those fears, Chernin suggests, stem from daughters' feelings in infancy that by suckling, they were depleting their mothers of nourishment. For some, gaining weight may be a way of avoiding successful relationships with men in order to avoid surpassing their mothers. For others, the urge to overeat may be a way of symbolically making up for nurturing they

feel is missing in their lives. *The Hungry Self: Women, Eating and Identity* (Harper and Row, 1985).

For still other women, gaining weight may represent an attempt to hold onto their mothers—either through being fed, or as psychologist Stiver suggests, by sharing their mothers' obsession with food. Another possible explanation is that women maintain excess weight to avoid the ire of mothers—real or internalized—who might feel angry or hurt if their daughters become autonomous, successful, sexual women.

22. Epstein, "Positive Effects of the Multiple Negative," p. 932; J. C. Lovelace, "Career Satisfaction and Role Harmony in Afro-American Women Physicians," *Journal of the American Medical Women's Association* 40 (1985) pp. 4–8; cited in Roselyn Payne Epps, "The Black Woman Physician—Perspectives and Priorities," *Journal of the National Medical Association* 78:5 (1986) p. 379; Cheryl Bernadette Leggon, "Black Female Professionals: Dilemmas and Contradictions of Status," in *The Black Woman*, edited by La Frances Rodgers-Rose, pp. 189–202; Malcolm et al., *The Double Bind*, 34.

23. From S. Steptoe, "Strangers in a Strange Land," *Wall Street Journal*, "A Special Report—the Corporate Woman," March 24, 1986, pp. 22–23, in Nkomo, "Race and Sex: The Forgotten Case of the Black Female Manager," p. 138; Simpson, "The Daughters of Charlotte Ray," p. 168.

24. Roberta Morse, *The Black Female Professional* (Washington, D.C.: Mental Health Research and Development Center, Institute for Urban Affairs Research, Howard University, occasional paper no. 21, 1983) p. 13, citing R. Staples *The Black Woman in America: Sex, Marriage and the Family* (Chicago: Nelson Hall, 1973); P. J. Andrisani and M. B. Shapiro, "Women's Attitudes Toward Their Jobs: Some Longitudinal Data on a National Sample," *Personnel Psychology*, 31:1 (1978) pp. 15–35.

25. Simpson, "The Daughters of Charlotte Ray," pp. 136, 138.

26. Farah A. Ibrahim, "A Course on Asian-American Women: Identity Development Issues," *Women Studies Quarterly* 1992, 1&2, pp. 41–58; quotes on p. 50. Ibrahim draws on the work of S. Mazumdar, "General Introduction," Deborah Woo, "The Gap Between Striving and Achieving: The Case of Asian-American Women," and Kesaya E. Noda, "Growing Up Asian in America," all in *Making Waves: An Anthology*, edited by Asian Women United of California (Boston: Beacon Press, 1989) pp. 1–24, 185–196, 243–350; and on R. Josselson, *Finding Herself* (San Francisco: Jossey Bass, 1987).

27. Noda, "Growing Up Asian in America," in *Making Waves*, p. 248.

28. Denise A. Segura and Jennifer L. Pierce, "Chicana/o Family Structure and Gender Personality: Chodorow, Familism, and Psychoanalytic Sociology Revisited," *Signs* 19:11 (1993) pp. 76–77; Malcolm et al., *The Double Bind*, p. 34.

29. Ibrahim, "A Course on Asian-American Women: Identity Development Issues," pp. 50–51.

30. Roger L. Gould, *Transformations, Growth and Change in Adult Life* (New York: Simon and Schuster, 1978) pp. 96–105.

Chapter 8

1. Mary Frances Berry, *Why ERA Failed: Politics, Women's Rights and the Amending Process of the Constitution* (Bloomington: Indiana University Press, 1986) pp. 114, 115; E. J. Dionne, "Both Parties Using Family and Moral Issues," *New York Times*, September 28, 1987, pp. A1, 30; No byline, "Influencing Government Policy, Left and Right Fight for Custody of 'Family' Issue," *New York Times*, August 20, 1987, p. B12.

2. Judy Klemesrud, "Americans Assess 15 Years of Feminism," *New York Times*, Dec. 19, 1983, p. 1.

3. U.S. Bureau of the Census, "Detailed Occupations of the Experienced Civilian Labor Force by Sex for the U.S. and Regions: 1980 and 1970," Census of Population, 1980, Supplementary Report, PC 80-S1-15 (Washington, D.C.: U.S. Government Printing Office, 1980, 305-40212 B57A) in Suzanne Bianchi and Daphne Spain, *American Women in Transition* (New York: Russell Sage Foundation, 1986) p. 160; Susan Fraker, "Why Women Aren't Getting to the Top," *Fortune* 16 (April 1984) p. 40; Ann M. Morrison, Randall P. White, and Ellen Van Velsor, and the Center for Creative Leadership, *Breaking the Glass Ceiling: Can Women Reach the Top of America's Largest Corporations?* (Reading, Mass.: Addison Wesley Publishing Company, Inc., 1987) p. 155; Suzanne Keller, "Women in the Twenty-First Century: Summing Up and Going Forward," Address to The Radcliffe Conferences on Defining the Challenge: Emerging Needs and Constraints, Radcliffe College, Dec. 2, 1988.

4. Keller, "Women in the Twenty-First Century," Daphne Spain, "Women's Demographic Past, Present, and Future," Radcliffe Conferences, Dec. 2, 1988. Whereas in 1950, one in four working women were clerical workers, in 1988, the figure was one in three. Leonard Silk, "Women Gain but at a Cost," *New York Times,* Feb. 6, 1987, p. D2.

5. Doreen Weisenhaus, "Still a Long Way to Go for Women and Minorities," *National Law Journal* (Feb. 8, 1988) pp. 1, 48, 50, 53 and Lawrence K. Altman, with Elisabeth Rosenthal, "Changes in Medicine Bring Pain to Healing Profession, *New York Times,* Feb. 18, 1990, pp. A1, A34; Gwyned Simpson, "Black Women in the Legal Profession," unpublished manuscript, New York City, in Natalie Sokoloff, *Black Women and White Women in the Professions: Occupational Segregation by Race and Gender, 1960–1980* (New York: Routledge Press, 1992) pp. 76, 129; Roselyn Payne Epps, M.D., "The Black Woman Physician—Perspectives and Priorities," *Journal of the National Medical Association* 78:5 (1986) p. 378.

6. Shirley M. Tilghman, "Science vs. the Female Scientist," *New York Times,* January 25, 1993, p. A17; Associated Press, "Women Scientists Lagging in Industry Jobs," *New York Times,* January 18, 1994, p. C5.

7. Associated Press, "Women Said to Be Kept From Top Media Posts," *New York Times,* March 2, 1988, p. B5; Elizabeth M. Fowler, "Careers: Optimism on Women Engineers," *New York Times,* July 21, 1987, pp. D17, 57, 61; Robert Reinhold, "Women in Electronics Find Silicon Valley Best and Worst," *New York Times,* March 2, 1984, pp. A1, A12; Jane Meredith Adams, "Giving up the Dream," *Boston Globe,* March 21, 1986, p. 43. This story reports on a trend in which women who found the going rough in corporations were quitting to start their own companies; Ann M. Morrison, Randall P. White and Ellen Van Velsor, in "Executive Women: Substance Plus Style," *Psychology Today* 21:8 (August 1987) p. 20; Sandra Salmans, "Top Tiers Still Elude Corporate Women," *New York Times,* August 17, 1987, p. B4; Suzanne G. Haynes and Manning Feinleib, "Women, Work and Coronary Heart Disease," in *American Journal of Public Health* 70 (1980) pp. 133–141, and Peggy Thoits, "Multiple Identities: Examining Gender and Marital Status Differences in Distress," *American Sociological Review* 51 (1986) pp. 259–272, in Arlie Hochschild, *The Second Shift* (New York: Avon Books, 1990) p. 4.

8. Jane Gross, "Single Women Coping With A Void," *New York Times,* April 28, 1987, p. A1; Gwyned Simpson, "The Daughters of Charlotte Ray: The Career Development Process During the Exploratory and Establishment Stages of Black Women Attorneys," *Sex Roles: A Journal of Research* (New York: Plenum, July 1984) Vol. 11. p. 134; Epps, "The Black Woman Physician," p. 381. Megan Marshall, *The Cost of Loving: Women and the New Fear of Intimacy* (New York: Putnam, 1984); Barbara Ehrenreich, "A Feminist's View of the New Man," *New York Times Magazine,* May 20, 1984, p. 36.

9. Haynes and Feinleib, "Women, Work and Coronary Heart Disease," pp. 133–141,

and Thoits, "Multiple Identities: Examining Gender and Marital Status Differences in Distress," pp. 259–272, cited in Hochschild, *Second Shift,* pp. 4, 255, 2, 286, 289; Simpson, "The Daughters of Charlotte Ray," p. 35.

10. Lenore Weitzman, *The Divorce Revolution* (New York: Macmillan, The Free Press, 1985) pp. xi, xii, x–xiii; New York attorney Julia Perles, quoted in Georgia Dullea, "Divorce Law is Called Unfair by Bar and Women's Groups," *New York Times,* August 5, 1985, p. 1.

11. Forty to fifty percent of children born in the 1970s would spend part of their youth in a female-headed household. The average income of a single mother was $9,000 a year, 57 percent of female-headed households were "poor," as were 22 percent of all American children, as opposed to 14 percent ten years earlier. Sylvia Ann Hewlett, *A Lesser Life: The Myth of Women's Liberation in America* (New York: Warner Books, 1987) p. 109, citing: Select Committee on Children, Youth and Families, *U.S. Children and their Families: Current Conditions and Recent Trends* (Washington, D.C.: U.S. Government Printing Office, May 1983) p. 6; and National Citizen's Board of Inquiry into Health in America, *Health Care USA* (October 1984) Vol. 1, p. 1; *Money, Income and Poverty Status of Persons and Families in the U.S. 1983,* Current Population Reports, Series P-60 (Washington, D.C.: Bureau of the Census, 1984).

12. Helen Blank, testimony of the Children's Defense Fund Before the Joint Economic Committee Concerning Child Care Problems Faced by Working Mothers and Pregnant Women, April 3, 1984; Lunette Long and Thomas Long, *The Handbook for Latchkey Children and Their Parents* (New York: Arbor House, 1983) p. 174, both in Hewlett, *A Lesser Life,* pp. 118, 124.

13. Daphne Spain, "Women's Demographic Past, Present and Future," talk delivered at Conference on Women in the Year 2000, Dec. 2, 1988; Suzanne Bianchi and Daphne Spain, *American Women in Transition,* for the National Committee for Research on the 1980 Census (New York: Russell Sage Foundation, 1986) p. 3.

14. Diana Dill, "Understanding Women's Achievement, Sex Differences in the Structuring of Achievement Situations," talk at Henry A. Murray Research Center, Radcliffe College, Oct. 15, 1985; Diana Zuckerman, "Medical School Plans and Other Life Goals of Students at the Seven Colleges," *Seven College Macy Study,* talk at Henry A. Murray Center, Radcliffe College, March, 1983. At Barnard College in New York City, women students expressed deep conflicts concerning careers and definitions of femininity. Mirra Komarovsky, *Women in College: Shaping Feminine Identities* (New York: Basic Books, 1985). Karen D. Arnold, "Academically Talented Women in the 1980s: The Illinois Valedictorian Project," in *Women's Lives Through Time: Educated American Women of the Twentieth Century,* edited by Kathleen Day Hulbert and Diane Tickton Schuster (San Francisco: Jossey-Bass Inc. Publishers, 1993) pp. 398–399.

15. Susan Jacoby, "Hers," *New York Times,* April 14, 1983, p. C2; see also Susan Bolotin, "Voices from the Post-Feminist Generation," *New York Times Magazine,* October 17, 1982, Section 6, pp. 28–31, 103–117. *Seventeen Magazine* told advertisers that its average reader cooked an average of five meals a week for her family, eleven meals a week for herself. "She's one of 80 percent of young women who shop for family food, 90 percent of whom make brand decisions" a full-page ad states. "If you're not reaching her, you're missing the other female head of the household." Advertisement in *New York Times,* Jan. 13, 1988, D. 28, citing Seventeen Food Survey, 1986; TRU Fall 1987, Triangle Communications, Inc. 1988.

16. Sandra Blakeslee, "Female Sex Hormone Is Tied to Ability to Perform Tasks," *New York Times,* Nov. 18, 1988, pp. A1, D20; David Gelman, with John Carey, "Just How the Sexes Differ," *Newsweek Magazine* 98 (May 18, 1981) pp. 72–81.

17. V. E. Schein, "The Relationship Between Sex-role Stereotypes and Requisite Management Characteristics," *Journal of Applied Psychology* 57 (1973) pp. 95–100; also, V. E. Schein, "Relationships Between Sex-role Characteristics and Requisite Management Characteristics Among Female Managers," *Journal of Applied Psychology* 60 (1975) pp. 340–344; D. M. Haccoun, R. R. Haccoun, and G. Sallay, "Sex Differences in the Appropriateness of Supervisory Styles: A Nonmanagement View," *Journal of Applied Psychology* 63 (1978) pp. 124–127; Marilyn Loden, *Feminine Leadership, or How to Succeed in Business without Being one of the Boys* (New York: Times Books, 1985), cited in Ann M. Morrison, Randall P. White, Ellen Van Velsor, and the Center for Creative Leadership, *Breaking the Glass Ceiling, Can Women Reach the Top of America's Corporations?* (Reading, Mass.: Addison Wesley, 1987) p. 49.

18. Sara Ruddick, *Maternal Thinking: Toward a Politics of Peace* (Boston: Beacon Press, 1989); Suzanne Gordon, *Prisoners of Men's Dreams: Striking Out for a New Feminine Future* (Boston: Little Brown, 1991).

19. Simpson, "The Daughters of Charlotte Ray," p. 137.

20. Epps, "The Black Woman Physician," p. 381; B. M. Campbell, "To Be Black, Gifted and Alone," *Savvy* 67:74 (May 1984) p. 62, cited in Stella M. Nkomo, "Race and Sex: The Forgotten Case of the Black Female Manager," in *Women's Careers: Pathways and Pitfalls*, edited by S. Rose and L. Larwood (New York: Praeger, 1989) p. 138.

21. Simpson, "The Daughters of Charlotte Ray," p. 37.

22. Abigail Stewart, "Personality to Life Outcomes among College-Educated Women," Doc. diss. 1975, Murray Center Archives; Alexandra Symonds, "The Wife as the Professional," *The American Journal of Psychoanalysis* 39:1 (1979) pp. 61–62.

23. Carol Nadelson, M.D., "'Normal' and 'Special' Aspects of Pregnancy: A Psychological Approach," in *The Woman Patient: Medical and Psychological Interfaces, Vol. 1, Sexual and Reproductive Aspects of Women's Health Care,* edited by Malkah T. Notman, M.D., and Carol C. Nadelson, M.D. (New York: Plenum Press, 1978) pp. 74–75.

24. Nancy Richardson, "Developmental Shifts in Constructions of Success," Doc. diss., Harvard University, 1981, Henry A. Murray Research Center, Radcliffe College.

25. Susan Brownmiller, *Femininity* (New York: Linden Press, 1984) pp. 16–18; Sarah Ruddick, *Maternal Thinking;* Gordon, *Prisoners of Men's Dreams.*

26. Irene Stiver, interview with author, May 18, 1988; Elizabeth Debold, Marie Wilson, and Idelisse Malave, *Mother Daughter Revolution: From Betrayal to Power* (Reading, Mass.: Addison Wesley, 1993); Ruthellen Josselson, *Finding Herself: Pathways to Identity Development in Women* (San Francisco: Jossey-Bass, 1987) pp. 44–54.

27. Although the judge, persuaded of real and fundamental differences between men and women, found in Sears' favor, Joan Wallach Scott and others have since suggested that framing the debate in terms of male/female differences did not allow for solutions providing for variation of preference within the genders. Rosalind Rosenberg, "What Harms Women in the Workplace," Feb. 27, 1986, *New York Times,* p. A23; Samuel G. Freedman, "Of History and Politics, Bitter Feminist Debate," *New York Times,* June 6, 1986, pp. B1, B4; Joan Wallach Scott, *Gender and the Politics of History* (New York: Columbia University Press, 1988) chapter 4, discussion of the decision, p. 171.

28. Robert Pear, "Administration May Challenge Equal Pay Rule," *New York Times,* January 22, 1984, p. A1; Robert Pear, "Equal Pay is Not Needed for Jobs of Comparable Worth, U.S. Says," *New York Times,* June 18, 1985, p. A12.

29. Some opponents of pregnancy leave legislation, however, feared it would favor middle-class employees who could afford to take time off, or that it would discourage companies from hiring women, who would be the likeliest to take advantage of it. A Swedish study showed that while in that country, family leave was offered to all employees, men

rarely used it. Stuart Taylor, "Justices Hear Debate Over Pregnancy Leave," *New York Times,* October 9, 1986, p. A30. Linda Greenhouse, "Momentum and 'Family Leave,'" *New York Times,* February 3, 1987, p. A18.

30. Clifford Krauss, "Senate Passes Bill Setting Up Leaves for Family Needs," *New York Times,* Oct. 3, 1991, pp. 1, 20. The Swedish Institute, "Child Care Programs in Sweden: Fact Sheets on Sweden," Stockholm, September 1984, in Barbara Bergmann, *The Economic Emergence of Women* (New York: Basic Books, 1986) p. 214.

31. "Editorial," *New York Times,* March 27, 1984, p. A30; No byline, "Women's Groups Consider a Plan to Overturn Sex-based Disability Rate," *Wall Street Journal,* April 17, 1994, p. 1.

32. Geneva Overholser, "What Post-Feminism Really Means," *New York Times,* September 19, 1986, p. A34.

33. Irene Stiver, interview with author, September 17, 1988.

Chapter 9

1. Tim Bovee, "Census Study Sees Reshaped US by 2050," *Boston Globe,* September 29, 1993, p. 1, citing U.S. Bureau of the Census Projections.

2. Charles Westoff, "Marriage Fertility in the Developed Countries," *Scientific American* 239 (Dec. 1978) pp. 51–57, cited in Andrew Cherlin, *Marriage, Divorce and Remarriage* (Cambridge: Harvard University Press, 1981) p. 45.

3. Carl Degler, *At Odds: Women and the Family in America from the Revolution to the Present* (New York: Oxford University Press, 1981) pp. 188–189, 194–202, 257–259. Sara M. Evans, "Women in the Twentieth Century, An Overview," in *The American Woman, 1987–88, A Report in Depth,* edited by Sara E. Rix (New York: Norton, 1987) p. 33.

4. Marcia Guttentag and Paul Secord, *Too Many Women, The Sex Ratio Question* (Beverly Hills: Sage Publications, 1983); David Herlihy, *Medieval Households* (Cambridge: Harvard University Press, 1985) pp. 50–52, 100.

5. Richard Easterlin, *Birth and Fortune, The Impact on Personal Welfare* (New York: Basic Books, 1980); Easterlin, personal interview for MacNeil-Lehrer Report, Anita Harris and Shirley Wershba, "Will There Soon Be Another Baby Boom?" aired May 9, 1977.

6. Susan Faludi, *Backlash: The Undeclared War Against American Women* (New York: Crown Publishers Inc., 1991); Jean Lipman-Blumen, "Ideology, Social Structure and Crisis," Paper presented at the American Sociological Association 69th Annual Meeting, Montreal, Quebec, Canada, August 25–29, 1974. Lewis Feuer, *The Conflict of Generations: The Character and Significance of Student Movements* (New York: Basic Books, 1969); Arthur Schlesinger Jr., *The Cycles of American History* (Boston: Houghton Mifflin, 1986); and William Strauss and Neil Howe, *Generations: The History of America's Future: 1584–2069* (New York: William Morrow, 1991) suggest alternative cyclic theories.

7. "The Waiting Game: Women Make Strides But Men Stay Firmly in Top Company Jobs," *Wall Street Journal,* March 29, 1994, p. A1.

8. Los Angeles Times (no byline) "Conference of women ends with protest by workers," in *Boston Globe* (no author), July 13, 1992, p. 16, referring to International Women's Summit in Dublin. Challenge to speakers from members of the audience, Radcliffe College Panel on Mary Wollstonecraft, March 6, 1992; Suzanne Gordon, *Prisoners of Men's Dreams: Striking Out for a New Feminine Future* (Boston: Little Brown, 1991). *Time*/Cable News Network Poll by Yankelovich Clancy Shulman, in Nancy Gibbs, "Telephone poll of 625 American women," *Time,* March 9, 1992, p. 54; Jane Gross, "Patricia Ireland, President of N.O.W.: Does She Speak for Today's Women?" *New York Times Magazine,* March 1,

1992, pp. 16–18, 38, 54. Anthony Flint, "New Breed of Feminist Challenges Old Guard," *Boston Globe,* May 29, 1994, pp. 1, 14.

9. Gibbs, "The War Against Feminism," pp. 50–57; Eileen McNamara, "The Myth of Sisterhood," *Boston Globe Magazine,* January 5, 1992, pp. 13, 18–32; Michael Specter, "Feminists Painfully Watching Holtzman and Ferraro Battle," *New York Times,* March 14, 1992, p. A1; Jane Gross, "Women, Where Ambition Meets Opportunity," describing California senatorial race, *New York Times,* May 29, 1992, p. A19; Suzanne Gordon, "Every Woman for Herself," *New York Times,* August 19, 1991, p. A15; "Do Women Help Women? Don't Bet on Some at Top," No byline, *Wall Street Journal,* March 29, 1994, p. A10.

10. Alecia Swasy, "Stay-at-Home Moms Are Fashionable Again in Many Communities," *Wall Street Journal,* July 23, 1993, p. A1.

11. Bonita L. Betters-Reed and Lynda L. Moore, "Managing Diversity: Focusing on Women and the Whitewash Dilemma," in *Womanpower: Managing in Times of Demographic Turbulence,* edited by Uma Sekaran and Frederick T. L. Leong (Newbury Park, Calif.: Sage Publications, Inc., 1991) pp. 31–58; Bonita Betters-Reed, and Lynda Moore, "Valuing Differences, Valuing Diversity," Social Science Faculty Talk, Simmons College, Boston, Mass., April 29, 1992; Steven A. Holden, "Survey Finds Minorities Resent One Another Almost as Much As They Do Whites," *New York Times,* March 3, 1994, p. B8, citing L. H. Research Survey conducted for the National Conference of Christians and Jews.

12. Barbara Presley Noble, "At Work: Interpreting the Family Leave Act," *New York Times,* August 8, 1993, p. A23. In 1993, 44 percent of women (23.5 million) worked in technical, sales, and administrative support jobs according to Barbara Presley Noble, "The New Equality in Hard Times, Some Stats From the Bottom Line," in "At Work," *New York Times,* August 8, 1993, p. F25, based on statistics released by Women's Bureau of the Bureau of Labor Statistics, Summer 1993; Peter T. Kilborn, "More Women Take Low-Wage Jobs Just So Their Families Can Get By," *New York Times,* March 13, 1994, p. 24.

13. Between 1979 and 1990, poor children grew poorer and children living in poverty increased 22 percent. From 1979 to 1990, the median income of families with children adjusted for inflation fell by 5 percent, while families without children saw a 7 percent increase in their income. Average income of families in the bottom fifth income bracket fell 12.6 percent, while average income in the top fifth bracket increased 9.2 percent between these same years, to $70,000.

Births to single teenagers rose 14 percent, children in single-parent families increased 123 percent, the violent deaths of teenagers aged fifteen to nineteen increased 11 percent, and the juvenile incarceration rate rose 10 percent, in 33 states, in which 82 percent of American children live. The rise in deaths among teenagers was led by a rise in suicides and homicides.

White single girls accounted for the majority of teenagers having babies and showed the most significant rate of increase. While the infant mortality rate improved 22 percent, a black baby was twice as likely as a white baby to die in the first year after birth. Study by Annie E. Casey Foundation and the Center for the Study of Social Policy, reported in *New York Times,* no byline, "Report Says Poor Children Grew Poorer in 1980s," March 24, 1992, p. A22; Susan Chira, "Study Confirms Worst Fears on U.S. Children," *New York Times,* April 12, 1994, p. A1, reporting on Carnegie Commission, "Starting Points: Meeting the Needs of Our Youngest Children (New York, 1994).

14. Susan Chira, "Bias Against Girls is Found Rife in Schools, With Lasting Damage," *New York Times,* February 12, 1992, p. A1; Bob Herbert, "Battered Girls in School," *New York Times,* November 24, 1993 pp. A1, A23.

15. *Boston Globe,* no author, "The Day Care Hunt," May 10, 1992, p. 38, drawing on

Hewitt Associates survey of 1,006 large employers. Diane E. Lewis, "Fast Track, News in the Workplace," *Boston Globe,* March 23, 1992, citing The Conference Board, "Work-Family Roundtable: Flexibility," Vol 1, No. 1, *The Conference Board* (Dec. 1991) p. 17; Sue Shellenbarger, "As More Pregnant Women Work, Bias Complaints Rise," *Wall Street Journal,* December 6, 1993, p. B1; Rochelle Sharpe, "Family Friendly Firms Don't Always Promote Females," *Wall Street Journal,* March 29, 1994, p. B4.

16. Madeline Drexler, "Medicine Woman," *The Boston Globe Magazine,* March 29, 1992, pp. 18, 27–39, describing the appointment of Dr. Vivian Pinn as head of the new national Office of Research in Women's Health; Carol Stocker, "The A Group," *Boston Globe,* Jan. 14, 1992, pp. A25, 29.

17. Bruce McCabe, "Helping lawyers face family life," *Boston Globe,* Dec. 3, 1991, p. 61.

18. Nancy Gilson, interview with author, Simmons College, Boston, Mass., November 18, 1991.

19. Barbara Bergmann, "Policy Agenda for the Sex Role Revolution," talk delivered at Radcliffe College Conference on Women in the Year 2000, Dec. 2, 1988; Kilborn, "More Women Take Low-Wage Jobs Just so Their Families Can Get By," p. A24.

20. Martha Minow, *Making All the Difference: Inclusion, Exclusion and American Law* (Ithaca, N.Y.: Cornell University Press, 1991) pp. 59, 74; Kathleen Sullivan, "Constitutional and Legal Issues Facing Women in the 21st Century," talk at Conference on Women in the Year 2000, Radcliffe College, Dec. 2, 1988; Fred Strebeigh, "Defining Law on the Feminist Frontier," *New York Times Magazine,* October 6, 1991, pp. 28–31, 50–56.

21. Minow, *Making All the Difference,* p. 59; Beth B. Hess, "Aging Policies and Old Women: The Hidden Agenda," in *Gender and the Life Course,* edited by Alice Rossi (New York: Aldine Publishing Company, 1985) pp. 321–323.

22. Sullivan, Dec. 2, 1988.

23. Rosabeth Moss Kanter, "Structuring the Inside: The Impact of Organizations on Sex Differences," in *Outsiders on the Inside,* edited by B. Forisha and B. Goldman (Englewood Cliffs, N.J.: Prentice-Hall, 1981) pp. 75–83.

24. Bergmann, Dec. 2, 1988; see also Barbara Bergmann, *The Economic Emergence of Women* (New York: Basic Books, 1986); Juliet Schor, *The Overworked American* (New York: Basic Books, 1991).

25. Nicholas Beutell and Jeffrey Greenhaus, "Balance Acts: Work-Family Conflict and The Dual Career Couple," in *Not as Far As You Think: The Realities of Working Women,* Lynda L. Moore (Lexington Mass.: Lexington Books, 1986) pp. 149–162. As of 1991, some 10 percent of America's large companies had embraced flexible scheduling and a range of assistance programs to support workers juggling family demands: Sue Shellenbarger and Timothy D. Schellhardt, "Is a Dream Workplace Any Closer to Reality," *Wall Street Journal,* Oct. 18, 1991, p. B4; Survey by Hewitt Associates, an Illinois-based benefits consulting firm, described in Diane F. Lewis, "A helping hand in the balancing act," *Boston Globe,* Nov. 30, 1991, p. 3.

26. For a description of various forms, see Judith Stacey, *Brave New Families: Stories of Upheaval in Late Twentieth Century America* (New York: Basic Books, 1990).

27. Bell Hooks, "Black Women: Shaping Feminist Theory," in Hooks, *Feminist Theory from Margin to Center* (Boston: South End Press, 1984) pp. 1–15; Johnnetta B. Cole, "Commonalities and Differences," in *All American Women,* edited by Johnnetta B. Cole (New York: Free Press, 1986) pp. 1–30; Peggy McIntosh, "White Privilege and Male Privilege: A Personal Account of Coming to See Correspondence Through Work in Women's Studies," paper, Wellesley College Center for Research on Women, Wellesley, Mass., 1988; Betters-Reed and Moore, "Managing Diversity," pp. 231–258.

28. Betters-Reed and Moore, "Managing Diversity," pp. 46–47; McIntosh, "White Privilege and Male Privilege"; Claudia Deutsch, "Don't Forget the White Males," *New York Times,* Dec. 8, 1991, p. 29.

29. Bonita Betters-Reed, interview with author, Simmons College, April 6, 1992; Bruce Butterfield, "Xerox makes it work," *Boston Sunday Globe,* Oct. 20, 1991, p. A33, 37.

30. Betters-Reed and Moore, "Managing Diversity," p. 32.

31. Frances Fox-Piven, "Women and the State: Power, Ideology and the Welfare State," in *Gender and the Life Course,* edited by Alice Rossi, pp. 265–287, 282–284. Fox-Piven describes how, with the erosion of the traditional family and women's power within it, the welfare state has generated "powerful cross-class ties" among the different groups of women who have stakes in protecting it.

BIBLIOGRAPHY

Books

Allen, Frederick Lewis, *Only Yesterday, An Informal History of the Nineteen Twenties* (New York: Harper and Brothers, 1931; New York: Harper and Row, 1959).

Allport, Gordon, *Pattern and Growth in Personality* (New York: Holt, Rinehart and Winston, 1961).

Asian Women United of California, eds., *Making Waves: An Anthology* (Boston: Beacon Press, 1989).

Bardwick, Judith, ed., *Readings on the Psychology of Women* (New York: Harper and Row, 1972).

Bardwick, Judith, and Elizabeth Douvan et al., eds., *Feminine Personality and Conflict* (Belmont, California: Brooks Cole, 1970).

Bataille, Gretchen M., ed., *Native American Women* (New York: Garland Publishing Company, 1993).

Bergmann, Barbara R., *The Economic Emergence of Women* (New York: Basic Books, 1986).

Berry, Mary Frances, *Why ERA Failed, Politics, Women's Rights and the Amending Process of the Constitution* (Bloomington: Indiana University Press, 1986).

Bianchi, Suzanne, and Daphne Spain, *American Women in Transition* (New York: Russell Sage Foundation, 1986).

Boydston, Jeanne, *Home and Work: Housework, Wages and the Ideology of Labor in the Early Republic* (New York: Oxford University Press, 1990).

Brownmiller, Susan, *Femininity* (New York: Linden Press, 1984).

Burns, Edward M., Robert E. Lerner, and Standish Meacham, *Western Civilizations: Their History and Their Culture,* Vol. 1 (New York and London: W. W. Norton and Co., 1984).

Caplow, Theodore, Howard M. Bahr, Bruce A. Chadwick, Reuben Hill, Margaret Holmes Williamson, *Middletown Families, Fifty Years of Change and Continuity* (Minneapolis: University of Minnesota Press, 1982).

Carter, Betty, and Monica McGoldrick, eds., *The Family Life Cycle* (New York: Gardner Press, 1980).

Chafe, William, *Women and Equality, Changing Patterns in American Culture* (New York: Oxford University Press, 1979).

———, *The American Woman: Her Changing Social, Economic and Political Roles, 1920–1970* (New York: Oxford University Press, 1974).

Cherlin, Andrew, *Marriage, Divorce and Remarriage* (Cambridge: Harvard University Press, 1981).

Chernin, Kim, *The Hungry Self: Women, Eating and Identity* (New York: Harper and Row, 1985).

———, *The Obsession* (New York: Harper and Row, 1981; Harper Colophon, 1982).

Chodorow, Nancy, *The Reproduction of Mothering: Psychoanalysis and the Sociology of Gender* (Berkeley: University of California Press, 1978).

Cole, Johnnetta, ed., *All American Women: Lines That Divide, Ties That Bind* (New York: Free Press, 1986).

Cott, Nancy, *The Bonds of Womanhood: "Women's Sphere" in New England, 1780–1835* (New Haven: Yale University Press, 1977).

———, *The Grounding of Modern Feminism* (New Haven and London: Yale University Press, 1987).

———, ed., *Root of Bitterness: Documents of the Social History of American Women* (New York: Dutton, 1972).

Cott, Nancy, and Elizabeth Pleck, eds., *A Heritage of Her Own: Families, Work and Feminism in America* (New York: Touchstone Books, 1980).

Debold, Elizabeth, Marie Wilson, and Idelisse Malave, *Mother Daughter Revolution: From Betrayal to Power* (Reading, Mass.: Addison Wesley Publishing Company, 1993).

Degler, Carl, *At Odds: Women and the Family in America from the Revolution to the Present* (New York: Oxford University Press, 1981).

Deutsch, Helene, *The Psychology of Women,* Vols. 1 and 2 (New York: Grune and Stratton, 1945; Bantam, 1973).

Drachman, Virginia, *Women Lawyers and the Origins of Professional Identity in America: The Letters of the Equity Club, 1887–1890* (Ann Arbor: University of Michigan Press, 1993).

Easterlin, Richard, *Birth and Fortune, The Impact on Personal Welfare* (New York: Basic Books, 1980).

Eichenbaum, Luise, and Susie Orbach, *Understanding Women, A Feminist Psychoanalytic Approach* (New York: Basic Books, 1983).

Elder, Glen H., Jr., *Children of the Great Depression: Social Change in Life Experience* (Chicago: University of Chicago Press, 1974).

Epstein, Cynthia Fuchs, *Woman's Place: Options and Limits in Professional Careers* (Berkeley: University of California Press, 1971).

———, *Women in Law* (New York: Basic Books, Inc., 1981).

Erikson, Erik H., *Childhood and Society* (New York: Norton, 1970).

———, *Identity, Youth and Crisis* (New York: W. W. Norton Co., 1968).

Evans, Sara M., *Born for Liberty: a History of Women in America* (New York: Free Press, 1989).

———, *Personal Politics: The Roots of Women's Liberation in the Civil Rights Movement and The New Left* (New York: Random House, 1980; first published by Knopf, 1979).

Faludi, Susan, *Backlash: The Undeclared War Against American Women* (New York: Crown Publishers, Inc., 1991).

Fass, Paula, *The Damned and the Beautiful: American Youth in the 1920s* (Oxford University Press, 1979).

Bibliography

Fernandez, John P., *Racism and Sexism in Corporate Life: Changing Values in American Business* (Lexington, Mass.: Lexington Books, 1981).

Feuer, Lewis, *The Conflict of Generations: The Character and Significance of Student Movements* (New York: Basic Books, Inc., 1969).

Filene, Peter, *Him/Her/Self: Sex Roles in Modern America* (New York: Harcourt, Brace, Jovanovich, 1975; New American Library, pb. 1976; Second Ed., Baltimore: Johns Hopkins University Press, 1986).

Forisha, Barbara L. and Barbara H. Goldman, eds., *Outsiders on the Inside* (Englewood Cliffs, N.J.: Prentice-Hall, 1981).

Fox-Genovese, Elizabeth, *Feminism without Illusions, A Critique of Individualism* (Chapel Hill: University of North Carolina Press, 1991).

Friday, Nancy, *My Mother/Myself: The Daughter's Search for Identity* (New York: Delacorte Press, 1977; Dell, 1982).

Friedan, Betty, *The Feminine Mystique* (New York: Dell Publishing Co., 1983; New York: Norton, 1963).

——, *The Second Stage* (New York: Summit Books, 1981).

Friedman, Jane, *America's First Woman Lawyer: The Biography of Myra Bradwell* (Buffalo: Prometheus Books, 1993).

Gay, Peter, *Education of the Senses* (New York: Oxford University Press, 1984).

Gilligan, Carol, *In A Different Voice* (Cambridge: Harvard University Press, 1982).

Gilligan, Carol, Nona P. Lyons, and Trudy J. Hanmer, *Making Connections: The Relational Worlds of Adolescent Girls at Emma Willard School* (Troy, New York: Emma Willard School, 1989).

Gilligan, Carol, Janie Victoria Ward, and Jill McLean, with Betty Bardige, eds., *Mapping the Moral Domain* (Cambridge: Center for the Study of Gender Education and Human Development, Harvard University Graduate School of Education, distributed by Harvard University Press, 1988).

Ginsberg, Eli, *Lifestyles of Educated Women* (New York: Columbia University Press, 1966).

Gitlin, Todd, *The Sixties: Years of Hope, Days of Rage* (New York: Bantam, 1987).

Glazer, Pnina M. and Miriam Slater, *Unequal Colleagues, 1890–1940* (New Brunswick, New Jersey: Rutgers University Press, 1987).

Gordon, Suzanne, *Prisoners of Men's Dreams: Striking Out for a New Feminine Future* (Boston: Little Brown, 1991).

Gould, Roger, *Transformations, Growth and Change in Adult Life* (New York: Simon and Schuster, 1978).

Guttentag, Marcia, and Paul Secord, *Too Many Women: The Sex Ratio Question* (Beverly Hills: Sage Publications, 1983).

Harris, Barbara, *Beyond Her Sphere: Women and the Professions in American History* (Westport, Conn.: Greenwood Press, Inc., 1978).

Hennig, Margaret, and Anne Jardim, *The Managerial Woman* (New York: Doubleday, 1976).

Herlihy, David, *Medieval Households* (Cambridge: Harvard University Press, 1985).

Hewlett, Sylvia Ann, *A Lesser Life: The Myth of Women's Liberation in America* (New York: Warner Books, 1987).

Hine, Darlene Clark, ed., *Black Women in America, An Historical Encyclopedia* (Brooklyn, New York: Carlson Publishing Company, 1993).

Hochschild, Arlie R., *The Second Shift* (New York: Avon Books, 1989).

Hooks, Bell, *Ain't I a Woman: Black Women and Feminism* (Boston: South End Press, 1981).

——, *Feminist Theory from Margin to Center* (Boston: South End Press, 1984).

Hulbert, Kathleen Day and Diane Tickton Schuster, eds., *Women's Lives Through Time: Educated American Women of the Twentieth Century* (San Francisco: Jossey-Bass, Inc., Publishers, 1993).

Hummer, Patricia, *The Decade of Elusive Promise, Professional Women in the United States 1920–1930* (Ann Arbor: U.M.I. Research Press, 1979).

Hymowitz, Carol, and Michaele Weissman, *A History of Women in America* (New York: Bantam, 1979).

Jordan, Judith V., Alexandra G. Kaplan, Jean Baker Miller, Irene P. Stiver, and Janet L. Surrey, *Women's Growth in Connection: Writings from the Stone Center* (New York: The Guilford Press, 1991).

Josselson, Ruthellen, *Finding Herself: Pathways to Identity Development in Women* (San Francisco: Jossey-Bass, 1987).

Kaminer, Wendy, *A Fearful Freedom: Women's Flight from Equality* (Reading, Mass.: Addison Wesley, 1990).

Kanter, Rosabeth, *Men and Women of the Corporation* (New York: Basic/Colophon Books, 1977).

Kaplan, Louise J., *Oneness and Separateness: From Infant to Individual* (New York: Simon and Schuster, 1978).

Keniston, Kenneth, *The Uncommitted: Alienated Youth in American Society* (New York: Harcourt Brace Jovanovich, 1965).

———, *Young Radicals: Notes on Committed Youth* (New York: Harcourt Brace and World, 1968).

———, *Youth and Dissent: The Rise of a New Opposition* (New York: Harcourt, Brace, Jovanovich, 1971).

Kessler-Harris, Alice, *Out to Work: A History of Wage-Earning Women in the United States* (New York: Oxford University Press, 1982).

King, Mary, *Freedom Song: A Personal Story of the 1960s Civil Rights Movement* (New York: William Morrow 1987).

Klein, Ethel, *Gender Politics: From Consciousness to Mass Politics* (Cambridge: Harvard University Press, 1984).

Komarovsky, Mirra, *Women in College: Shaping Feminine Identities* (New York: Basic Books, 1985).

Kraditor, Aileen, *Up From the Pedestal, Selected Writings in the History of American Feminism* (Chicago: Quadrangle Press, 1968).

Kuhn, Thomas, *The Structure of Scientific Revolutions* (Chicago: University of Chicago Press, 1962).

Lasch, Christopher, *The Culture of Narcissism: American Life in the Age of Diminishing Expectations* (New York: W. W. Norton and Co, 1979).

———, *The New Radicalism in America 1889–1963: The Intellectual as Social Type* (New York: Alfred A. Knopf, 1966).

Lemons, James Stanley, *The Woman Citizen: Social Feminism in the 1920s* (Urbana: University of Illinois Press, 1973).

Lerner, Gerda, *The Creation of Patriarchy* (New York, Oxford: Oxford University Press, 1986).

Levinson, Daniel, with Charlotte N. Darrow, Edward B. Klein, Maria H. Levinson, and Braxton McKee, *The Seasons of a Man's Life* (New York: Ballantine Books, 1978).

Lifton, Robert Jay, ed., *The Woman in America* (Boston: Beacon Paperback, 1967).

Lipset, Seymour Martin, *Rebellion in the University* (Boston: Little Brown, 1971).

Lipset, Seymour Martin, and Philip G. Altbach, eds., *Students in Revolt,* (Boston: Houghton Mifflin, 1969).

Bibliography

McAdam, Doug, *Freedom Summer* (New York: Oxford University Press, 1988).

McGoldrick, Monica and Randy Gerson, *Genograms in Family Assessment* (New York: Norton, 1985).

MacKinnon, Catherine, *Sexual Harassment of Working Women* (New Haven: Yale University Press, 1979).

Mahler, Margaret, Fred Pine, and Anni Bergman, *The Psychological Birth of the Human Infant: Symbiosis and Individuation* (New York: Basic Books, Inc., 1975).

Mansbridge, Jane, *Why We Lost the ERA* (Chicago: University of Chicago Press, 1986).

Margolis, Maxine, *Mothers and Such: Views of American Women and Why They Changed* (Berkeley: University of California Press, 1984).

Marshall, Megan, *The Cost of Loving: Women and the New Fear of Intimacy* (New York: Putnam, 1984).

Mattfeld, Jacqueline A. and Carol G. Van Aken, eds., *Women in the Scientific Professions* (Cambridge, Mass: Massachusetts Institute of Technology Press, 1965).

May, Elaine Tyler, *Homeward Bound: American Families in the Cold War Era* (New York: Basic Books, 1988).

Meyerowitz, Joanne J., *Women Adrift: Independent Wage Earners in Chicago, 1880–1930* (Chicago and London: University of Chicago Press, 1988).

Miller, Jean Baker, *Toward a New Psychology of Women* (Boston: Beacon Press, 1976).

Minow, Martha, *Making All the Difference: Inclusion, Exclusion and American Law* (Ithaca, N.Y.: Cornell University Press, 1991).

Mintz, Steven, *A Prison of Expectations, The Family in Victorian Culture* (New York and London: New York University Press, 1983).

Mintz, Steven and Susan Kellogg, *Domestic Revolutions: A Social History of American Family Life* (New York: The Free Press, 1988).

Money, John and Anke Ehrhardt, *Man & Woman, Boy & Girl, The Differentiation and Dimorphism of Gender Identity from Conception to Maturity* (Baltimore: Johns Hopkins University Press, 1972; Signet, 1974.)

Moore, Lynda L., ed., *Not As Far As You Think: The Realities of Working Women* (Lexington, Mass.: Lexington Books, 1986.)

Morantz, Regina Markell, Cynthia Stodola Pomerleau, and Carol Hansen Fenichel, *In Her Own Words, Oral Histories of Women Physicians, Contributions in Medical History,* Number 8 (Westport, Conn.: Greenwood Press, 1982).

Morantz-Sanchez, Regina Markell, *Sympathy and Science: Women Physicians in American Medicine* (New York: Oxford University Press, 1985).

Morrison, Ann M., Randall P. White, Ellen Van Velsor, and the Center for Creative Leadership, *Breaking the Glass Ceiling: Can Women Reach the Top of America's Largest Corporations?* (Reading, Mass.: Addison Wesley Publishing Company, Inc., 1987).

Norton, Mary Beth, *Liberty's Daughters: The Revolutionary Experience of American Women 1750–1800* (Boston: Little Brown, 1980).

Notman, Malkah and Carol Nadelson, *The Woman Patient,* Vol. 1, Medical and Psychological Interfaces (New York: Plenum Press, 1978).

O'Neill, William, *Everyone Was Brave: The Rise and Fall of Feminism in America* (Chicago: Quadrangle Press, 1969).

Rix, Sara E., ed., *The American Woman, 1987–88, A Report in Depth* (New York: Norton, 1987).

Roland, Alan, and Barbara Harris, eds., *Career and Motherhood, Struggles for a New Identity* (New York: Human Sciences Press, 1979).

Rosenberg, Charles E., ed., *The Family in History* (Philadelphia: University of Pennsylvania Press, 1975).

————, *No Other Gods: On Science and American Thought* (Baltimore: Johns Hopkins University Press, 1976).

Rosenberg, Rosalind, *Beyond Separate Spheres: Intellectual Roots of Modern Feminism* (New Haven: Yale University Press, 1982).

Rossi, Alice, ed., *The Feminist Papers from Adams to Beauvoir* (New York: Bantam Books, 1973).

————, ed., *Gender and the Life Course* (New York: Aldine Publishing Co., 1985).

Rossiter, Margaret, *Women Scientists in America: Struggles and Strategies to 1940* (Baltimore: Johns Hopkins University Press, 1982).

Rothman, Sheila, *Women's Proper Place: A History of Changing Ideals and Practices 1870 to the Present* (New York: Basic Books, 1978).

Rubin, Lillian, *Intimate Strangers: Men and Women Together* (New York: Harper and Row, 1983).

Ruddick, Sara, *Maternal Thinking: Toward a Politics of Peace* (Boston: Beacon Press, 1989).

Ruddick, Sara and Pamela Daniels, *Working It Out: 23 Women Writers, Scholars, Scientists and Scholars Talk About Their Lives and Work* (New York: Pantheon, 1977).

Ryan, Mary P., *Womanhood in America: From Colonial Times to the Present* (New York: New Viewpoints, 1975).

Scarf, Maggie, *Unfinished Business: Pressure Points in the Lives of Women* (New York: Doubleday, 1980).

Schlafley, Phyllis, *The Power of the Positive Woman* (New Rochelle, N.Y.: Arlington House, 1977).

Schlesinger, Arthur M., Jr., *The Cycles of American History* (Boston: Houghton Mifflin, 1986).

Schor, Juliet B., *The Overworked American* (New York: Basic Books, 1991).

Scott, Joan Wallach, *Gender and the Politics of History* (New York: Columbia University Press, 1988).

Sheehy, Gail, *Passages: Predictable Crises of Adult Life* (New York: E. P. Dutton and Co., 1974, 1976).

Showalter, Elaine, ed., *These Modern Women: Autobiographical Essays from the Twenties* (Westbury, New York: The Feminist Press, 1978).

Smith, Jessie Carney, ed., *Notable Black American Women* (Detroit: Gale Research, Inc., 1992).

Smith-Rosenberg, Carroll, *Disorderly Conduct: Visions of Gender in Victorian America* (New York: Alfred A. Knopf, 1985).

Sokoloff, Natalie, *Black Women and White Women in the Professions: Occupational Segregation by Race and Gender, 1960–1980* (New York: Routledge Press, 1992).

Stacey, Judith, *Brave New Families: Stories of Upheaval in Late Twentieth Century America* (New York: Basic Books, 1990).

Stage, Sarah, *Female Complaints: Lydia Pinkham and the Business of Women's Medicine* (New York: W. W. Norton, 1979).

Stone, Lawrence, *The Family, Sex and Marriage in England, 1500–1800* (New York, Harper and Row, 1977).

Strauss, William and Neil Howe, *Generations: The History of America's Future: 1584–2069* (New York: William Morrow, 1991).

Theodore, Anthena, ed., *The Professional Woman* (Cambridge, Mass.: Schenkman Publishing Co., 1971).

Theriot, Nancy, *The Biosocial Construction of Femininity: Mothers and Daughters in Nineteenth Century America* (Westport, Conn.: Greenwood Press, 1988).

Bibliography

Ulrich, Laurel Thatcher, *Good Wives: Image and Reality in the Lives of Women in Northern New England 1650–1750* (New York: Vintage Books, 1991; first published, 1980).

Vaillant, George, *Adaptation to Life* (Boston: Little Brown, 1977).

Walsh, Mary Roth, *Doctors Wanted: No Women Need Apply. Sexual Barriers in the Medical Profession, 1835–1975* (New Haven: Yale University Press, 1977).

Weitzman, Lenore, *The Divorce Revolution* (New York: Macmillan, The Free Press, 1985).

Wisconsin Department of Public Instruction, *Women of Color Forum, A Collection of Readings,* Wisconsin Department of Public Instruction, Nov. 1979, Bulletin #404.

Articles, Dissertations, Interviews, Speeches

Adams, Jane Meredith, "Giving Up the Dream," *Boston Globe,* March 21, 1986, pp. 43, 53.

Altman, Lawrence K. with Elisabeth Rosenthal, "Changes in Medicine Bring Pain to Healing Profession," *New York Times,* Feb. 18, 1990, pp. A1, A34.

Associated Press, "Women Said to Be Kept From Top Media Posts," *New York Times,* March 2, 1988, p. B5.

———, "Women Scientists Lagging in Industry Jobs," *New York Times,* January 18, 1994, p. C5.

Baruch, Grace, "Maternal Influences Upon Women's Attitudes Toward Career Achievement," Doc. diss., Bryn Mawr, 1970, Henry A. Murray Research Center Archives.

Bergmann, Barbara, "Policy Agenda for the Sex Role Revolution," talk delivered at Radcliffe College Conference on Women in the Year 2000, Dec. 2, 1988.

Bernstein, Doris, "Female Identity Synthesis," in *Career and Motherhood, Struggles for a New Identity,* edited by Alan Roland and Barbara Harris (New York: Human Sciences Press, 1979) pp. 103–124.

Betters-Reed, Bonita, interview with author, Simmons College, Boston, Mass., April 6, 1992.

Betters-Reed, Bonita, and Lynda L. Moore, "Valuing Differences, Valuing Diversity," social science faculty talk delivered at Simmons College, Boston, Mass., April 29, 1992.

———, "Managing Diversity: Focusing on Women and the Whitewash Dilemma," in *Womanpower: Managing in Times of Demographic Turbulence,* edited by Uma Sekaran and Frederick T. L. Leong (Newbury Park, Calif.: Sage Publications, Inc., 1991) pp. 31–58.

Beutell, Nicholas and Jeffrey Greenhaus, "Balance Acts: Work-Family Conflict and The Dual Career Couple," in *Not as Far As You Think: The Realities of Working Women,* edited by Lynda L. Moore (Lexington, Mass.: Lexington Books, 1986) pp. 149–162.

Bieri, James, "Parental Identification, Acceptance of Authority and Differences in Cognitive Behavior," *Journal of Abnormal and Social Psychology* (1960) p. 60.

Blakeslee, Sandra, "Female Sex Hormone Is Tied to Ability to Perform Tasks," *New York Times,* Nov. 18, 1988, pp. A1–D20.

Bolotin, Susan, "Voices from the Post-Feminist Generation," *New York Times Magazine,* October 17, 1982, pp. 28–31, 103–117.

Boston Globe, no byline, "The Day Care Hunt," May 10, 1992, p. 38.

Bovee, Tim, "Census Study Sees Reshaped US by 2050," *Boston Globe,* September 29, 1993, pp. 1, 6.

Butterfield, Bruce, "Xerox Makes It Work," *Boston Globe,* Oct. 20, 1991, p. A37.

Carr, Louis Green, and Lorena S. Walsh, "The Planter's Wife: The Experience of White Women in Seventeenth Century Maryland," *William and Mary Quarterly* 3d series, 34 (1977) p. 552.

Caspi, Avshalom, and Glen H. Elder, Jr., "Emergent family patterns: The intergenerational

207

construction of problem behaviour and relationships," in Robert Hinde and Joan Stevenson-Hinde, eds., *Relationships Within Families* (Oxford: Oxford University Press, 1988) pp. 218–240.

Chira, Susan, "Bias Against Girls is Found Rife in Schools, With Lasting Damage," *New York Times,* Feb. 12, 1992, p. A1.

———, "Study Confirms Worst Fears on U.S. Children," *New York Times,* April 12, 1994, pp. A1, A13.

Cole, Johnnetta B., "Commonalities and Differences," in *All American Women,* edited by Johnnetta Cole (New York: Free Press, 1986) pp. 1–30.

Costello, Nancy, "Moving from Homosocial to Heterosexual Relationships in the Early 1900s: Women's Gain or Loss," Unpublished paper, Harvard University Extension School, 1984.

Deutsch, Claudia, "A Darker Side to Women's Success," *New York Times,* September 19, 1986, pp. C1, C10.

———, "Don't Forget the White Males," *New York Times,* Dec. 8, 1991, p. 29.

Dill, Diana, "Understanding Women's Achievement: Sex Differences in the Structuring of Achievement Situations," talk at Henry A. Murray Research Center, Radcliffe College, October 15, 1985.

Dionne, E. J., "Both Parties Using Family and Moral Issues," *New York Times,* September 28, 1987, pp. A1, A30.

Drachman, Virginia, Brown Bag Lunch Talk delivered at Henry A. Murray Research Center, Radcliffe College, Cambridge, Mass., May 13, 1986.

Drexler, Madeleine, "Medicine Woman," *The Boston Globe Magazine,* March 29, 1992, pp. 18, 27–39.

Dullea, Georgia, "Divorce Law is Called Unfair by Bar and Women's Groups," *New York Times,* August 5, 1985, p. A1.

Easterlin, Richard, "Will There Soon Be Another Baby Boom?" interview with author and Shirley Wershba on *MacNeil-Lehrer Report* (Public Broadcasting System, May 9, 1977).

Ehrenreich, Barbara, "A Feminist's View of the New Man," *New York Times Magazine,* May 20, 1984, p. 36.

Ehrhardt, Anke, "Psycholobiology of Gender," in *Gender and the Life Course,* edited by Alice Rossi (New York: Aldine Publishing Co., 1985) pp. 82–93.

Elder, Glen H., Jr., "Women's Work in the Family Economy," *Journal of Family History* 4 (Summer 1979) pp. 153–176.

Elder, Glen H., Jr., Geraldine Downey, and Catherine Cross, "Family Ties and Life Chances: Hard Times and Hard Choices in Women's Lives Since the 1930s," in Nancy Datan, Anita L. Greene, and Hayne W. Reese, eds., *Life Span Developmental Psychology: Intergenerational Relations* (Hillsdale, N.J.: Lawrence Erlbaum Associates, 1986) pp. 151–183.

Elder, Glen H., Jr., and Jeffrey K. Liker, "Hard Times in Women's Lives: Historical Influences across Forty Years," *American Journal of Sociology* 88:2 (1982) pp. 241–269.

Elder, Glen H., Jr., T. Nguyen, and A. Caspi, "Linking Family Hardship to Children's Lives," *Child Development* (1985) 56, pp. 361–375.

Epps, Roselyn Payne, "The Black Woman Physician—Perspectives and Priorities," *Journal of the National Medical Association,* 78:5 (1986) pp. 375–381.

Epstein, Cynthia Fuchs, "Positive Effects of the Multiple Negative: Explaining the Success of Black Professional Women," *The American Journal of Sociology,* 78:4 (January 1973) Columbia University Bureau of Applied Social Research Reprint # A662, pp. 912–935.

Bibliography

Evans, Sara M., "Women in the Twentieth Century, An Overview," in *The American Woman 1987–1988, A Report in Depth,* edited by Sara E. Rix (New York: Norton, 1987), pp. 33–66.

Flint, Anthony, "New Breed of Feminist Challenges Old Guard," *Boston Globe,* May 29, 1994, pp. 1, 14.

Fowler, Elizabeth, "Careers: Optimism on Women Engineers," *New York Times,* July 21, 1987, pp. D17, D57, D61.

Fox-Piven, Frances, "Women and the State: Power, Ideology and the Welfare State," in *Gender and the Life Course,* edited by Alice Rossi (New York: Aldine Publishing Co., 1985) pp. 265–287.

Fraker, Susan, "Why Women Aren't Getting to the Top," *Fortune* 16 (April 1984) p. 40.

Freedman, Samuel G., "Of History and Politics, Bitter Feminist Debate," *New York Times,* June 6, 1986, pp. B1, B4

Gelman, David, with John Carey, "Just How the Sexes Differ," *Newsweek* 98 (May 18, 1981) pp. 72–81.

Gibbs, Nancy, "The War Against Feminism," *Time,* March 9, 1992, pp. 50–57.

Gilligan, Carol, interview with author, Bunting Institute, Radcliffe College, Cambridge, Mass., November 4, 1982.

———, "The Relational Worlds of Adolescent Girls," talk delivered at the Bunting Institute, January 14, 1981.

Gilson, Nancy, interview with author, Simmons College, Boston, Mass., November 18, 1991.

Glass, Jennifer, Vern L. Bengston, and Charlotte Chorn Dunham, "Attitude Similarities in Three Generational Families: Socialization, Status Inheritance or Reciprocal Influence?" *American Sociological Review* 51 (Oct. 1986) pp. 685–698.

Gluck, Nora R., Elaine Dannefer, and Kathryn Miles, "Women in Families," in *The Family Life Cycle,* edited by Betty Carter and Monica McGoldrick (New York: Gardner Press, 1980) pp. 295–327.

Gordon, Suzanne, "Every Woman for Herself," *New York Times,* August 19, 1991, p. A15.

Graham, Patricia, "Women in Academe," in *The Professional Woman,* edited by Athena Theodore (Cambridge, Mass.: Schenkman Publishing Co., 1971) pp. 720–740.

Greenhouse, Linda, "Momentum and 'Family Leave,'" *New York Times,* February 3, 1987, p. A18.

Gross, Jane, "Patricia Ireland, President of N.O.W.: Does She Speak for Today's Women?" *New York Times Magazine,* March 1, 1992, pp. 16–18, 38, 54.

———, "Single Women Coping with A Void," *New York Times,* April 28, 1987, p. A1.

———, "Where Ambition Meets Opportunity," *New York Times,* May 29, 1992, p. A19.

Haccoun, D. M., R. R. Haccoun, and G. Sallay, "Sex Differences in the Appropriateness of Supervisory Styles: A Nonmanagement View," *Journal of Applied Psychology* 63: (1978) pp. 124–127.

Harlan, Carol Anne and Carol Weiss, "Moving Up: Women in Managerial Careers," Working Paper, #86, Wellesley College Center for Research on Women, 1981.

Helson, Ravenna, "Women Mathematicians and the Creative Personality," *Journal of Consulting and Clinical Society,* 36:2 (1971), reprinted in *Readings on the Psychology of Women,* edited by Judith Bardwick (New York: Harper and Row, 1972) pp. 93–100.

Herbert, Bob, "Battered Girls in School," *New York Times,* November 24, 1993, pp. A15, A25.

Herman, Judith Lewis, and Helen Block Lewis, "Anger in the Mother Daughter Relationship," in *The Psychology of Today's Woman: New Psychoanalytic Visions,* edited by Toni Bernay and Dorothy Cantor (Hillsdale, New Jersey: Analytic Press, 1986) pp. 139–163.

Hess, Beth B., "Aging Policies and Old Women: The Hidden Agenda," in *Gender and the Life Course,* edited by Alice Rossi (New York: Aldine Publishing Co., 1985) pp. 319–332.

Hilly, Dorothy, conversation with author, New York, N.Y., December 31, 1986.

Holden, Steven A., "Survey Finds Minorities Resent One Another Almost as Much As They Do Whites," *New York Times,* March 3, 1994, p. B8.

Hooks, Bell, "Black Women: Shaping Feminist Theory," in *Feminist Theory from Margin to Center,* by Bell Hooks (Boston: South End Press, 1984).

Horner, Matina, "Femininity and Successful Achievement: A Basic Inconsistency," in *Feminine Personality and Conflict,* edited by Judith Bardwick and Elizabeth Douvan et al. (Belmont, California: Brooks Cole, 1970), Ch. 3.

———, "The Motive to Avoid Success and Changing Aspirations of College Women," in *Readings on the Psychology of Women* edited by Judith Bardwick (New York: Harper and Row, 1972) pp. 62–67.

Hurtado, Aida, "Relating to Privilege: Seduction and Rejection in the Subordination of White Women and Women of Color," *Signs: Journal of Culture and Society* 14:4 (University of Chicago, Summer 1989) pp. 833–855.

Ibrahim, Farah A., "A Course on Asian-American Women: Identity Development Issues," *Women's Studies Quarterly* 1 & 2 (Spring and Summer 1992) pp. 41–57.

Jacoby, Susan, "Hers," *New York Times,* April 14, 1983, p. C2.

Kanter, Rosabeth Moss, "Structuring the Inside: The Impact of Organizations on Sex Differences," in *Outsiders on the Inside,* edited by Barbara Forisha and Barbara Goldman (Englewood Cliffs, N.J.: Prentice-Hall, 1981) pp. 75–83.

Keller, Suzanne, "Women in the Twenty-First Century: Summing Up and Going Forward," Address to The Radcliffe Conferences, Defining the Challenge: Emerging Needs and Constraints, Radcliffe College, Dec. 2, 1988.

Keniston, Kenneth, "Radicals: Renewal of the Tradition," "Radicals Revisited, Some Second Thoughts," and "You Have to Grow Up in Scarsdale," in his collection *Youth and Dissent: The Rise of a New Opposition* (New York: Harcourt Brace Jovanovich, 1971) pp. 213–229, 269–286, 303–317.

Keniston, Kenneth, and Michael Lerner, "The Unholy Alliance," in Keniston's *Youth and Dissent: The Rise of a New Opposition* (New York: Harcourt Brace Jovanovich, 1971) pp. 352–369.

Kilborn, Peter T., "More Women Take Low-Wage Jobs Just So Their Families Can Get By," *New York Times,* March 13, 1994, pp. A11, A24.

Klemesrud, Judy, "Americans Assess 15 Years of Feminism," *New York Times,* Dec. 19, 1983, p. A1.

Korn/Ferry International, "Profile of Women Senior Executives" (New York: Korn Ferry International, 1982).

Krauss, Clifford, "Senate Passes Bill Setting up Leaves for Family Needs," *New York Times,* Oct. 3, 1991, pp. A1, A20.

Leggon, Cheryl Bernadette, "Black Female Professionals: Dilemmas and Contradictions of Status," in *The Black Woman,* edited by La Frances Rodgers-Rose (Beverly Hills, California: Sage Publications, Inc., 1980) pp. 189–202.

Leon, Carol Boyd, "Occupational winners and losers: who they were during 1972–80," *Monthly Labor Review* (June 1982) pp. 18–28.

Lerner, Gerda, "The Lady and the Mill Girl: Changes in the Status of Women in the Age of Jackson, 1800–1840," in *A Heritage of Her Own,* edited by Nancy Cott and Elizabeth Pleck (New York: Touchstone Press, 1980) pp. 182–196.

Levinson, Daniel, "A Conception of Adult Development," *American Psychologist* 41:1 (January 1986) pp. 3–13.

Lewis, Diane E., "A Helping Hand in the Balancing Act," *Boston Globe,* Nov. 30, 1991, p. 3.

———, "Fast Track, News in the Workplace," *Boston Globe,* March 23, 1992, p. 17.

Lipman-Blumen, Jean, "The Development and Impact of Female Role Ideology," prepared for conference on Resources for a Changing World, Radcliffe Institute, 1972.

———, "Ideology, Social Structure and Crisis," paper presented at the American Sociological Association 69th meeting, Montreal, Quebec, Canada, August 25–29, 1974.

Los Angeles Times, no byline, "Conference of Women Ends with Protest by Workers," in *Boston Globe,* July 13, 1992, p. 16.

McCabe, Bruce, "Helping lawyers face family life," *Boston Globe,* Dec. 3, 1991, p. 61.

Maccoby, Eleanor, "Sex Differences in Intellectual Functioning," in *Readings on the Psychology of Women,* edited by Judith Bardwick (New York: Harper and Row, 1972) pp. 34–43.

McIntosh, Peggy, "White Privilege and Male Privilege: A Personal Account of Coming to See Correspondence Through Work in Women's Studies," paper, Wellesley College Center for Research on Women, Wellesley, Mass., 1988.

McLaughlin, Steven D., John O. Billy, Terry R. Johnson, Barbara Melber, Linda D. Winges, and Denise M. Zimmerle, *The Cosmopolitan Report on the Changing Life Course of American Women* (Seattle, Washington: Batelle Human Affairs Research Centers, 1985).

McNamara, Eileen, "The Myth of Sisterhood," *Boston Globe Magazine,* January 5, 1992, pp. 13, 18–32.

Malcolm, Shirley Mahaley, Paula Quick Hall, and Janet Welsh Brown, eds., *The Double Bind: The Price of Being a Minority Woman in Science* (Washington, D.C.: American Association for the Advancement of Science, Report No. 76-R-3, April 1976).

Menaker, Esther, "Some Inner Conflicts of Women in a Changing Society," in *Career and Motherhood: Struggles for a New Identity,* edited by Alan Roland and Barbara Harris (New York: Human Sciences Press, 1979) pp. 87–102.

Milkman, Ruth, "Women's Work and the Economic Crisis," in *A Heritage of Her Own: Families, Work and Feminism in America,* edited by Nancy Cott and Elizabeth Pleck (New York: Touchstone Books, 1980) pp. 507–541.

Miller, Jean B., "The Development of Women's Sense of Self," *Work in Progress #12,* Stone Center for Developmental Services and Studies, Wellesley College, Wellesley, Mass., 1985.

Morrison, Ann M., Randall P. White, and Ellen Van Velsor, "Executive Women: Substance Plus Style," *Psychology Today* 21:8 (August 1987).

Morse, Roberta, "The Black Female Professional," Occasional Paper No. 21, Mental Health Research and Development Center (Washington, D.C.: Institute for Urban Affairs and Research, Howard University, 1983).

Ms. Magazine, no byline, "How Optimistic Are American Women?" 16:1,2 (July, August 1987) pp. 172, 174–176.

Nadelson, Carol, "'Normal' and 'Special' Aspects of Pregnancy: A Psychological Approach," in *The Woman Patient: Medical and Psychological Interfaces Vol. I: Sexual and Reproductive Aspects of Women's Health Care,* edited by Malkah T. Notman and Carol C. Nadelson (New York: Plenum Press, 1978) pp. 73–86.

New York Times, advertisement, Jan. 13, 1988, p. D28, citing Seventeen Food Survey, 1986; TRU Fall 1987, Triangle Communications, Inc., 1988.

New York Times, no byline, "Report Says Poor Children Grew Poorer in 1980s," March 24, 1992, p. A22.

Noble, Barbara Presley, "The New Equality in Hard Times, Some Stats From the Bottom Line," in "At Work," *New York Times,* August 8, 1993, p. F25.

Noda, Kesaya E., "Growing Up Asian in America," in *Making Waves: An Anthology,* edited by Asian Women United of California (Boston: Beacon Press, 1989) pp. 243–250.

Nkomo, Stella M., "Race and Sex: The Forgotten Case of the Black Female Manager," in *Women's Careers: Pathways and Pitfalls,* edited by Suzana Rose and Laurie Larwood (New York: Praeger, 1989) pp. 135–147.

Notman, Malkah, M.D., conversation with author, Henry A. Murray Research Center, A Center for the Study of Lives, Radcliffe College, Cambridge, Mass., April 5, 1994.

Overholser, Geneva, "What Post Feminism Really Means," *New York Times,* September 19, 1986, A34.

Pear, Robert, "Administration May Challenge Equal Pay Rule," *New York Times,* January 22, 1984, p. A1.

———, "Equal Pay is Not Needed for Jobs of Comparable Worth, U.S. Says," *New York Times,* June 18, 1985, p. A12.

Peterson, Richard E., "The Student Left in American Higher Education," in *Students in Revolt,* edited by Seymour Martin Lipset and Philip G. Altbach (Boston: Houghton Mifflin, 1969) pp. 202–234.

Powers, Sally, interview with author, Henry A. Murray Research Center: A Center for the Study of Lives, Radcliffe College, Cambridge, Mass., Nov. 14, 1985.

Reinhold, Robert, "Women in Electronics Find Silicon Valley Best and Worst," *New York Times,* March 2, 1984, pp. A1, A12.

Richardson, Nancy, "Developmental Shifts in Constructions of Success," Doc. diss., Harvard University, 1981.

Rosenberg, Rosalind, "What Harms Women in the Workplace," *New York Times,* Feb. 27, 1986, p. A23.

Rossi, Alice, "Barriers to the Career Choice of Engineering, Medicine, or Science Among American Women," in *Women in the Scientific Professions,* edited by Jacqueline A. Mattfeld and Carol G. Van Aken (Cambridge: M.I.T. Press, 1965) pp. 51–130.

———, "Equality Between the Sexes: An Immodest Proposal," in *The Woman in America,* edited by Robert J. Lifton (Boston: Beacon Paperback, 1967) p. 116. First published in *Daedalus,* Spring, 1964, pp. 99–140.

Ryder, Norman B., "The Cohort as a Concept in the Study of Social Change," *American Sociological Review* 30:6 (Dec. 1965) pp. 841–861.

Salmans, Sandra, "Top Tiers Still Elude Corporate Women," *New York Times,* August 17, 1987, p. B4.

Schein, V. E., "The Relationship Between Sex-Role Stereotypes and Requisite Management Characteristics," *Journal of Applied Psychology* 57 (1973) pp. 95–100.

———, "Relationships Between Sex-Role Characteristics and Requisite Management Characteristics Among Female Managers," *Journal of Applied Psychology* 60 (1975) pp. 340–344.

Scott, Joan Wallach, "The Mechanization of Women's Work," *Scientific American* (September 3, 1982) pp. 167–185.

Segura, Denise, and Jennifer L. Pierce, "Chicana/o Family Structure and Gender Personality: Chodorow, Familism, and Psychoanalytic Sociology Revisited," *Signs: Journal of Women in Culture and Society* 19:1 (1993) pp. 62–90.

212

Bibliography

Sharpe, Rochelle, "Family Friendly Firms Don't Always Promote Females," *Wall Street Journal,* March 29, 1994, pp. B1, B5.

Shellenbarger, Sue, "As More Pregnant Women Work, Bias Complaints Rise," *Wall Street Journal,* December 6, 1993, pp. B1, B2.

Shellenbarger, Sue and Timothy D. Schellhardt, "Is a Dream Workplace Any Closer to Reality," *Wall Street Journal,* Oct. 18, 1991, p. B4.

Silk, Leonard, "Women Gain but at a Cost," *New York Times,* Feb. 6, 1987, p. D2.

Simpson, Gwyned, "The Daughters of Charlotte Ray: The Career Development Process During the Exploratory and Establishment Stages of Black Women Attorneys," *Sex Roles: A Journal of Research* 11:1 and 2 (New York: Plenum, July 1984) pp. 113–139.

Spain, Daphne, "Women's Demographic Past, Present, and Future," talk at Radcliffe Conference on Women in the Year 2000, Defining the Challenge: Emerging Needs and Constraints, Dec. 2, 1988.

Specter, Michael, "Feminists Painfully Watching Holtzman and Ferraro Battle," *New York Times,* March 14, 1992, p. A1.

Stewart, Abigail, "Personality to Life Outcomes among College-Educated Women," Doc. diss., Harvard University, 1975, Murray Center Archives.

Stewart, Wendy, "A Psychosocial Study of the Formation of the Adult Life Structure in Women," Doc. diss., Harvard University, 1976, Murray Center Archives.

Stiver, Irene P., interviews with author, McLean Hospital, Belmont, Mass., November 3, April 20, 1983; informal conversations, 1983–1994.

———, "Work Inhibitions in Women," Stone Center for Developmental Services and Studies, Wellesley College No. 82-03, 1983, also in Judith Jordan, Jean Baker Miller, Irene P. Stiver, and Janet L. Surrey, eds., *Women's Growth in Connection, Writings from the Stone Center* (New York: The Guilford Press, 1991) pp. 223–236.

Stocker, Carol, "The A Group," *Boston Globe,* Jan. 14, 1992, p. 25.

Stone, Lawrence, "The Rise of the Nuclear Family in Early Modern England: The Patriarchal Stage," in *The Family in History,* edited by Charles Rosenberg (Philadelphia: University of Pennsylvania Press, 1975) pp. 13–57.

Strebeigh, Fred, "Defining Law on the Feminist Frontier," *New York Times Magazine,* October 6, 1991, pp. 28–31, 50–56.

Sullivan, Kathleen, "Constitutional and Legal Issues Facing Women in the 21st Century," talk at Conference on Women in the Year 2000, Radcliffe College, Dec. 2, 1988.

Surrey, Janet, "The Self in Relation: A Theory of Women's Development," in *Women's Growth in Connection,* edited by Judith Jordan et al. (New York: Guilford Press, 1991), pp. 51–66.

Swasy, Alecia, "Stay-at-Home Moms Are Fashionable Again in Many Communities," *Wall Street Journal,* July 23, 1993, pp. A1, A4.

Symonds, Alexandra, "The Wife as the Professional," *American Journal of Psychoanalysis* 39:1 (1979) pp. 55–63.

Tangri, Sandra, "Role Innovation in Occupational Choice Among College Women," Doc. diss., University of Michigan, 1969 (reprinted by University Microfilms Ltd., 1970, 1979).

Taylor, Stuart, "Justices Hear Debate Over Pregnancy Leave," *New York Times,* October 9, 1986, p. A30.

Tilghman, Shirley M., "Science vs. the Female Scientist," *New York Times,* January 25, 1993, p. A17.

Turner, Ralph H., "Some Aspects of Women's Ambition," in *The Professional Woman,* edited by Athena Theodore (Cambridge, Mass.: Schenkman Publishing Co., Inc., 1971), pp. 227–251.

U.S. Department of Labor, Bureau of Labor Statistics Bulletin 2080, Table 11, "Employment of Women in Selected Occupations, 1950, 1960, 1970 and 1979," *Data book, Bulletin 2080, 1980.*

Wall Street Journal, no byline, "Do Women Help Women? Don't Bet on Some at Top," March 29, 1994, p. A10.

———, no byline, "The Waiting Game: Women Make Strides but Men Stay Firmly in Top Company Jobs," March 29, 1994, p. A1.

Wall Street Journal, no byline, "Women's Groups Consider a Plan to Overturn Sex-based Disability Rate," April 17, 1994, p. A1.

Weisenhaus, Doreen, "Still a Long Way to Go for Women and Minorities," *National Law Journal* (Feb. 8, 1988) pp. 1, 48, 50, 53.

Witt, Shirley Hill, "Native American Women in the Workforce," speech delivered at the U.S. Department of Labor Conference on Native American Women and Equal Opportunity: A Federal Training Seminar, November 13, 1978, published in *Women of Color Forum, A Collection of Readings,* Wisconsin Department of Public Instruction, Nov. 1979, Bulletin #404.

Woo, Deborah, "The Gap Between Striving and Achieving: The Case of Asian American Women," in Asian Women United of California, eds. *Making Waves, An Anthology* (Boston: Beacon Press, 1989) pp. 185–196.

Zuckerman, Diana, "Medical School Plans and Other Life Goals of Students at the Seven Colleges," Seven College Macy Study, talk delivered at Henry A. Murray Center, Radcliffe College, March, 1983.